Aug. 8, 2007

Carolyn —
Hope you enjoy my book.

B. Spark

Rare Personal Accounts
of
Abraham Lincoln

Rare Personal Accounts
of
Abraham Lincoln

✧

by John E. Boos

Edited by William R. Feeheley & Bill Snack

Published by Rail Splitter Publishing

©2005

Rare Personal Accounts of Abraham Lincoln
By John E. Boos

Copyright ©2005 by Rail Splitter Publishing, LLC

All Rights Reserved

No part of this book may be reproduced in any form or by any electronic or mechanical means, including information storage and retrieval systems, without written permission from the publisher, except by a reviewer who may quote passages in a review.

Cover design by Rail Splitter Publishing, LLC

Book design and typesetting by JustYourType.biz

Edited by William R. Feeheley & Bill Snack

Published by Rail Splitter Publishing, LLC
5321 W. Lake Mitchell Drive
Cadillac, Michigan 49601

Printed in the U.S.A.

First Edition Printing 2005

ISBN # 0-9772672-0-2

Dedication

Earl Eugene (Gene) Snack

This book is dedicated to my brother, Gene Snack, who spent most of his life collecting historic memorabilia. The "Rare Personal Accounts of Abraham Lincoln," can be published today because Gene saw their value and preserved the aged, handwritten documents.

For 35 years, Gene was a respected, well-known educator in the Decatur, Illinois school system. Now retired, his many hobbies include horticulture, painting with oils and water colors and photography. One of seven children of Dorothy and Earl Snack, Gene was born in the small town of Sidell, Illinois in 1928. He graduated from Eastern Illinois University and later received his Master of Arts degree from the University of Illinois. During World War II, he served as a medic and was stationed in Germany.

—Bill Snack

"What constitutes the bulwark of our own liberty and independence? It is not our frowning battlements, our bristling sea coasts, the guns of our war steamers, or the strength of our gallant and disciplined army. These are not our reliance against a resumption of tyranny in our fair land. All of them may be turned against our liberties, without making us stronger or weaker for the struggle. Our reliance is in the love of liberty which God has planted in our bosoms. Our defense is in the preservation of the spirit which prizes liberty as the heritage of all men, in all lands, every where. Destroy this spirit, and you have planted the seeds of despotism around your own doors."

– *Abraham Lincoln*
From the September 11, 1858 Speech at Edwardsville

CONTENTS

INTRODUCTION ix

PART ONE: The Lincoln-Douglas-Debates
   Scene of the Debates
   Ottawa, Aug. 21st 1858
      E.H. Straight 16
      William M. Morris 19
   Freeport, Aug. 27th 1858
      W.V. Lucas 23
   Jonesboro, Sept. 15th 1858
      Captain J.W. King 26
   Charleston, Sept 18th 1858
      George A.J. Colgan 29
      Henry S. Scofield 34
   Galesburg, Oct. 7th
      Mrs. Isabella Wright 35
      Dr. Homer Mead 38
   Quincy, Oct. 13th 1858
      Edward Jonas 40
      Admiral G.W. Beaman 43
   Alton, Oct. 15th 1858
      William H. Heath 48
   N.Y. Times Editorial

PART TWO: Speeches and Debates
   Lewiston
      J.M. Graham 51
   A Debate Witness
      T.G. Martin 55
      Samuel E. Morison 57
      E.H. Straight 58
   Then Lincoln went to Freeport
      James A. Cartwright 62
      The Speech at Clinton
      Isaac H. Crim 63
   Jonesboro
      General A.A. Harbeck 66

That Third Debate, Jonesboro
   William L. Robinson 70
Madison Wisconsin
   Arthur Gleason 74
Charleston
   S.W. Fordyce 76
Toulon
   Andrew S. Whitaker 78
Galesburg, the Fifth of the Debates
   Charles A. Blanchard 82
The Debaters Spoke at Rockport
   Mr. I.W. Swan 85
The Debate is Renewed at Quincy
   Jonathan Labrant 90
At Urbana
   Mrs. A.A. Glass 93
The Last of the Great Debates
   G.W. Beaman 96
A Debate at Macomb
   Thomas Gilmore 100

PART THREE: Lincoln's Farewell Address to Springfield
   Dr. Preston Bailhache 105

PART FOUR: Gen. Thomas
   Gen. William T. Sherman 107
   Hon. B.F. Fade 123
   James C. Blaine 125
   John L. Stahl 131
   William J. Kay 134
   Sidney W. Day 137
   Gen. Gordon Granger 140
   James W. White 140
   A.D. French 143
   M.B. Willis 145
   Charles W. Bennett 147
   Samuel L. Harman 149
   F.J. Young 149
   W.W. Roberts 151
   R.R. Graham 153
   W.A. Marietta 155
   Arthur E. West 157
   Enoch F. Byng 160
   Joseph A. Barrall 162

George H. Thomas 163
S. McAulliff 166
W.H. Bisbee 167

PART FIVE: The Lincoln Guards
George C. Ashmun 170
Henry G. Baird 173
William R. Bogardus 174
William M. Clarke 177
William B. Cary 179
Horace E. Clough 182
Col. W.H. Crook 184
William E. Patterson 185
Smith Stimmel 188
A.M. White 191
Henry M. Kieffer 193
Dr. A.H. See 197
A.P. Simmons 199
Robert A. Smith 201
George E. Smith 203
Samuel R. Fisher 216
George E. Seymour 218
Justice Foote 220
Dr. Daniel M. Fiske 221
Homer B. Sprauge 222
Ira B. Webster 226
Senator Simeon D. Fess 229

PART SIX: Johnson Brigham
"That Man saw Lincoln" 247
"Memory Pictures of Lincoln" 247
Mr. Kearney 257

PART SEVEN: The Failed Assassination Attempt
Edward K. Black 265
Daniel Yarman 278

PART EIGHT: The Lincoln Assassination and Funeral
Henry Clay Ford 283
Jennie Gourly-Struthers 285
Jacob J. Soles 289
Oran J. Randlett 291
Corporal James Tanner 292
John Flaherty 298
Henry C. Rankin 299

Henry W. Littlefield	301
Calvin L. Vincent	305
C.D. Curtis	306
John B. Patrick	308
Harlan G. Mendenhall	311
P.E. Harrington	314
Charles D. Beldon	317
Charles H. Porter	320
Edward Godfrey	322
Robert B. Dickie	324
H.R. Wright	325
James H. Kenny	327
Dr. C.R. Pontius	330
Cornilius Van Dyck	333
Charles Blodgett	334
George A. Jewett	336
Peter Yeager	338
Hugh A. Cummings	341
Joseph Ruff	343
M.D. Vance	346
M.B. Lessier	347
Henry R. Rathbone	354

Introduction

John E. Boos

John E. Boos, author and avid Lincoln collector, was born on September 3, 1879, in Albany, New York. He died on January 12, 1974. His works include local histories of Albany; such as, "The Sacandga Valley," "Landmarks of the Capital District," "Ramblings with Jerry" and "Roaming near the Fireplace." By 1935, few eye witnesses or personal acquaintances of Abraham Lincoln were still living. Author John E. Boos believed he had collected the stories and signatures of most of these people. Collectors Gene and Bill Snack have uncovered the letters and content in "Rare Personal Accounts of Abraham Lincoln" and restored them to legible documents. Now for the first time, RailSplitter Publishing has published the "Rare Personal Accounts of Abraham Lincoln."

In his quest to learn more about Lincoln, Boos conducted face-to-face interviews and correspondence with people by mail throughout the United States. His strategy for selecting people to contact was based on the assumption that all living Union Civil War veterans and others that could have had personal contact with Lincoln. We are uncertain as to how many living veterans and non-veterans Boos actually reached in this endeavor, but considering the communication and travel options available during this period, his efforts had to have been extraordinary. He visited people near his home in Albany, N.Y. and traveled to places as far away as Fargo, North Dakota, Santa Cruz, California, and cities in Kansas, Florida, and Pennsylvania. Between 1912 and 1940, Boos collected anecdotes from people who actually knew or had personal encounters with Lincoln. These stories take the reader back in time and give fresh insight as to the real Lincoln - how he lived, his values and depict various points in time in the life of Lincoln.

Boos was an avid Republican. He believed that Lincoln, perhaps more than any other dignitary in history, embodied the ideals of the Republican Party. His personal goal was to demonstrate that Lincoln embraced individual liberty as ordained by the founding fathers of the United States Constitution. Boos dedicated nearly three decades of his life persistently pursuing information on Lincoln to help prove and preserve this history for future generations. The effort put forth by Boos was not about personal gain nor being in the good graces of those in political power, but rather to keep the principles alive that he believed necessary to maintain the freedom that so many died in the Civil War to win.

One might argue that many historians have written about Lincoln and that his history has been well documented; however, the "Rare Personal Accounts of Abraham Lincoln" captures rich insight into the character of the man that could be revealed only through people who actually knew Lincoln. The interview style used by Boos was simple: He merely asked, "Did you know Lincoln?" As the stories unfolded, Boos listened and scribed as people spoke. Many of the individuals interviewed were unaware of each other, yet their stories revealed similar conclusions.

These stories express Lincoln's oratorical ability, the quality of his character and the influence he had on the lives of people. Considerable detail is revealed, even down to the mud on his boots. Historical facts are also corroborated with a remarkable degree of objectivity and voiced in tones often lacking in writings by some historians who have attempted to explain history from the perspective of their own era. Some accounts may also shed new light on the Lincoln assassination and other important historical events. It is this uniqueness that makes reading "Rare Personal Accounts of Abraham Lincoln" a wonderful experience for the casual reader and historian alike.

"Rare Personal Accounts of Abraham Lincoln" enables the reader to experience on a personal level the Lincoln-Douglas debates, the "Farewell to Springfield" speech, the Lincoln family train ride to Washington D.C., the failed assassination attempt, the White House years and ultimately the assassination and 21-day funeral procession to Springfield, IL. Lincoln admirers were saddened by his assassination, while many that were not fond of him feared his death might jeopardize the reconstruction effort or even mean a return to war.

Boos understood that many people fiercely opposed Lincoln's beliefs. Today, we do not know if Boos actually interviewed these individuals; if he did, this opposition was not revealed in "Rare Personal Accounts of Abraham Lincoln." Even though most accounts are from Union loyalists, Boos collected stories that highlight the sense of loss felt by the entire country after the assassination. Perhaps it was the tenets Lincoln held dear, the love he showed for people and the freedom he defended, that Boos wanted to keep alive by preserving the memories of Lincoln. The love people had for Lincoln can be sensed in these documents.

New York Times Editorial, 1939

Boos' praised the following New York Times Editorial in 1939:

Ever since Stanton said the words, early in the morning of Saturday, April 15th, 1865, the American people have known that Abraham Lincoln belonged to the ages. He has been more than ever in our minds during the last year or two, because we live in a time of crisis in which much depends upon whether or not the things he said stood for are true.

In one of his debates with Douglas, Lincoln declared: "No man is good enough to govern another man without that man's consent." If he was right, democracy, with its elections to express the will of the majority and its constitutional guarantees to protect the minority, is right. If he was wrong, then, of course, Hitler and Mussolini and Stalin are right. Old things are being said in new ways, but this is the issue, as it was in Lincoln's day.

Lincoln would be the first to say that the issue is more important than the man. Stanton, Seward, or Chase might have done most of the practical things he did. We believe now that slavery was wasteful as well as unjust, and was therefore doomed by its own weight; and that the North, having more resources, more men and heavier artillery, was bound to subdue the South. But Lincoln did, for his own generation and for ours, what no other man could have done so well. He had a mystic insight which enabled him to look beyond the crudities of a democratic society. He made democracy poetic, beautiful, majestic.

The poignant cadences of the Gettysburg Address and the Second Inaugural fall with an everlasting music on our ears. The certainties which they express came from a heart wrung by nights and days of agony, warm with compassion for friends and enemies alike, infinitely tender, full of the sad laughter of one who knew the worst of human nature and hoped for the best, incapable of pettiness or hate. In the well-ordered, simple words was the rhythm of the pioneer's axe in the deep forest, of the horses straining at the plow, of cart-wheels in the mud, of hammers nailing log-cabins together, or folk stories and folk songs, of the language spoken by a people who had dreamed a heroic dream. The symbols have changed. Our days grow metallic, noisy, furious. But the meanings abide.

We have in our generation seen conquerors in their pride. But here was no ruthless commander, smirking in victory. Here was a man who had suffered with both sides in a great civil war and who had compassion for both. Here was one who prayed for peace, not for revenge. Here was one who would gladly have put his power aside and gone back to Springfield, as he intended, to practice law with Billy Herndon. The common clay of Kentucky and Illinois was on the boots with which he walked, with that awkward, majestic stride of his, to immortality. There was, and is, no one too humble to say with confidence, Lincoln was one of us, yet during all the years the Republic shall last we shall be struggling to make a nation in his image.

But we must not lose ourselves in the admiration of a single personality. Lincoln survives because his words were true and right. The tall figure in the frock coat and plug hat, stooped a little under his heavy burden and the better to hear the petition of the condemned soldier's mother or the sorrowing wife in Mississippi, walks among us, invisible, forever, because he expressed and embodied an undying aspiration toward justice, mercy, and freedom.

R.E. Ruff, 1939

The New York Times
TIMES SQUARE, NEW YORK, N.Y.
LACKAWANNA 4-1000

May 23/1929

Dear Mr. Boos —

 Many thanks! Please note this is NOT "The Editor" but a humble staff contributor who, nevertheless, is touched by your appreciation.

Sincerely,
R.L. Duffus

N.Y. Times Editorial

Part One: THE LINCOLN-DOUGLAS DEBATES

Did you boys ever read about Daniel Boone, Buffalo Bill, or Grover Cleveland in school? If you did, I won't have to tell you they were great hunters. You remember Boone shot the bear and deer in the dark and bloody ground; Buffalo Bill killed all the buffaloes on the Great Plains, and Grover Cleveland shot all the ducks in Virginia. They were great hunters, and their names deserve to be in the story books. But I know a gallant son-of-a-gun who never made headlines, because he dreaded the limelight, but he has killed every woodchuck in the Sand Maine, every fox, mink, wildcat and mastodon in Albany County and every crow in the village of west Albany.

To prove his membership he took me on a trip one zero day many years ago in Muckle's Dead Horse Farm on the old Tunnel Trail. He waded through snow waist deep for miles, crawled to the crest of many sand dunes, the valley between being filled with carcasses of dead horses, and covered with crows, who loved to feed on carrion. After steady aim my ears fired; and we crawled and fired all day. When we went to bag our catch, marry a crow could we find. The great hunter insisted some animal that eats crown atole them, but I must confess I did not see one fall, though the gun did make a tremendous racket. He is a great hunter just the same, and were it not for his old reliable and good aim, the land might be filled with the elephant and kangaroos.

Did you ever see him in his Hunting togs? A khaki cap with a couple of badges on it, four or five sweaters under a hunting coat whose pockets bulge sweaters under a hunting coat whose pockets creel filled with a lunch, and double-barreled shot gun? The clothes make him look as wide as he is long, and the yellow hair-now very much thinned-sticking out from under the cap makes him look like a Scandanavin-Polick, but he is a good hunter and a good photo-engraver.

I can say a lot more about the whale-John Appel calls him that-but I had better quit and tell you his name is George Karl. He was born among the cattle yards in the West Albany, not far from the railroad works, on June 4, 1883. George thought his college degree was earned when he left grammar school and became an apprentice in the Austin Engraving Co., when Teddy Roosevelt was running up San Juan Hill in 1898. He is a member of St. John's Lutheran Church, holds a card in the Masons, the Chapter, the Shrine, the West End and the Colony Gun Clubs, and in a number of other societies to conserve the wild life.

I want to dedicate this book to that old friend.

SCENE OF THE DEBATES

It is October, just before the date of the Galesburg Debate seventy-seven years ago. The trees are splashed with Autumn colors. The mountains are gay in bright and deep green, orange, red and brown, while here and there a great black mass of rock juts out, too barren to give roots a chance to take hold, and in time mourish a tree to grow big and high, that its colors might hide the sore and add beauty to its massive side. The air is raw, just as raw as it was that historic day of the Debate, and while I enjoy the heat of the log sputtering on the andirons, I am glad I am not in the shivering crowd, as much as I would have loved to hear the speakers had I lived at that time. Though the clouds hang low, and the rain beats hard on the rough, they cannot hide the beauty of the superb lake of the Sacandaga stretching from the length of the valley from Conklingville to Northville, and almost entirely surrounded by mountains.

I can see a long stretch of the lake from the camp window, and many of the mountains, though some of the crests are hidden in the midst. I can hear twittering of birds in the nearby birches, the rasping "Caw" of the crows in the fields, and the call of the wild ducks flying over the water, but that is the only evidence I have of their nearness, because the rain, and darkness of low hanging clouds hide them from my sight.

The leaves are quiet, the lake is calm, the drops come down as though weighted with lead, and the mist keeps rising, then lowering again over the high peaks

> James M Gale,
> "Late Captain Co 'E'"
> 28th Regiment Illinois
> Infantry Volunteers.
> Heard Mr Lincoln
> speak during the Lincoln-
> Douglas debates, and
> attended his funeral —
> Bushnell Illinois

rising, then lowering again over the high peak directly across. There is stands; massive, invincible, unmovable, majestic, awe-inspiring. I ponder over the great mass of rock; wonder if it has thoughts, and has an opinion of man, and if man, with all his craftiness and power, understands and appreciates the mountain.

Speaking of the high hills, Ethel Romig

Fuller says,–

> "Who knows a mountain?
> One who has gone
> To worship its beauty
> In the dawn;
> One who has slept
> On its breast at night,
> One who has measured
> His strength to its height;
> One who has followed
> Its longest trail,
> And laughed in the face
> Of its fiercest gale;
> One who has scaled its peaks,
> And has trod
> Its cloud-swept summits
> Alone with God."

According to the political program, Stephen A. Douglas was nominated for the United States Senate by the Democratic Party, and Abraham Lincoln was put forward by the Republicans. Douglas was running for re-election and he was confident of success, while the Republicans were exerting every effort to gain enough votes in the legislature to elect their candidate, the leaders not alone having confidence in Lincoln, but they gave him the credit of being the leading exponent of principles of the new Party of the West.

The candidates had been speaking in different parts of the State for more than a month, when Lincoln, on July 24, 1858, sent a letter to Douglas in which he said, "Will it be agreeable to you to make an arrangement for you and myself to divide time, and address the same audiences is the perfect canvas?"

Douglas answered the same day, as the letter had been handed to him by a close friend of Lincoln's, Mr. Judd. The answer was very critical, and, in parts, insulting, but he concluded by saying he would be willing to speak in one town in seven counties of the nine congressional districts, naming the cities.

On the 29th Lincoln answered the criticisms and agreed to the proposal. The very next day Douglas named Ottawa, Freeport, Jonesboro, Charlestown, Galesburg, Quincy and Altona as the places for the meetings, saying, "I will speak at Ottawa an hour; you can reply, occupying an hour and a half, and I will then follow for half an hour. At Freeport you shall open the discussion and speak one hour, I will follow for an hour and a half, and you can then reply for half an hour. We will alternate in like manner in each successive place."

Lincoln accepted on the 31st, the first debate to take place August 21st. The two candidates spoke almost daily, and as the time drew near for the contest, the public became more interested, and though little attention was paid to the series out side of the State, within its borders every citizen was anxious to hear, or read of them.

Ottawa, Aug. 21st 1858

E.H. STRAIGHT

When the day came, great crowds filled Ottawa, and the weather having been dry for days, everything was covered with dust, from the people moving through the streets, and from the vehicles. The houses of the town were covered with bunting; cannons roared and bands played. Great processions met the speakers; Lincoln at the railroads station; Douglas at the border of the town, and they were escorted to the platform amid the cheers of each debater's friends.

The public square was crowded, the committees had a task to reach the platform, and it took some time to clear it, every inch of the floor and roof being packed with boys and men. At last the platform was clear, but the roof gave away, and the crowd of young men and boys fell to the platform, but fortunately no one was badly hurt. Another delay was experienced until the wreckage was cleared, the bands and cheer leaders keeping the crowds good natured.

When the Little Giant climbed on the platform, the crowd "A short, thickest, burly man, with large, round head, heavy hair, dark complexion, and fierce bulldog look. Strong in his own real power, and skilled by a thousand conflicts in all the strategy of a hand-to-hand, or a general fight; of towering ambition, restless in his determined desire for notoriety, proud, defiant, arrogant, audacious, unscrupulous, 'Little Doug' ascended the platform and looked out impudently and carelessly on the immense throng which surged and struggled before him."

Then the Railsplitter mounted the platform, "In physique the opposite to Douglas. Build on the Kentucky type, very tall, slender, and angular, awkward even in gait and attitude. His face is sharp, large-featured, and unprepossessing. His eyes are deep-set under heavy brows, his forehead is high and retreating, and his hair is dark and heavy. In repose, I must confess that 'Long Abe's' appearance is not comely. But stir him up and the fire of his genius plays on every feature. His eyes glow and sparkles; every lineament, now so ill-formed, grows brilliantly and expressive, and you have before you a man of rare power and strong magnetic influence."

Leads of both parties filled the platform when the chairman introduced Senator Douglas. The crowd paid close attention to his remarks, applauding at times. During his speech he said,

"This doctrine of Mr. Lincoln, of uniformity among institutions of the different States, is a new doctrine, never dreamed of by Washington, Madison, or the framers of the government. Mr. Lincoln and the Republican Party set themselves up as wiser than these men who made this government, which has flourished for seventy years under the principle of popular sovereignty, recognizing the right of each State to do as it pleased."

Then Lincoln rose to answer the many arguments put forth, saying at one time, "There is a physical difference between the races, which, in my judgment, will probably forever forbid their living together upon the footing of perfect equality; and inasmuch as it becomes a necessity that there must be a difference, I, as well as Judge Douglas, am in favor of the race to which I belong having the superior position. I have never said anything about to the contrary, but I hold that, notwithstanding all this, there is no reason in the world why the negro is not entitled to all the natural rights enumerated in the Declaration of Independence-the right to life, liberty, and pursuit of happiness. I hold that he is as much entitled to these as the white man. I agree with Judge Douglas he is not my equal in many respects-certainly not in color, perhaps not in moral or intellectual endowment. But in the right to eat the bread, without the leave of anybody else, which his own hand earns, he is my equal and the equal of Judge Douglas, and the equal of every living man."

Writing of the debate years later, E.H. Straight said,–

"Lincoln and Douglas came on the same train. There was a large crowd to meet them and escort the candidates to the speaker's stands in the public park at Ottawa. This was about 1 p.m. The speaking commenced soon and lasted until 4 p.m.

"As to Mr. Douglas, everyone knew he was something of a drinker, and he looked it on the stand. When Mr. Lincoln spoke there was some hooting and handicapping at times, but not much interruption. When Douglas got to talking, everything was quiet. Along in his winding up he accused Lincoln of being a saloon keeper and bar tender. After he finished, Lincoln got up to reply and said, 'Ladies and Gentlemen, Mr. Douglas tells you I was a bar tender. I acknowledge the truth of it, but while I was officiating on the side of the bar, Mr. Douglas was a constant attendant on the other side.' I can still hear the clapping and shouting for at least five minutes. At the end there was a great rush to shake hands with Mr. Lincoln. I did not get a chance to shake his hand because three or four other men put him on their shoulders and carried him about a block to the Mayor's residence where there was quite a demonstration. It was getting late and our crowd of fifteen had to go eighteen miles in a farm wagon drawn by four horses, so we did not stay to see the end of the celebration."

> Dear Mr Boos   July 17 28
>
> will answer your Requests as I can Remember its about 70 years ago Lincoln and Douglas come on the same Train there was a large crowd to meet them at the Train and Escort them to the Speakers Stand in the Public Park this was about one P m the Speaking commenced very soon and lasted until 4 P m or after as to Mr Douglas every one knew he was something of a Drinker and he looked it on the Stand Mr Lincoln Spoke first some hooting and hand clapping at times but not much interruption then Douglas got to talking everything was quiet along in his winding up he accused Lincoln of being a Saloon keeper and Bar Tender after he finished Lincoln got up to reply and said Ladies and Gentlemen Mr Douglas tells you I was a Sloon keeper and Bar tender and I acknowledge the truth of it that while I was officiating on one side of the Bar Mr Douglas was a constant attendent on the other Side now listen I can still hear the clapping and Shouting for at least five minutes it was great at the end there was a great rush to get to shake hands with Mr Lincoln I did not get to him to shake hands but

William M. Morris

William M. Morris wrote to me this fine, long letter about that first Debate at Ottawa. The letter rambles, and is rather mixed in places, but you must realize it was written by a very old man who had been through the Civil War, and whose memory was getting as feeble as his body.

Of the speakers appearance he said,–

"Douglas was a pompous little fellow and a great orator. Lincoln was quite common, dressed in Kentucky jeans clothes."

> Colorodo Springs, Colo., Jan. 23, '15
>
> Mr. J. E. Boos,
>
> Dear Sir:–Just received yours of the 18th, asking for my autograph and anecdotes of Abraham Lincoln, so I have written out the following.
>
> At Ottowa Ills, Judge Douglass and Lincoln were in joint discussion for U. S. Senator. Douglass was a pompous little fellow and a great orator. Lincoln was quite common, dressed in Kentucky jeans clothes. The Judge was to open the debate, and he commenced by reducing Lincoln as common stock; said the first time I saw my opponent was at a little town in this state called Salem/ He was selling Whiskey, and went on at a great rate with his slang. Lincoln gets up, and after viewing the crowd, said; fellow citizens my Opponent, would have you believe that I am of very low character and Classes me as a bar keeper. Now the facts are these. I taught school at Salem at that time and on Saturdays I used to audit the accounts for the merchants, who some times sold Whiskey. One of the merchants said to me Mr. Lincoln I wish you would run my business to-day as I have

2

to go away. Lincoln said he would do what he could for him, so the merchant left early in the day, up steps a pompeous looking man to the counter and said; Whiskey. I fumbled over the different bottles, finally found the whiskey bottle, he filled the tumbler and down she went, he then paced the floor, then came up for another Whiskey, filled her up again, down she went. Now fellow citizens do you know he has never paid for that Whiskey yet. Now which is the worst, he that never paid for it, or I, that never drank the vile stuff. The crowd yelled themselves hoarse and Lincoln was the favorite in the Debate.

While Lincoln was county surveyor at the same place. One day on the road out in the Country, met a stylish Kentucyan with a fine blooded horse who had come over to hunt the Country at that time was full of game. Lincoln had a tough looking nag, he said you have a good horse, Lincoln said he is not good looking but he is a fine hunter. Oh indeed (Lincoln had learned the horse a trick by raising his heel to his flank and pressing gently the horse would stop and squat) as they were going along the the road a Rabbit crossed over, the horse at once squatted, and the man said what is the matter with the horse. There is game here, he is as good as a pointer dog for game. Why the man said, a Rabbit just crossed the road. That accounts for it, the horse must have seen it when he squatted. This made the young man anxious for a trade. How will you trade as I want a hunting horse. If I would trade this horse my wife would broomstick me. This made the young man more anxious, so Lincoln said, you have fancied the horse much. I will stand the broomsticking and will give you an even trade both keep our saddles. So the trade was made at once each one mounted his new horse. As they rode along they came to a swollen stream, Lincoln pushed ahead and crossed over, the young man had lifted his feet to prevent them from getting wet and had touched the horse's flank and the horse squatted and stopped in the middle of the stream, and the young man hollored,

Davis & Lincoln lived then at Springfield Ills.

what is the matter with this horse. Oh, says Lincoln, he is just as good for fish as he is for game.

Wm. M. Morris

All of Lincoln's early career was from 1850 to 1860, when he was Elected President U.S Against Douglas and Breckenridge I am indebted to Judge David Davis who was Lincoln's Law partner, and afterwards U.S. Senator from Illinois. Davis said Lincoln, was most honest man, he never could charge enough for fees, they had a large case with Rail-Roads & they won the case. Davis said Mr Lincoln, let me do the Collecting in this case, so one day Davis came in, and placed $350- on the table Lincoln looked at it, that is for both of us, Davis said no its your, mine is in the Bank, Oh Lincoln said Mr Davis how could you get the heart to charge so much, it is to much. Davis said he had hard work to perswade him not to take part of the money back, Davis said Lincoln was trying a case against a most wilful liar, the fellow said it was pitch dark Lincoln in his argument to the jury pulled out an Almanack and showed to the jury that it was full moon and won the case. Lincoln always looked sad except when he was telling a humorus anacdote or making a pun when his face gleemed with delight yours Wm M Morris

Freeport, Aug. 27th 1858

W.V. LUCAS

Excerpts of the Debate were printed in papers throughout the country, and when the second of the series took place at Freeport on August 27th, there was nationwide interest in the outcome. In the meantime the two men were not idle, they speaking in different places every day, and the crowd around the speaker's platform was even greater and more enthusiastic then at Ottawa. Again processions escorted them through the crowds, and again there was much delay making room for the speakers.

It was at Freeport that Lincoln asked Douglas the following question,–"Can the people of a United States Territory, in any lawful way, against the wish of any citizen of the United States, exclude slavery from its limits, prior to the formation of a State Constitution?"

"Douglas answered 'Yes', and Lincoln's friends left the Debate, knowing with a certainty that their cause was lost. He had been begged not to put the question, but he insisted if Douglas won the election he would surely be defeated for the Presidency two years hence, because nearly every pro-slavery man though different. "To draw an affirmative answer from Douglas on this question was exactly what he wanted, and that his object was to make it impossible for Douglas to get the vote to the Southern States in the next Presidential election. He considered the fight much more important than the present one, and he would be willing to loose this in order to win that."

Douglas' answers at this Debate was the beginning of the split in the Democratic Party, and two years later, the Southern Wing nominated John C. Brackenridge, and the Northern nominated Douglas, thereby making the election of a Republican candidate a certainty.

W.V. Lucas was Captain of Company B, 14th Iowa Infantry from 1862 to 1865, moving after the War to Santa Cruz, California, and when I asked him about his experience with the great War President, he said,–

"I first saw Abraham Lincoln in Henry, Marshall Co., Ill, and heard him make a speech in September, 1856 at that place in company with Hon. W.D. Kellogg who was a candidate for Congress. The next and last time I saw him was at Freeport, Ill., in a joint debate with Hon. Stephen A. Douglas. At this time I shook hands with him. When I first saw him he had no more than a local reputation, and I was impressed by him as a queer looking man before he spoke. After hearing him I thought he was the most remarkable man I had ever seen or heard. I was then twenty years old. I went 120 miles to hear the joint debate, at the conclusion of which I believed Mr. Lincoln to have been inspired and the greatest man I had ever seen or heard, and as the years go by I am confirmed in the opinion I then formed concerning him."

W. T. Lucas
   Santa Cruz Calif.

I was Capt Co "B" 14" Iowa Inft from 1862 to 1865. I saw Abraham Lincoln the first time in Henry, Marsall Co Ill. and heard him make a speech in Sept 1856 at that place in company with Hon W. D. Kellogg who was a Candidate for Congress. The next, and last, time I saw Mr Lincoln was at Freeport Ill. in joint debate with Hon Stephen A. Douglass. At this time I shook hands with him. When I first saw him he had no more than a local reputation and I was impressed by him as a queer looking man before he spoke, after hearing him I thought the most remarkable man I had ever seen or heard. I was then 20 years old.

I went 120 miles to hear the joint debate between him and Judge Douglas, at the conclusion of which I believed Mr Lincoln to have been inspired and the greatest man I had ever seen or heard, and as the years go by I am confirmed in the opinion I then formed concerning him.

Abraham Lincoln belongs to the ages in general and to the United States in particular.

Very Respectfully

W. V. Lucas
Capt Co "B" 14" Iowa Inft.

Jonesboro, Sept. 15th 1858

Captain J.W. King

The third Debate was at Jonesboro on September 15th. The crowd was very small, hardly 1,500 people attending, nearly three railroad carloads coming from Cairo to cheer for Douglas. There was very little cheering, although the crowd gave close attention to every word spoken. The country was strongly Democratic, but anti-Douglas and bitter anti-Republican. Lincoln accused Douglas of repeating false statements about him, and of saying he, Lincoln had to be carried from the platform at the end of the Ottawa speech, ending with, "I don't want to quarrel with him,–to call him a liar,–but when I come square up to him I don't know what else to call him, if I must tell the truth out. I want to be at peace, and reserve all my fighting powers for necessary occasions."

Douglas answered by saying,–"I did say there in a playful manner that when I put these questions to Mr. Lincoln at Ottawa, he failed to answer, and that he trembled, and had to be carried off the stand, and required seven days to get up a reply. That he did not walk off from that stand he will not deny. That when the crowd went away from the stand with me, a few persons carried him home on their shoulders and laid him down, he will admit. I wish to say to you that whenever I degrade my friends and myself by allowing them to carry me on their backs along through the public streets, when I am able to walk, I am willing to be deemed crazy."

Douglas took many unfair thrusts at Lincoln during the campaign, but not in his opponent's presence.

Captain J.W. King was in the crowd that day, and he afterward he said,–"One thing I am proud of, I heard him and Douglas make one of their famous speeches in 1858 at Jonesboro. At that time Union County and almost the entire southern part of the State was filled with Douglas Democrats. Union County was not only Democrat, it was a Rebel Hole. It raised a regiment that was a disgrace to the State. They were dishonorably discharged, though the few loyal members were assigned to the 111th Illinois Volunteers."

General Land office
Washington D.C. Jun 5th
1914

Mr Baas. I willingly send you my signature but am extremely sorry I know so little personally about the great Emancipator Lincoln although he was from my state Ill. One thing I am proud of I heard him and Douglas make one of their famous Speeches in 1858 at Jonesboro Union Co Ill. At that time that Co + almost the entire Southern part of the State was Douglas democrats, Union Co was not only democratic it was a Rebel hole. It raised a Reg't that was a disgrace to the state. They were dishonorably discharged most of them. One Co. was assigned to the 111th Ill. Vol. & a few from other Cos. I think it was the 109 or 110. Ill. I am sending you the envelope your letter came in to show what a round it had to find me. Sincerely Yours, J. W. King

Late Capt. Co. 120th Ill. Inf. Vol.

Charleston, Sept. 18th 1858

GEORGE A.J. COLGAN

The fourth debate took place September 18th at Charleston, Coles County. A great crowd welcomed the speakers, because the contest had become of nationwide interest. Both speakers left the train at Mattoon, ten miles away, that their followers might have a parade moved over the dusty roads with banners flying high, drums beating and the marchers cheering the whole distance. There were floats, one of which contained thirty-two young ladies, representing the States of the Union, each carrying a flag with the name of the commonwealth she sponsored. Behind, a lady on horse-back, waved a flag which read, "Kansas-I will be Free."

The Douglas procession was also large, and had floats, they, too, marching the ten miles through ankle-deep dust. A large crowd lined the main street of Charleston, cheering their respective champions, and when the platform was reached, the addition of the parades made a dense thong, the bands and cheering making a thunderous racket. At last quiet was restored and Lincoln opened the debate by declaring and showing proof that Douglas was one of a group of Senators that introduced a bill in the Senate to pass a constitution for the State of Kansas, and not submit it to a vote of the people.

Douglas, in his answer hotly denied the charge, but would not satisfactorily explain it, ending his flow of oratory by accusing Lincoln of favoring negro equality. "In conclusion let me ask you why should this government be divided by geographical line-arraying all men North in one great hostile party against all men South? Mr. Lincoln tells you, in his speech at Springfield, that a house divided against itself; that this government divided into free and slave states, cannot endure permanently; that they must either be all one thing or all the other. Why cannot this government endure divided into free states and slave states, as our fathers made it?"

Lincoln, in his summing up, answered this charge by saying,–"While I am here perhaps I ought to say a word if I have the time, in regard to the latter portion of the Judge's speech, which was a sort of declamation in reference to my having said I entertained the belief that this government would not endure half slave and half free. I have said so, and I did not say it without what seemed to me to be good reasons. It perhaps would require more time than I have now to set forth these reasons in detail; but let me ask you a few questions. Have we ever had any peace on this slavery question? When are we to have peace upon it if it is kept in the position it now occupies? How are we ever to have peace upon it? That is an important question. To be sure, if we will all stop and allow Judge Douglas and his friends to march on in their present career until they plant the institution all over the nation, here and wherever else our flag waves, and we acquiesce in it, there will be peace. But let me ask Judge Douglas how he is going to get the people to do that? They have been wrangling over this question for at least forty years. This was the cause of the agitation resulting in the Missouri Compromise; this produced the troubles at the annexation of Texas, in the acquisition of this was the trouble which was quieted by the compromise of 1850, when it was settled 'forever', as both the great political parties declared in their national conventions. That 'forever' turned out to be just four years, when Judge Douglas himself opened it."

"When is it likely to come to an end." Lincoln had the best of the argument, and the meeting broke up with his friends well pleased, and Douglas' followers rather crestfallen.

George A.J. Colgan saw Lincoln about that time and he wrote the following story about him sixty-five years later.

"In the month of May, 1858, I ran away from home in the Town of Hillsburgh, Ill., where I was bound out with another boy to a farmer by the name of Willis Simmons, who beat me because he said I had told him a lie. My chum and I lost each other and I never met him afterwards. I went to work on a farm owned by a widow lady named Crest. I stopped there until October and then tramped to the town of Litchfield, where a man by the name of Clark Swift let me do chores at his hotel, which was called the Montgomery House. On the night of October 9th, I think it was, Mr. Lincoln, Stephan Douglas and Senator Trumbull, stopped after they had spoken in town. I had just brought in an armful of wood, and like a boy I was whistling. Mr. Swift, who was talking with Lincoln, said, 'Boston, stop that noise.' Boston was my nickname. Lincoln then said, 'Clark, let the boy enjoy himself.' This incident occurred after one of the famous debates but I have forgotten which one.

"I returned to my home in Boston just before the War started and on the night of April 15th, I enlisted in the 6th Massachusetts. On the 19th, I was knocked out in the streets of Baltimore and was taken to a Washington hospital with the other wounded of the Regiment where I again saw Lincoln when he came to shake hands with the patients."

On October 7th, the political interest of the State was centered on Galesburg, the largest crowd of the series of Debates filling Knox College grounds to hear it. The friends of each candidate tried to out do the other towns in the size of the parades, and though the day was very cold and raw, they stood three hours in a cutting wind, listening with intense interest to every word. It was really a hardship for many, they coming from long distances in open wagons, and they were compelled to return home in the dark over rough roads. It was nearly dark when the debate was over, and so great was the interest in the speakers, they stayed to the end.

Douglas was the first speaker, and nearing the end of his time said, "I tell you that this Chicago doctrine of Lincoln's–declaring that negro and the white man are made equal by the Declaration of Independence and by Divine Providence,–is a monstrous heresy. The signers of the Declaration of Independence never dreamed of the negro when they were writing that document. They referred to white men, to men of European birth and European descent, when they declared the equality of all men. I see a gentleman there in the crowd shaking his head. Let me remind him that when Thomas Jefferson wrote that document he was the owner, and so continued to his death, of a large number of slaves. Did he intend to say in that Declaration that his negro slaves, which he held and treated as property, were created his equals by divine law, and that he was violating the law of God everyday of his life by holding them as slaves? It must be borne in mind when the Declaration was put forth, every one of the thirteen Colonies, and every man who signed that instrument represented a slave-holding constituency. Recollect, also, that no one of them emancipated his slaves, much less put them on an equality with himself, after he signed they signed the Declaration. One the contrary, they all continued to hold their negroes as slaves during the Revolutionary War. Now, do you believe,–are you willing to have it said,–that every man who signed the Declaration of Independence declared the negro his equal, and then was hypocrite enough to continue to hold him as a slave, in violation of what he believed to be the divine law? And yet when you say that the Declaration of Independence includes the negro, you charge the signers of it with hypocrisy."

When Lincoln's turn came, he immediately answered this charge by saying,– "The Judge has alluded to the Declaration of Independence, and insisted that negroes are not included in that Declaration; and that it is a slander upon the framers of that instrument to suppose that negroes were meant therein; and he asks you; 'Is it possible that Mr. Jefferson, who penned the immortal paper, could have supposed applying the language of that instrument to the negro race, and yet held a portion of that race in slavery? Would he not at once freed them?' I have only to remark upon this part of the Judge's speech, that I may believe the entire records of the world, from the date of the Declaration up to within three years ago, may be searched in vain for one single affirmation, from one single man, that the negro was not included in the Declaration of Independence; I think I may defy Judge Douglas to show that he ever said so, that Washington ever said so, that any member of Congress ever said so, or that any living man ever said so, until the necessities of the present policy of the Democratic party in regard to slavery had to invent that affirmation. And I will remind Judge Douglas and the audience that while Mr. Jefferson was the owner of slaves, as undoubtedly he was, in a speaking upon the very subject, he used the strong language that, 'he trembled for his country when he remembered that God was just'; and I will offer the highest premium in my power to Judge Douglas if he will show that he, in all his life, ever uttered a sentiment at all akin to that of Jefferson."

The Republicans were overjoyed at Lincoln's answers, and the way the crowd reasoned to them, his friends were sure he had the best of the argument.

1602 Dor Ave
10/8/25

John E. Boos Esq
My Dear Sir.
You ask me where I first met that Great Man Abraham Lincoln. to my mind the Grandest and best President we ever had. Well in month of May 1858. I ran away from Home and in the Town of Hillsborough Ill. was bound out with another Boy to a Farmer by the name of Willis Simmons. who beat me for he said I told him a Lie, which was falsh. My Chum and I lost Each other, and I never met afterwards. I then went to work on a Farm owned by Widow Lady by the name of Crest. where I stopped till October 1858, I then Tramped to the Town of Litchfield Ill, and kind Man by the name of Clark Swift took me to do Chores at the Hotel which he was the owner. Called the Montgomery House. and on the night of November 9d 1858 I think it was. Mr Lincoln. Stepher Douglass and Senator Trumble, stopped. after they had Spoke waiting for the Train to take them away. the Speaches was about the Senator's fight. I had just brought in an Arm full of wood. and like I was a Boy I was whistling when Mr Clark Swift to was talking with Mr Lincoln said to me Boston stop that noise. Boston was they used to call me, and as near as I can remember this late day, Mr Lincoln said Clark let the Boy enjoy himself I was called and Mr Lincoln asked I came out there he just said to me be a good Boy and mind Mr Swift. that was all, I was only 14 Years. Old then the next Sunday Morning when I was cleaning out the Office

next sheet

about 9 o'clock Mr Swift called to him and said Boston would you like to go to Work in the Rail Road Shops. I told him I would he then gave me a letter and you go over to morrow which was monday give this letter to Mr Seath who was the master Mecanic of the Tere Haut and alton Shops in the Town, I did and was to serve 5 years, in later Part of 1860 I think it I got letter from Boston Stating if I wanted to see my Father befor he didd to come home, I got a Pass for 40 Days, but I did not get back, and on the night of April 15st 1861. I answered President first call, and the 19th of april I got my Knock out in the Streets of Baltimore a High Private in Co K Old 6 th Co K Old 6th Regt of Mass. the first armed Regt to get to President, the next time that I saw that great man he was President, and it was when came with Genl Scott and Maj McDowl to visit the wounded in the Hospital 36 of the Boys, he shook hands with them all, and when he came to me, he said when got well he would send me Home to my Mother, I dont Know what Put it to my Head, I said you did not send me Home from Litchfield Ill. he sat down beside me and what I ment. and told him I was the Boy called Boston. At the Montgomry House, he then Told the major to muster me in while he held my.

That is all Excuse Poor Writing I am now 82 years old. and not very strong,

Respectfully Yours
Geo A, J, Colgan,
High Private Co K Old 6th Mass Regt

Henry S. Scofield

After the Civil War, Henry S. Scofield lived in Troy, N.Y., he having been a private in the 112th Illinois Volunteers. His family were anti-slavery, and he told me one day that "The Party of which I was a member traveled twenty miles in a lumber wagon to hear the speaking. It was in the open, and the crowd was so large, it was impossible for those on the outskirts to hear the speaking."

Galesburg, Oct. 7th 1858

Mrs. Isabella Wright

Mrs. Isabelle Wright said,–"I can still see Honest Old Abe as they used to call him. I was one of the lucky ones present at the City of Galesburg on that day in 1858 to shake hands with that great and noble man, Abraham Lincoln. I was a little girl, born in 1846, and when I stepped up, he said, 'Good luck little girl, and God bless you.'"

Six days later, on October 13th, the battle-ground was at Quincy and another great crowd greeted the opponents. The Republican procession was headed by a live raccoon on a pole, while the Democrats had a dead coon suspended from a pole to head their procession. The rivalry was intense, but no disorderly acts were committed, cat-calls and jeers being the harshest words shouted at the paraders. It was a beautiful day and everybody was in good humor.

It was Lincoln's turn to open the debates and he as given a long cheer, his followers now confident he was sure to be the winner in the contests. A large part of the speech was about the Dred-Scott decision, and in one paragraph he said,– "We oppose the Dred-Scott decision in a certain way, upon which I ought perhaps to address you a few words. We do not propose that when Dred-Scott had been decided to be a slave by the court, we, as a mob, will decide him to be free. We do not propose that, when any other one, or one thousand shall be decided by that court to be slaves, we will be in any violent way disturb the rights of property thus settled; but we nevertheless do oppose that decision as a political rule, which shall be binding on the voter to vote nobody who thinks it wrong, which shall be binding on the Member of Congress or the President to favor no measure that does not actually concur with the principles of that decision. We do not propose to be bound by it as a political rule in that way, because we think it lays the foundation not merely of enlarging and spreading out what we consider an evil but it lays the foundation for spreading that evil into the States themselves. We propose so resisting it as to have it reversed if we can, and a new judicial rule established on this subject."

Plymouth
Ills
Hancock
Co

Dear Sir

Receive Mr Clauns
letter & will try
to state as best I
can as it has ben a
so meney years. But
I can see Him mist
old Abe as they they
yoast to call Him
I was one at the Lockey
ones to Bo Present
at the City of Gailesbog
on the ddy 1857-8. tos Shake
Hands with that Grate
& noble man Abraham
Lincoun the Futhear of
our Conlry & the Brave
I yurst to Hear aften

as I hade a persole in the war that Are Lincan & I Rember when I Stept up & takes his good Luck & Prosperdy. Smiling God Bless you. I was a little Girl as I was Boreed in the yeare of 1846 But I was Geone a lang time before I was & you mite think — I am olde now but I dont etend to git old gad helping me I mae a Pore pen I am sory as I would of liked to shore in Betor I have a brother Lafs with the Story so why osen him I hop you will be able to read this with the best wishes pleased to hear from you Mrs Isabelle, Mrs Isabelle

Dr. Homer Mead

Before Lincoln could be seated, Douglas strode to the edge of the platform and commenced to storm back at him over the decision. In one of his statements he said,–"He tells you that he does not like the Dred Scott decision. Suppose he does not, how is he going to help himself? He says that he will reverse it? I know of but one way of reversing judicial decisions, and that is by appealing from the inferior to the superior court. But I have never yet learned how or where an appeal could be taken from the Supreme Court pronounced by the highest tribunal on earth. From that decision there is no appeal this side of heaven. Yet Mr. Lincoln says he is going to reverse the decision. By what tribunal will be reverse it? Will he appeal to a mob? Does he intend to appeal to violence, to lynch-law? Will he stir up strife and rebellion in the Land, and overthrow the court by violence? He does not deign to tell you how he will reverse the Dred Scott decision, but keeps appealing each day from the Supreme Court of the United States to political meetings in the country. He wants me to argue with you the merits of each point of that decision before this political meeting. I say to you, with all due respect, that I choose to abide by the decisions of the Supreme Court as they are pronounced. It is not for me to inquire after a decision is made, whether I like it in all the points or not."

Dr. Homer Mead of Augusta, stood in the crowd, and he afterward wrote,–"At eleven years of age, holding my father's hand, I stood amid the throng where the large boulder in the park marks the spot of the famous Debate between Lincoln and Douglas at Quincy, Illinois, in the Fall of 1858, and there I saw the immortal Abraham Lincoln."

At eleven years of age, holding my father's hand, I stood amid the throng where the large boulder in the park marks the spot of the famous debate between Lincoln and Douglas at Quincy Illinois, in the fall of 1858, and there I saw the immortal Abraham Lincoln.

Although but a youth, I succeeded in Aug 1863, in getting accepted in Co K 8th Iowa Cav. Our regiment brought on the first battle of Sherman one hundred consecutive days fighting at Varnell Station, we remained with him, until the confederates evacuated Atlanta then opposed Hood's crossing of the Tennessee river at Muscle Shoals, fought in the bloody battle of Franklin Tenn. and with General Thomas at Nashville Tenn. — And on General Wilson Alabama raid, was the "Lost Brigade" and roamed alone all over what was left of the southern Confederacy, and was at Macon Ga and participated in the night hunt when Jeff Davis was captured.

   Homer Mead M D
    Augusta, Illinois
K Co 8th Iowa Cav.

Quincy, Oct. 13th 1858

Edward Jonas

The family of Edward Jonas were very close friends of Lincoln. Writing of his life he said,– "I was a private at first in the 50th Illinois Infantry, later was aid to Generals Prentice, Hurlburt, and finally to G.M. Dodge, commanding 16th Corps, Army of Tennessee. Was Captain and Brevet Lieutenant Colonel with Presidential appointment and have Mr. Lincoln's signature upon my Captain's commission.

"Mr. Lincoln and my father were personal friends. Had served in the legislature and practiced law together. If you have ever seen Carl Schurz's reminiscences you will not as one of the illustrations my father's office in Quincy as Mr. Lincoln's headquarters. My father was this A. Jonas to whom Mr. Lincoln's political letters which Theodore Roosevelt quotes frequently in his speeches were addressed.

"I saw Mr. Lincoln first in my father's home in Quincy during the great Douglas-Lincoln Debates and during the same period, my father, who was taking part in the campaign took me with him to various points where Mr. Lincoln was present. I was only thirteen years old and it was I think either at Augusta or Newcomb, Illinois. While my father was speaking, I, with a boy's curiosity was strolling about the speakers platform on a tour of investigation when I suddenly felt a tickling behind my ear. Thinking it a bug or fly I slapped vigorously, but upon its being repeated several times, I became suspicious and turned suddenly and caught the fly. It was Mr. Lincoln with a straw in his hand. He made it all right at once by catching me with his long arm, drawing me to his side and talking to me very entertainingly until his turn came to address the assemblage.

"The last time I saw Mr. Lincoln was in October, 1862, when I was in Washington with Gen. Prentiss and others on my way home from Southern prisons."

The day after the Quincy Debate, Lincoln, Douglas, and a great many of their friends took the steamer City of Louisiana to Alton, where the last of the series was to take place on the 15th. The day was very pleasant, but the crowd was small, the big parades and excitement of most of the other Debates were lacking, and to those who had gone from town to town, the whole affair seemed very tame.

Rev J. E. Boos

Dear Sir
Yours of Nov 16th rec'd. I am glad to be able to respond. I was a private at first in the 50th Illinois Inf'y; later was Ady - to Generals Prentiss, Haveled & finally to Gen. G. M. Dodge com'g 16th Corps Army of the Tenn., was Capt. & Bvt. Lt. Col. with incidents efforts about Mr Lincoln's inequality when my Captain Commission

Mr Lincoln & my father were personal friends had lived in the Capitals of various law schools. Reminiscences you will note as one of the illustrations my father offers in Quincy at Mr Lincoln's & Douglas in Lacon, my father was this A. Jonas to welcome Mr Lincoln's [?] before which Mr Lincoln greated [?] his speech was addressed.

I saw Mr Lincoln first in my father's home in Lacon during the great Lincoln debates, & during the same period my father who was taking part in the campaign took me with him to various point where Mr Lincoln was present. I was only thirteen years old - I was then either at Augusta & Macomb Illinois while my father was speaking. I with a boy's curiosity was strolling about the speakers platform on a tour of investigation where I suddenly felt a tickling behind my ear. Thinking it a bug, or fly I slapped vigorously but upon it's being repeated several times, I became suspicious & turned suddenly & caught the fly. It was the Presdt. with a straw in his hand, he made it all right at once by entertaining me with his long anecdote inviting me to his side, & telling to eat until his turn came to address the Assemblage.

The last time I saw the Presdt. was in Oct 1862 where I was in Washington with Genl Prentiss & others on our way home from Southern prisons

Very truly
Edward Jonas.
Capt & Bvt Lt. Col & ant
Lieut vols

Alton, Oct. 15th 1858

Admiral G.W. Beaman

Admiral G.W. Beaman was one of the fortunate young men to be in that crowd, and writing of the scene more than sixty-five years afterward, said,–

"I have very vivid remembrances of a pleasant Autumn afternoon, in October, 1858, when I had the pleasure of listening to the Debate at Alton. Enroute Boston to St. Louis, I had stopped over a day at Alton for the sole purpose of listening to this Debate. Through the favor of a friendly newspaper man I had a seat on the platform. When, after some delay, the speakers appeared, I received a shock that for the moment was almost overpowering. The great Lincoln, tall, gaunt, his rugged face exhibiting slight traces of tonsorial care for some time previously, and wearing a long linen duster, which had evidently been on the circuit for a prolonged period, served to increase the wearer's height to seven feet, at least. But what served to impress me were his eyes, which at rest seemed to have a far-away, dreamy, almost sad expression. As from time to time he recognized some old acquaintance among the audience, they lighted up with a most kindly expression. As to speaking of the Debate, history has recorded it well."

Douglas opened, and during his remarks, said,–

"The Abolition Party really think that under the Declaration of Independence the negro is equal to the white man, and that negro equality is an inalienable right conferred by the Almighty, and hence that all human laws in violation of it are null and void. With such men it is no use for me to argue. I hold that the signers of the Declaration of Independence had no reference to negroes at all when they declared all men to be created equal. They did not mean negroes, nor the savage Indians, nor the Feejee Islanders, nor any other barbarous race. They were speaking of white men. They alluded to men of European birth and European decent-to white men and to none others, when they declared that doctrine. I hold that this government was established by white men, for the benefit of white men and their posterity forever, and should be administered by white men and none others. But it does not follow, by any means, that merely because the negro is not a citizen, and merely because he is not our equal, that therefore he should be a slave. On the contrary, it does follow that we ought to extend to the negro race, and to all other dependent races, all the rights, all the privileges, and all the immunities which they can exercise consistently with the safety of society. Humanity requires that we should give them all those privileges; Christianity commands that we should extend those privileges to them. The question then arises. What are those privileges, and what is the nature and extent of them? My answer is that is a question each State must answer for itself."

Douglas had been using a like argument in most of the Debates, and, Lincoln, rather ruffled in temper when he arose said in answer,–"At Galesburg the other day,

I said in answer to Judge Douglas, that three years ago there never had been a man, so far as I knew or believed, in the whole world, who had said that the Declaration of Independence did not include negroes in the term 'all men.' I reassert it to-day. I assert that Judge Douglas and all his friends may search the whole records of the country, and it will be a matter of great astonishment to me if they shall be able to find that one human being three years ago had ever uttered the astounding sentiment that the term 'all men' in the Declaration did not include the negro. Do not let me be misunderstood. I know that more than three years ago there were men who, finding this assertion constantly in the way of their schemes to bring about the ascendancy and perpetuation of slavery, denied the truth of it. I know that Mr. Calhoun, and all the politicians of his school denied the truth of the Declaration. I know that it ran along in the mouths of some Southern men for a period of years, ending at last in that shameful though rather forcible declarations of Pettit of Indiana, upon the floor of the United States Senate, that the Declaration of Independence was that respect 'a self evident lie,' rather than a self-evident truth. But I say, with a perfect knowledge of all this hawking at the Declaration without directly attacking it, that three years ago there had never lived a man who had ventured to assail it in the sneaking way of pretending to believe it and then asserting it did not include the negro. I believe the first man who ever said it was Chief Justice Taney in the Dred Scott case and next to him was our friend Stephan A. Douglas. And now it has become the catchword of the entire party. I would like to call upon his friends everywhere to consider how they have come in so short a time to view this matter in a way so entirely different from their former belief; to ask whether they are not being borne along by an irresistible current-whither they know not."

The debates were ended. Many of the Democrats believed Lincoln had bested his opponent, but when the ballots were counted, there were fifty-four Democrats and forty-six Republicans who would vote when the House of Representatives and the State Senate came together in joint session to elect a United States Senator, and when the roll was called, Douglas was re-elected, and Lincoln had won nation wide notice.

One writer said everybody but Lincoln was worn out when the last Debate closed. Douglas' voice became so husky he could hardly be heard, but Lincoln's was as fresh and strong as it was at the start.

J. E. Boos,

    Dear Sir:

        In response to your enquiry I may say that it is somewhat singular, (for during the Civil War I was quite frequently in Washington,) I never saw President Lincoln. I have however, a very vivid remembrance of a pleasant Autumnal afternoon, in October, 1858, when I had the pleasure of listening to the joint debate between Lincoln and Douglass, at Alton, Illinois. These debates were extended to all parts of the State, and as is well known, did much to call the attention of the country to Mr. Lincoln's great ability as a public speaker. The fact that his antagonist was Senator Douglass, the author of the bill repealing the Missouri Compromise and perhaps its most powerful advocate, served to excite great interest in the canvas for the Illinois Senatorship throughout the entire country, north and south.

    En route from Boston to St. Louis, I had stopped over a day at Alton for the sole purpose of listen-

ing to this debate. It was my first visit to the
West. For a young man I was quite familiar with the
public speakers of New England and New York, with the
result that, not unnaturally, I had looked forward
to seeing men more or less of the eastern type, come
forward on that rude platform. The characteristics
of a typical western audience might have sufficed to
advise me to the contrary before the speakers appeared,
but it had not. I looked for men of the type of
Wendell Phillips, Charles Sumner, Geo. W. Curtis,
Edward Everett, clad in the conventional broadcloth
of their day. Through the favor of a friendly newspaper
man I had a seat on the speakers' platform.
When, after some little delay, the two speakers
appeared, young Boston received a shock that for the
moment was almost overpowering. The great Lincoln,
tall, gaunt, his rugged face exhibiting slight
traces of tonsorial care for some time previously,
and wearing a long linen duster, which had evidently
been on the circuit for a prolonged period, served

is now a matter of history. The discussions in this canvass were all, I think, quite fully reported and are available in good libraries.

Cambridge, Mass., Feb. 12, 1915.

Dear Sir:

Having been a little bit under the weather I have not until now got around to a response to your note of the 30th ult.

I do not precisely understand what you are going to do with this autograph collection, but the evident pains you are taking in the matter of binding etc., has induced me to re-read my manuscript to see if I had not done something worse than to intrench on the margins! I find an clumsy sentence toward the end of the last page which I have modified somewhat, and if it does not give you too much bother I should be glad to have corrected.

Very truly etc.

Mr. J. E. Boos

WILLIAM H. HEATH

William H. Heath was a first Lieutenant in the 18th Illinois Volunteers, and was mustered out at the end of the war as Lieutenant-Colonel of the 33rd Missouri Volunteers. Writing of the Debate, he said, "I saw Lincoln but once. It was at his closing Debate with Senator Douglas at Alton, Illinois. I was then a boy of eighteen. An old gentleman who stood beside me at the foot of the platform from which the addresses were delivered, he made a remark at the close of the Debate that I never forgot. He said, 'they call Douglas 'the Little Giant', I wonder what they will call the other fellow?'"

William L. Heath

Private 3rd U. S. Reserve Corps of Missouri.
1st Lieut Co J. 18th Ills Inf.
Aide & Acting Commissary Genl McClernand's Staff.
Acting Commissary on Staff of Genl U. S. Grant.
Adjutant 18th Ills Infy,
Major 33d. Missouri Infy
Lt Col 33d " "
Brevet Col. Volunteers.

I saw Mr Abraham Lincoln but once. It was at his closing debates with Senator Stephen A. Douglas. at Alton Ills, in the fall of 1858, nearly three years before our Civil war. I was then a boy of 18. An old gentleman, who stood beside me, at the foot of the platform from which the addresses were delivered, made a remark at the close of the debate that I never forgot. He said: "They call Douglas the little Giant, I wonder what they will call the other fellow?"

Part Two: Speeches and Debates

Lewiston

J.M. Graham

Of all the great Debates in American history the outstanding one is the series which took place between Abraham Lincoln and Stephan A. Douglas in the Summer and Fall of 1858. Before they ended the whole nation was interested, and as time passed, more and more people read them, and they are still interesting and widely read. The dates and places for the seven Debates were picked up by Douglas on July 30th, the first to be at Ottawa on August 21st. In the meantime both leaders spoke in different towns, and on August 17th, Lincoln spoke at Lewiston, and in the course of his speech said,–

"Now, my countrymen, if you have been taught doctrines conflicting with the great landmarks of the Declaration of Independence; if you have listened to suggestions which would take away from its grandeur and mutilate the fair symmetry of its proportions; if you have been inclined to believe that all men are not created equal in those inalienable rights enumerated by our chart of liberty, let me entreat you to come back.

"Return to the fountain whose waters spring close by the blood of the Revolution. Think nothing of me-take no thought for the political fate of any man whomsoever,–but come back to the truths that are in the Declaration of Independence. You may do anything with me you choose, if you will but heed these sacred principles. You may not only defeat me for the Senate, but you may take me and put me to death. While pretending no indifference to earthly honors, I do claim to be actuated in this contest by something higher than an anxiety for office. I charge you to drop every paltry and insignificant thought for any man's success. It is nothing; I am nothing; Judge Douglas is nothing. But do not destroy the immortal emblem of humanity-the Declaration of Independence."

It was a warm day, and a large crowd stood around the platform to hear the address. They listened to every word and cheered the speech at every telling point. It was only four days before the first of the Debates the people of Illinois were so anxious to hear and to read about, and the excitement was very intense. The Lincoln partisans cheered him at every mass meeting, while Douglas' friends were doing the same when he spoke, each side sure its champion would win the contest for the Senatorship.

J.M. Graham stood in the crowd, and though but a boy, he was an enthusiastic follower of the Republican candidate. Three years later, when the Debater he had cheered so lustily for, called for 75,000 volunteers to defend the Union, he immediately enlisted, his papers showing the date of April, 1861. The young soldier became a member of the band of the 17th Illinois Volunteers.

Speaking of that day at Lewiston, he said,–

"I was a member of the band , and we met Lincoln at the edge of the town, where I shook hands with him, and we led the procession to the stand. We roused the crowd with our music and I stood close to the platform through the whole speech. I again met him in the evening at a reception where he mingled with those present, talking and joking with everybody. I again heard him at Peoria, and as I am in my 87th year, I believe I am the only person living who heard him speak at both places."

Mr. Graham wrote these words in Berkeley, California in 1928 and no doubt he was the last of many that heard the great leader speak in those towns.

Mr. John E. Boos
  Albany
      N.Y.

Dear Sir —
   Replying to your request —
         Joseph M. Graham
Musician in Regimental Band, 17th reg't Illinois Vol. Infantry.
   Enlisted Apr. 1861 at Pres't Lincolns first call for 75000 volunteers.
   First met Abraham Lincoln Aug. 10" 1858 at Lewistown Ills — during Lincoln Douglas campaign.
   I was a member of a band

and met him at the edge of town where he shook hands with all of us.

Heard his address to the assemblage, also met him at the evening reception where we got a closer view of him.

Heard him again at the joint debate at Peoria. There are not many left now who heard those debates.

Sincerely
J. M. Graham
In 87th year.

Berkeley
Calif.
2510 College Ave.

A Debate Witness

T.G. Martin

T.G. Martin was fifteen years old when he heard some of the Debates, he having been born in Illinois in 1843.

"I distinctly remember the great discussion between Lincoln and Douglas; my parents being anti-slavery people I was a Republican rooter, and helped cheer Uncle Abe, booing and jeering at Douglas every time the crowd did, when he made an unpopular statement.

"I enlisted in the war on July 25, 1861, and was not mustered out until July 24th, 1865; never wounded and never sick, having served as Sergeant of Co. Ho., 40th Illinois Volunteers."

This letter was written in Salem, Illinois, when Mr. Martin was 74 years old.

Salem Ills Feb 26th 1917

J. E. Boos
  Albany N.Y.
    Dear Sir
       I Was raised in Illinois
And remember distinctly the
the great discussion between
Abraham Lincoln and Stephen
A Douglas,
       I have also visited his
birth place near Hodgenville Ky.
and the Tomb of his Mother
at Lincoln City Ind,
I also Served 4 years as a Soldier
under the Grand old man,
from July 25th 1861 to July 24th 1865 —
am now 74 years old,
       Yours Truly

         T. G. Martin Sergant
       Co. H. 40th Illinois

Samuel E. Morison

One day long ago I received a letter from Samuel E. Morison, the author, who described the scene of the first Debates, and I think it one of the finest descriptions I have ever read. Mr. Morison was born in Boston, Mass., July 9, 1887, so that he had to take his story from the writing of those who took part in, or heard the Debates, connecting the scanty stories to make a vivid whole. He received an A.B. Degree from Harvard in 1908, an A.M. from Oxford University in 1922, was professor of history at Harvard from 1915 to 1935; went to England a part of the years 1922 to 1935 to lecture at Oxford on history, joined the army in 1918 as a private in the World War, and in 1919 was attached to the Russian Division of the American Commission to negotiate Peace at Paris. He has written a number of books, and he was too cussed mean, or modest, to put more than his initials under the letter he sent me in 1935.

> Dickens had only visited Illinois in the summer of 1858! How he would have roared with laughter at the sight of the two champions--the frenzied gestures of Douglas, and Lincoln's awkward habit of bending his knees and then rising to his full height with a jerk, in order to enforce a point-- and how he would have listened to them in the end. For no recorded debate in the English language surpassed those between Lincoln and Douglas for keen give and take, vigorous Saxon language, and clear exposition of vital issues.
>
> S. E. Morison.

Darn his buttons!

E.H. Straight

It was a warm summer day, the 21st of August, 1858, and the public square was jammed with people,–partisans, I should say,–to hear the opening speeches of a series of debates, which became more widely read than the famous contest between Webster and Haynes on the floor of the United States Senate twenty-eight years before. Stump-speaking, they called it in those days, but before the seven debates ended, the whole nation was anxious to read what the speakers had said.

The Debates made the slavery question become an even more vital issue than it had been, and the leading thinkers realized it would have to be settled in a decade, either by a stricter enforcement of the fugitive slave laws, by secession, or by war.

When the series ended, it was agreed Lincoln had the better of the argument, but Douglas gained a majority of the seats in the legislature, and he was returned to the United States Senate. When the excitement had passed, the voters began to study those addresses, and two years later, when Lincoln and Douglas again appeared before the people, as candidates for the highest office in the land, the principles of many had changed, and The Little Giant stayed in the Senate, while Honest Abe went to the White House.

The band was still playing, and Douglas moved to the front of the platform amid the cheers of his friends,–and the cheers were thunderous. He waited for quiet; then in a clear, strong voice, the tone of which had impressed and won over many audience said,–"I appear before you today for the purpose of discussing the leading political topics which now agitate the public mind. By an arrangement between Mr. Lincoln and myself, we are present here today for the purpose of having a joint discussion, as the representatives of two great political parties of the State and Union, upon the principles in issue between those parties; and this vast concourse of people shows the deep feeling which pervades the public mind in regard to the questions dividing us."

He spoke in this manner for an hour, often interrupted by the applause of his friends, and then the sweating orator stepped back to allow his opponent to reply. The tall, slim, dark man stood at the very edge of the platform patiently waiting for his friends to stop their cheering, and then in a quiet voice, though clear and distinct, began his answer, which took an hour and a half, the vast throng listening intently to every word. I like to read passages of that address, and I wonder how Douglas and his partisans felt while they listened to the speech that put him and the whole Democratic Party on the defensive and which sent a wave of bitter resentment through the Slave States.

A seventeen year old boy stood in that crowd with his father, and they cheered the second speaker with the strength of their lungs. The boy was E.H. Straight, and just three years later, at the age of twenty, he put on a blue uniform to fight for the Union that Abraham Lincoln wanted to make safe for every man, regardless of color or creed.

He still lived near the scene of that first debate in Ottawa, Ill., in 1928, and writing of his early days he said,–"I was born in the township of Hume, Alleghany Co., N.Y., April 15, 1841 and came out West to La Salle County, Illinois, April 14, 1857, and worked on a farm by the month for thirteen dollars a month, until I enlisted in the Township of Northville, August 7, 1861, in company F, 36th Illinois Infantry. I was discharged from the army October 19, 1865. I was wounded five times, twice reported mortally wounded. My wounds have bothered me all these years.

"As to seeing Abraham Lincoln-I saw him at Ottawa, Ill., on August 21, 1858, at his and Senator Douglas's first speech making tour of the state. This was the only time I ever saw him as my regiment was always in the Western army and had no opportunity to meet him."

Mr. John E. Boos,
Albany, N.Y.

My Dear Sir;— I was born in the township of Hume, Alleghany County, New York, April 18, 1841, and came out west to La Salle Co. Illinois, April 14, 1857, and worked on a farm by the month, for thirteen dollars per month, until I enlisted in the township of Northville, La Salle County, Aug 7, 1861, in Company F, 36th, Illinois Infantry. I was discharged from the army October 19, 1865. I was wounded five times, twice reported mortally wounded. My wounds have bothered me all these years.

As to seeing Abraham Lincoln — I saw him at Ottawa, Ill. on Aug. 21, 1858 at his and Senator Douglas's first speech making tour of the state. This was the only time I ever saw him as my regiment was always in the western army and had no opportunity to meet him.

Very truly yours,
E. H. Strait

Then Lincoln went to Freeport

JAMES A. CARTWRIGHT

The two masters of oratory had fought a verbal battle before a great crowd at Ottawa, and six days later, on August 27th, they again prepared to face an even larger assemblage then had met them the Saturday before, and it was here at Freeport that Lincoln put Douglas on the defensive and made a permanent dent in his nationwide popularity. Lincoln's answer on that occasion has ever since been quoted, and is known as the Great Freeport Speech.

When the mass of people became quiet enough so that he could proceed, he being the first speaker, he began by saying, "On Saturday last, Judge Douglas and myself first met in public discussion," and then spoke on for an hour and a half, when the Judge had his turn of an hour, and Lincoln ended the debate of the day with a half-hour.

One of those who cheered Lincoln on was a 16 year old boy who came to Freeport that day to help the Republican cause. He was James H. Cartwright, who was born at Maquoketa, Iowa on December 1, 1842, and was then attending Rock River Seminary Free Soldier, and when graduated in 1862, he enlisted as a private in the 69th Illinois Volunteers, and two years later became a Captain in the 140th Illinois Infantry.

After the war the young man, now 25, returned to college and was given an LL.B. by the University of Michigan in 1867. He immediately opened a law office at Oregon, Illinois where he spent the rest of his life.

In 1888 the Captain became Judge of the 13th Judicial Circuit, and in 1891 was promoted to the Appellate Court, going from there to the Supreme Court, where he stayed almost to the time of his death. He was Chief Justice six different years, and was one of the outstanding legal minds of Lincoln's great State. He was very proud of his acquaintance with the great War President, and could tell many stories about him.

> James H. Cartwright
> 1862 Private 69th Ill. Inf
> 1864 Captain 140th Ill. Inf.
> Heard Lincoln – Douglas
> debate at Freeport, Illinois
> in 1858 –

The Speech at Clinton

Isaac H. Crim

The Freeport Debate was ended and the people were anxiously waiting for the two great speakers to meet again. In the interval, Lincoln spoke before a large crowd at Clinton. It was there he first uttered that famous expression, "You can fool all of the people some of time, and some of the people all the time, but you cannot fool all of the people all of the time."

The next day the Bloomington Pantograph said, "How any reasonable man can hear one of Mr. Lincoln's speeches without being converted to Republicanism is something we can't account for."

Isaac H. Crim, talking of the speech many years after had vivid remembrances of the excitement that day, and of how Lincoln impressed the crowd, a large majority of which lustily cheered him before he finished. They almost crushed him when they rushed forward to shake his hand when he stepped from the platform, many in the crowd knowing him well. The old soldier who had fought in the 141st Indiana Volunteers thought the date was in October, but the event took place on September 8th, about a week-and-a-half before the next debate at Jonesboro.

Mr. Crim met the President many times while in the army, and like all the old soldiers almost revered him.

Lincoln was against slavery, and he believed the slaveholders should loose their human property, but be paid for it by the government when it was freed. In 1862 the South was offered compensation for their chattels, but they refused to accept the offer and it has been howling about property rights ever since, never forgiving the negro because he had been given his freedom.

An article called the Mob Still Rides was printed in the World Film News in 1938, a paragraph telling how the South is still feeling towards the blacks.

"There are even more spectacular variations. One very good lynching, a year or two back, took the form of burning a schoolhouse, with the Negro chained to the roof. It was in the schoolhouse that he committed the crime, so the execution was not without poetic quality.

"Of course he was guilty. Every person lynched is guilty. He may, of course, be innocent of the crime he is accused of, but if so, he is guilty of something else. If he is a Negro, there is no need to split hairs, because the nature of the Negro is such that if he did not commit the crime, he nearly did, or at least might have, and in any case he was just about to commit another crime which was even worse. It all doubtful cases, the execution settles the matter for good and all; because when once the man is dead, the great principles can be quoted that he must have been guilty or he would not have been lynched."

I saw and heard Mr. Lincoln speak at Clinton, Ill., after his debate with Mr. Douglas in 1858. This was in October, but I do not remember the date. I again saw him at Harrisons Landing. I think it was in early part of August, 1862, when he came to visit Gen. McClellen and army while they were camped there.

I saw him many times in Washington during the Winter of 1862-3, while I was in the hospital after the battle of Antietam.

Mr. Lincoln visited our ward in the Patent Office building, speaking kind and encouraging words to the wounded. I saw him best on these occasions. When we were able we were permitted to go out in the city. We often went to LaFayette Park and watched for him to come out for his horse back ride. We saw him in this way quite often.

You may like to know I was a member of Co. C 141st Indiana Volunteers.

Isaac H Crim
M 13. 14 S—g
Bedford Ind

The Fifteenth of September, 1858

Jonesboro

GEN. A.A. HARBECK

Nearly three weeks had passed since the candidates met at Freeport, and the bands were again playing, two big parades were marching toward the stand at Jonesboro, and the great crowd was cheering, many for the Little Giant, and as many for the Railsplitter.

Douglas stepped to the front amid the tremendous cheers of his friends, it being minutes before he could start the third session of what would go down in history as the most famous series to take place in the Union.

He spoke a few sentences, almost unheard by the crowd, and then said, "Prior to 1854 this country was divided into two great parties known as the Whig and Democratic. These parties differed from each other on certain questions which were then deemed important to the best interests of the republic. Whigs and Democrats differed about a bank, the tariff, distribution, the specie circular, and the sub-treasury. On those issues we went before the country, and discussed the principles, objects, and measures of the two great parties. Each of the parties could proclaim its principles in Louisiana as well as in Massachusetts, in Kentucky as in Illinois. Since that period, a great revolution has taken place in the formation of parties, by which they now seem to be divided by a geographical line, a large party in the North being arrayed under the Abolition or Republican banner, in hostility to the Southern States, Southern people, and Southern institutions."

He went on in this way for an hour-and-a-half, and then Lincoln, cheered by his friends took Douglas' place, speaking for an hour, after which Douglas again spoke, this time for thirty minutes, and the debate of the day was ended.

Ending, Lincoln, said, his eyes aflame, and his frame quivering,–"The Judge has set about seriously trying to make the impression that when we meet at different places, I am literally in his clutches-that I am poor, helpless, decrepit mouse, and that I can do nothing at all. This is one of the ways he has taken to create that impression. I don't know any other way to meet it, except this. I don't want to quarrel with him,–to call him a liar,–but when I come square up to him I don't know what else to call him, if I must tell the truth out. I want to be at peace, and reserve all my fighting powers for necessary occasions. My time now, is very nearly out, and I give up the trifle that is left to the judge to let him set my knees trembling again-if he can."

"I was only a boy," wrote Gen. A.A. Harbeck, nearly sixty years later after the speech; "but I can recollect the smile that went around in the audience when the graceful figure of Mr. Douglas withdrew and the gaunt figure of Mr. Lincoln stepped to the front."

The General was born in Pennsylvania on August 14, 1841, moved to Illinois when a small boy, and when the war started he enlisted as a private in the 11th U.S. Infantry on May 7th, 1861. On June 11, 1862 he became a 2nd Lieutenant in the regiment and during the battle of Gettysburg, on July 2nd, 1863, became a 1st Lieutenant, serving with the regiment until he was transferred to the 20th United States Infantry on September 21, 1866. He fought in the Santiago campaign in Cuba in 1898, having slowly advanced to Lieutenant-Colonel, reaching the rank of Colonel on July 19, 1899. In March, 1902 he became Brigadier-General, and was retired on May 28th.

In 1927, the General was living in Santa Barbara, California.

John E. Boos,
Albany,
New York.

To Lexington Av

SANTA BARBARA CALIF
SEP 12 7-PM 1921

AFTER 5 DAYS, RETURN TO
C. C. [illegible]
1153 [illegible] Av
SANTA BARBARA, CALIFORNIA

I will try and give you what I recollect of personally seeing and hearing Abraham Lincoln in his debate with Stephen A. Douglas. I was only a boy, but I can recollect the smile that went around in the audience when the graceful figure of Mr. Douglas withdrew, and the gaunt figure of Mr. Lincoln stepped to the front. A smile that soon disappeared, and even I, as a boy, listened to what he had to say.

I next saw Mr. Lincoln as President, when he reviewed some troops in Washington, to which I belonged. I was on mustering duty at Harrisburg, Pa. when the news was received of his assassination, and was one of several officers to stand guard while the remains lay at the Capitol.

That Third Debate, Jonesboro

WILLIAM L. ROBINSON

It was more than two weeks after the debate at Freeport that the contestants met at Jonesboro. The date was September 15th, and it was Douglas' turn to speak first. Of the newly organized Republican Party, he said; "In 1854, certain restless, ambitious, and disappointed politicians throughout the land took advantage of the temporary excitement created by the Nebraska bill to try and dissolve the old Whig party and the Old Democratic party, to abolitionize their members, and lead them, bound hand and foot, captives into the abolition camp."

The Judge's Democratic friends cheered him to an echo, and Lincoln, when it was his turn to speak answered the statement by saying,–"I recollect in the presidential election of 1852, when we had Gen. Scott up for the presidency, Judge Douglas was around berating us Whigs as abolitionists, precisely as he does today-not a bit of difference. I have often heard him. We could do nothing when the Old Whig party was alive that was not abolitionism, but it has got an entirely good name since it has passed away."

I heard of an old soldier living in East Glouster, Mass., in 1929, and I wrote to him, asking if he had seen the great debater, and although he was nearly blind, he kindly answered but instead of him hearing the 3rd debate, he intently listened to the last one. His name was William L. Robinson, and he wrote,–"I am 91 years, sick and nearly blind. I first saw Abraham Lincoln at Alton when he and Stephen A. Douglas had their debate, which if I remember right was in the month of October, 1858. I enlisted at Springfield August 11, 1862 in Co. G, 7th Illinois Infantry and served three years lacking one month. I had a brother, John S. Robinson who was wounded in the battle of Allatoona Pass. A large minie ball had passed through his body and he died in the hospital at Chattanooga three months later. I had a twenty day furlough and went home and had him decently buried."

E. Gloucester Feb 14th 1929

John E. Boos

  Dear Sir,

I received your letter some time ago but on account of my age which is over 91 yrs and sick and nearly blind have neglected to answer before which I am very sorry. My wife is not well or she would have written to you before I hope it is not too late to send this. If it is not too late if you will let us know we will try and send more but will send a little now.

I first saw Abraham Lincoln at Alton

Illinoisville and Stephen and Douglas had their debate which I think of I remember right was in the month of Oct - 1858. I enlisted at Springfield Ill Aug 11th 1862 Co. G. 7th Ill. Infantry and served three (3) years packing on month. I had a brother - John O. Roteure who was wounded in the battle of Allatoona Pass. A large minnie ball passed through his body and he lived three (3) months. Died in the hospital at Chattanooga. I had a brother, day Pinsburgh and sent home and had him decently buried. I then went back to my regiment. I was in the Battle of Corinth

Oct 3 & 4 1862 had several close calls but escaped without a scratch. After the Battle of Corinth our regiment was mounted and served as mounted Infantry. I served as mounted Infantry, I served that of my time in the ranks of my company and also served as Fidelity Regimental Post Master. Hospital nurse... If you would like any further information of you will let me know I will gladly send to you. Please excuse all mistakes and also for the delay in not answering your letter. My younger Brother Daniel I Roteure enlisted near the close of the war.

Yours truly,
William L. Robinson
His Wife,
Mrs William L. Robinson

Mr Robinson is nearly blind and cannot see to read or write and does not know any one that comes to the house to see him. Please let me know if you would like any more. I hope this is not too late for you.

Madison Wisconsin

Arthur Gleason

Mr. Arthur Gleason was living in Los Angeles, California in 1927, he having served nearly three years in the army and was then a member of Stanton Post of the G.A.R. He heard Lincoln speak when he was a small boy in his home town, Madison, Wisconsin. I wondered why the debaters would be in that state, unless it was to help their friends who were running for office.

In the debate at Charleston, on September 18th, Lincoln said in his opening speech, "When Judge Trumbull returned to Illinois in the month of August, he made a speech at Chicago, in which he made what may be called a charge against Judge Douglas, which I understand to be very offensive to him. The judge was at that time out upon one of his speaking tours through the country, and when the news of it reached him, as I am informed, he denounced Judge Trumbull in rather harsh terms for having said what he did in regard to that matter. I was traveling at that time, and speaking at the same places with Judge Douglas on subsequent days."

From Lincoln's own statement he had been traveling and speaking with Douglas between debates and he no doubt went to Wisconsin to oppose Democratic speakers to help the Republican candidates running for office in that district.

"I am now in my 85th year, enlisted August 15, 1862 at Mineral Point, in Wisconsin, was a sergeant in Company B, 30th Wisconsin Volunteer Infantry. I saw Abraham Lincoln when I was living with my parents in Madison Wis. He was with Stephen A. Douglas on the speaking tour in 1858, they both were, I believe, candidates for the United States Senate. I heard Lincoln make his speech, and I have always, since my army experience, entertained a very high admiration of him. He was a wonderful character."

Los Angeles, California
May 23ᵈ 1927

Jno E. Boos Esq
    Albany N.Y.

Dear Sir:
Complying with yours of 6th will say: I am now in my 85th year, a native of Wisconsin. Enlisted Aug 15/62 at Mineral Pt Wis, was a seargent Co B. 30th Wis Vol Infty. served 34 mos.
  I saw Abraham Lincoln when I was living with my parents in Madison Wis. He was with Stephen A. Douglas on a speaking tour in 1858. They both were, I believe, candidates for U.S. Senate. I heard Lincoln make his speech, and I have always, since my army experience, entertained a very high admiration for him. He was a wonderful character.
  I thank you!

        Very Truly Yours
        Arthur Gleason

Charleston

S. W. FORDYCE

There had been three debates and Lincoln was conceded by nearly every student of the contest to be getting the best of the argument. Interest was increasing and when they met at Charleston on September 18th it had become more than a canvass for a Senatorship, it had become a nationwide course of lectures on political questions of much importance to the whole people.

A large crowd had gathered to hear the speakers, among them a member of correspondence of the leading papers. Douglas opened the second half of the debate by saying, "I had supposed that we assembled here today for the purpose of a joint discussion between Mr. Lincoln and myself, upon the political questions which now agitate the whole country. The rule of such discussion is, that the opening speaker shall touch upon all the points he intends to discuss, in order that his opponent, in reply, shall have the opportunity of answering them. Let me ask you what questions of public policy, relating to the welfare of this State or of the Union, has Mr. Lincoln discussed before you? Mr. Lincoln simply contended himself at the outset by saying, that he was not in favor of social or political equality between the white man and negro, and did not desire the law so changed as to make the latter voters or eligible for office. I am glad that I have at last succeeded in getting an answer out of him upon this subject of negro-citizenship and eligibility to office, for I have been trying to bring him to the point on it ever since this canvass commenced."

S.W. Fordyce was in the crowd. He afterward became an officer in the First Ohio Cavalry in the Army of Cumberland. Mr. Fordyce afterward said,–"During the years 1858, 1859 and until after Mr. Lincoln was nominated for the Presidency at Chicago in 1860, I attended school at Henry, Illinois. Was present at several of the joint debates between Mr. Lincoln and Judge Douglas in the contest for the United States Senate. Met and shook hands with Mr. Lincoln several times, and fell quite in love with him. He impressed me as one of the great men of the nation."

"And", said Mr. Fordyce; "Lincoln very pointedly answered that question of Douglas by saying, 'Judge Douglas has said to you that he was not been able to get from me an answer to the question whether I am in favor of negro citizenship. So far as I know, the Judge never asked me the question before. He shall have occasion to ever ask it again, for I tell him very frankly that I am not in favor of negro citizenship.'"

No doubt this soldier was a very young man when the debates took place and was much impressed by the speakers, more so by Lincoln than by Douglas, because he was in favor of the anti-slavery side and he may not have wanted to give the black man a vote, but he did want him to be free, and he proved his principles by putting on a blue uniform when the war commenced.

Mr. J. E. Boos,

    20 Dudley Heights,

        Albany, N.Y.

My dear Sir:

    Your polite note of the 11th inst. has been received and I am trying to comply with your request. I have made it as short as possible, thinking that this was what you desired.

    When your book is completed, if it is your desire to print other copies I would like very much to be advised, as I would gladly pay the price to get it. Please be kind enough to advise if and when the volume will be ready for sale and delivery.

                            Very truly yours,

    During the years 1858, 1859 and until after Mr. Lincoln was nominated for the Presidency at Chicago in 1860, I attended school at Henry, Illinois. Was present at several of the joint debates between Mr. Lincoln and Judge Douglas in their contest for the United States Senate. Met and shook hands with Mr. Lincoln several times, and fell quite in love with him. He impressed me as one of the great men of the Nation.

    My military service in the war between the States was as an Officer in the First Ohio Cavalry and later as an Assistant Inspector General of Cavalry in the Army of the Cumberland.

Toulon

Andrew S. Whitaker

When I read of the famous debates carried on by Lincoln and Douglas in the canvas for the United States Senate in 1858, I believed the contenders must have had constitutions of steel, they not alone facing each other and speaking for one hour-and-a-half, but they were constantly traveling and speaking in other towns, the two often being in the same town on the same day.

Lincoln was met on the prairie at Toulon while on his way to Galesburg, and he was induced to speak for two hours, the great crowd attentive to every word. A big procession was then formed, which escorted him through the village and cheered him on his way.

Andrew J. Whitaker was there, and writing from his home in Washington, D.C. in 1928, said "I heard Mr. Lincoln speak at Toulon, Stark Co., on the morning of October 7, 1858. There was a great enthusiasm when he appeared in the carriage occupied by him and the chairman of the meeting held on the Court House Square. The grand Marshall had formed a hollow square of about 10,000 people on the prairie two miles north of town accompanied by numerous bands of music and battalions of horseback riders and carriages, wagons and oxcarts while bedlam broke loose. The horses reared and plunged, but were soon calmed.

"The chairman, Mr. Henderson, said to Mr. Lincoln, 'Do you wish me to introduce you to the vast audience?'

"'Now, 'he said, 'if you have a speech prepared and want to fire it off, you fire it off; but I would a great deal rather have the time.'

"He had so much to say on the issues of the day, and only two hours to say it in.

"Mr. Lincoln went on to Galesburg that evening."

Whitaker,
  Andrew J.
Serving in Co H. 139th
  Ills. Vols.

Saw and heard
Lincoln speak at
Toulon. Stark Co. Ill
Oct 7. 1858 —
Douglass spoke
next day.
Large crowds from
all parts of the
country were
in evidence

Whitaker Andrew J.

There was great enthusiasm when Lincoln appeared in the carriage occupied by him and the chairman of the meeting held on the Court House square in Toulon. The Grand Marshal had formed a hollow square of about 10,000 people on the prairie 2 miles north of town accompanied by numerous bands of music, and battalions of horse back riders & carriages

Wagons and ox carts
when bedlam broke loose
the horses reared and
plunged but were soon
calmed.

The Chairman, Mr. Henderson,
said to Mr. Lincoln, "Do you
wish me to introduce you to
this vast audience?"
"No," he said, "if you have
a speech prepared and want
to fire it off, you fire
it off; but I would a great
deal rather have the
time."

He had so much to
say on the issues of
the day — and only
two hours to say it
in. —
    moving on to
Galesburg that evening.

Galesburg, the Fifth of the Debates

CHARLES A. BLANCHARD

The small boy had a fine time in Galesburg that October day in 1858 when Lincoln and Douglas drew great crowds to the city to hear them debate. He was everywhere in evidence, and he missed little of what was going on.

Charles A. Blanchard was born in that city on November 8, 1848 and he was barely ten years old when he squeezed through the great throng after following one of the parades to the platform, and he heard the two leaders speak.

Speaking at his home in Wheaton, Ill., sixty years after the event, he said,–"The day is very vivid in my memory. The hundreds of teams from all the country round about, from neighboring cities and towns, the bands of music playing as they came to town, the rough wooden platform on the south of the principal college building on which the debaters were to stand.

"I remember the different appearances of the men. Douglas short and fleshy, Mr. Lincoln tall, lean, and gaunt. I think I was chiefly impressed in the debate by the different ways in which the two debated addressed each other. Mr. Lincoln Spoke of Mr. Douglas as 'my opponent, the Senator, Senator Douglas,' etc. As I remember, Mr. Douglas's habitual designations for Mr. Lincoln were 'Old Abe, The Railsplitter, Abe Lincoln,' etc. Of course a boy of ten years of age does not take in a debate very thoroughly, but I received this impression that Mr. Lincoln was right, that he knew he was right and the Mr. Douglas knew he was right also, that therefore Mr. Lincoln was more kindly in his spirit than Mr. Douglas. As I recall it, Mr. Douglas seemed irritated, Mr. Lincoln at peace with himself.

"Mr. Douglas was dressed elegantly. Lincoln's clothing seemed as if he had never given it a thought. I doubt whether he did think very much about it. I do not mean to criticize Douglas as if he were giving too much attention to his apparel, but the difference in appearance of the two men as to clothes was very marked."

Dr. Blanchard graduated from Wheaton College in 1870, and almost immediately became an agent and lecturer of the National Christian Association. In 1872 he became an instructor at Wheaten College and later Professor of English Literature and Language, becoming in 1878, Vice-President, and in 1882, President of the College. He remained as President many years.

Wheaton, Ill.
April 10, 1917.

Mr. J. E. Boos,
    Albany, N.Y.
My dear Mr. Boos:-
        I am very glad to comply with your request to have written out for you what little I know concerning Mr. Lincoln. I think I never saw Mr. Lincoln but once. It was in Galesburg, Ill., on the occasion of his debate with Senator Douglass. I was at the time ten years old. The day is very vivid in my memory. The hundreds of teams from all the country round about, from neighboring cities and towns, the bands of music playing as they came to town, the rough wooden platform on the south of the principal college building on which the debaters were to stand.
        I am not quite sure of the things that proceeded the debate. My recollection is that as a boy I was around the town and that I saw Mr. Douglass in the hotel drinking at the bar. Possibly this is a trick of my memory. It seems to be correct. I remember the different appearances of the men. Douglass short and fleshy, Mr. Lincoln tall, lean and gaunt. I think I was chiefly impressed in the debate by the different ways in which the two debaters addressed each other. Mr. Lincoln spoke of Mr. Douglass as "my opponent", "the Senator," "Senator Douglass," etc. As I remember, Mr. Douglass's habitual designations for Mr. Lincoln were "Old Abe," "the rail splitter", "Abe Lincoln," etc., etc. Of course a boy ten years of age does not take in a debate very thoroly but I received this impression that Mr. Lincoln was right, that he knew he was right and that Mr. Douglass knew that he was right also, that therefore Mr. Lincoln was more kindly in his spirit than Mr. Douglass was. As I recall it, Mr. Douglass seemed irritated, Mr. Lincoln at peace with himself.
        I am not certain, it seems to me as if I once thereafter saw Mr. Lincoln standing on the rear platform of a NorthWestern train as he was moving out toward the northwest portion of the state. I am not certain of this. If it were true it was only for a moment as the train sped away. My recollection however is rather strong that I saw him standing on that platform. I think he had on a shawl to protect him from the cold.

The day he was killed I was plowing on my father's field and my brother Louis, who has now been many years with the Lord, came up and said to me "President Lincoln is killed." I thot at first he was joking but when he insisted that it was true the sky seemed to me to go dark altho it was a brilliant sunny April day. It seemed that all my joints lost their power to keep me in a standing position. I sank down on the ground, not as one takes his seat but sort of dropping in a heap as when one faints.
As years have passed he has grown greater and greater to me. I have always believed that Washington was the greatest American, that I believe still, but Lincoln seems to me to have been a worthy companion for the father of our country.

            Very truly yours,

CAB:MS   *Charles A. Blanchard*

P.S. I see I have said nothing about the dress of the two men. Mr. Douglass was dressed elegantly. Lincoln's clothing seemed as if he had never given it a thought. I doubt whether he did think very much about it. I do not mean to criticize Douglass as if he were giving too much attention to his apparel but the difference in the appearance of the two men as to clothes was very marked.

The Debaters Spoke at Rockport

MR. I.W. SWAN

A great many young men of Illinois had heard Lincoln speak during the years no man thought he would ever be a candidate for President. They were impressed with him, and when the time did come when banners bore the words "Lincoln for President," they helped form Wide Awake Clubs and were his enthusiastic followers. The interest did not stop with the election. When war came, they changed from the oilcloth cape and torch to a Blue uniform and a musket, marching proudly away to the tune of "The Girl I Left Behind Me." One of those boys was I.W. Swan, he having enlisted in the 13th Wisconsin Volunteers, and he marched and fought more than four years.

Lincoln and Douglas must have often stood in opposition on the same platform, Mr. Swan saying he heard them in the village of Rockford during the time of the debates. Writing from his home in Bellingham, Washington, in 1911, he sad;–"The only time I ever saw or heard the immortal Lincoln was in the fall of 1858 at Rockford, Ill., when those two greatest offhand debaters in America were the Democratic and Republican candidates for the United States Senate before the Illinois legislature. Douglas at this time was termed The Little Giant, and one of the most popular and widely known men in the country.

"Lincoln was little known outside Middle West, particularly before his famous 'A house divided itself cannot stand' speech, delivered a short time before at the Republican State convention at Springfield, which attracted the eyes of the entire country. I went early and secured a good seat well in the front.

What a contest between the two men as they appeared on the platform. Douglas, a short, stout, active, quick in speech, powerful and carried his audience by storm. Lincoln, tall, slender, and awkward, slow in movement and speech, and plain, simple language, and his plain, unpretending manner won its way to the hearts of the people. He was the one man Douglas feared.

"Lincoln could express more meaning and theme for thought in fewer words than any many I ever listened to, and he certainly proved more than a match for Douglas on this occasion."

Bellingham Wash. 2/14/14

I was a Member of Co K 13th Wisconsin Vol. Infantry, and served four years and three months in the Civil War, the greater portion portion of the time under Gen. Geo. H. Thomas in the army of the Cumberland.

The only time that I ever saw or heard the immortal Lincoln was in the Fall of 1858 at Rockford Ill, when there were two called off hand debators in America between the Democrats and Republican candidates for US Senator before the Ill State Legislature, Douglas at this time, was termed the Little Giant, and one of the most popular, and widely known men in the U.S. or America.

Lincoln outside the Middle West, particularly before his famous, A House divided against itself, can not stand speech, delivered a short time before at the Republican State convention at Springfield Ill which all created the expectations of the entire county at that time. I went early and secured a good seat well in front.

What a contrast physically between the two men as they appeared on the platform. Douglas short, stout, active, quick in speech, powerful and carried his audience by storm. Lincoln tall, slender and awkward, slow in movement and speech, used plain simple language and his plain unpretending manner won its way to the hearts of the people. [...] no one man Douglas feared.

Lincoln could express more meaning and thought for thought in fewer words than any man that I ever listened to, and he certainly proved more than a match for Douglas on this occasion. This discussion made him the logical candidate for the new party.

Bellingham J. W. Swan
Mass.   2731 Valletta St.

Bellingham Wash
2/16/14

Mr J E Boos
 Dear Sir
Enclosed please find my autograph &c as per your request. After first jotting down my reminiscence of the Lincoln and Douglas debate that I witnessed. My impressions of the two great men, at that time, who were undoubtly the two greatest off hand debaters in America, I found that I had written too much, about twice as much as would fill my allotted space, so I had to leave out sentences, and cut down.

So that what I am sending seems rather lame to me, And, does not do Lincoln Justice, does not give the political questions discussed. My impressions of the true men after hearing them need. But suffice it to say, that I was ever after hearing that discussion for Lincoln for president. I believed in his principles, his ability, his honesty, his judgement and that the old ship of State could be trusted in no safer hands.

Yours Respectfully,
O. W. Dixon

The Debate is Renewed at Quincy

JONATHAN LABRANT

Six days after the Galesburg Debate the candidates met at Quincy, with Lincoln having the better of the argument, but Douglas as confident he would get his opponent in serious difficulties as he was when he mounted the platform at Ottawa to open the series.

Lincoln was to open the debate, and when he stepped to the fore after the bands stopped playing and the crowd had become quiet, he commenced, and after answering a number of questions the Judge had put to him in the previous debate, accusing him of being on two sides of a question, he said, "We have in this nation the question of domestic slavery. It is a matter of absolute certainty that it is a disturbing element. It is the opinion of all great men who have expressed an opinion upon it, that it is a dangerous element. We keep up a controversy in regard to it. That controversy necessarily springs from difference of opinion, and if we can lean exactly-can reduce to the lowest elements-what that difference of opinion is, we perhaps shall be better prepared for discussing the different systems of policy that we would propose in regard to that disturbing element. I suggest that the difference of opinion, reduced to its lowest terms, is no other than the difference between the men who think slavery a wrong and those who do not think it a wrong. The Republican Party thinks it wrong-and we think it a moral, a social, and a political wrong. We think it is a wrong not confining itself merely to the persons or the States where it exists, but that it is a wrong which in its tendency, to say the least, affects the existence of the whole nation. Because we think it a wrong, we propose a course of policy that shall deal with it as a wrong. We deal with it as with it as with any other wrong, in so far as we can prevent its growing any larger, and so deal with it that in the run of time there shall be some promise of an end to it."

He went on in this way during most of the rest of his hour-and-a-half, and nearly everybody in the vast crowd seemed to agree with him, they seeming to be almost unanimous in their applause.

Then Douglas stepped quickly to the front and immediately began to accuse Lincoln of inconsistency, saying in one paragraph, "How does Lincoln propose to save the Union, unless by compelling all the states to become free, so that the house shall not be divided against itself? He intends making them all free; he will preserve the Union in that way; and yet he is not going to interfere with slavery anywhere it now exists. How is he going to bring it about? Why, he will agitate; he will induce the North to agitate until the South shall be worried out, and forced to abolish slavery. Let us examine the policy by which that is to be done. He first tells us that he would prohibit slavery everywhere in the Territories. He would thus confine slavery within its present limits. When he thus gets it confined, and surrounded, so that it cannot spread, the natural laws of increase will go on until the negroes will be so plenty that they cannot live on the soil. He will hem them in until starvation seizes them, and by starving them to death he will not put slavery in the course of ultimate extinction. If he is not going to interfere with slavery in the states, but in Territories, and thus smother slavery out, it naturally follows that he can extinguish it only by extinguishing the negro race; for his policy would drive them to starvation. This is the humane and Christian remedy that he proposes for the great crime of slavery."

When he had finished, after speaking in this manner for an hour, the crowd showed very little approval, because there was only scattered applause, and Lincoln came forward to continue for another half-hour.

In 1912, there lived in Kansas, a man named Jonathan Labrant who stood in the crowd, and who lustily cheered the Republican candidate. He was 22 years old and eligible to vote for that party's candidate. My old question of "Did you see Lincoln" brought forth "The only time I saw Abraham Lincoln was in Quincy when he and Stephen A Douglas were stumping the state as candidates for the U.S. Senate. Both were entertaining speakers and received equal applause. I was convinced Lincoln was right, voted the Abolition ticket, and when war came went into the army as a private in the 51st Illinois Volunteers. I was married in March, 1861, enlisted in December, and was not discharged until February 8, 1865."

Weir Kansas July 27. 1912

the first and only time that I Saw the Mortal Abraham Lincoln was in the Month of ~~September~~ October 1858, in the City of Quincy Ills, when he and Stephen. A. Douglas were Stumping the State as Candidates for the U.S. Senate, both were Entertaining Speakers, and recieved equal Applause, I was then 22 years of age and am now 76. I Enlisted Dec 1 1861 and Served My Country till Feb 8th 1865 was Married to Mary M. Willson March 26th 1861 having lived hapily together for over 51 years, and our health is fair for our years. Wife is 70 years old I will Sign My Name as it appears on the Muster Roll of the War Dep. late years I have mainly used the initials J.B. and use a capital B. in the last Sylable of Sir name we have 6 children 4 Boys & two Girls

Respectfully yours

Jonathan Labrant
Co. F. 58th Ills. vol. Inft

At Urbana

Mrs. A.A. Glass

My copy of Knickerbocker-News of March 31, 1939 had a large headline announcing the death of William Saxton, who was in charge of the military records in the Adjutant-General's office in the Albany capitol.

When I was a small boy, his father was Lieutenant-Governor, and a polished orator. He was a soldier in the Civil War, and naturally, a lover of Lincoln. I once heard him make a wonderful speech about the great Emancipator. When Governor Saxton was fighting for the Union, what is now the State of Washington was only a thinly settled territory and few in the East new much about it.

While I read the death notice, I thought of a dear old lady who had know Lincoln when she was a little girl and who had moved to the Pacific coast shortly after the territory had become a state. Sitting on her porch one warm afternoon in 1928, I listened to many stories of the early days in the Lincoln country and of the great faith and ability of the pioneers.

"I know Mr. Lincoln well when I was a girl," the gentle old lady said. "The first time I saw him was during the famous debates in 1858, when he and Douglas spoke from the same platform at Urbana. I saw him on the streets many times after that, he coming to our town to attend court; 'The Circuit,' as they called it in those days. That debate was never published with the series, but I heard every word of it. They spoke on the fugitive slave laws and squatter's rights. I listened closely as I despised slavery. Finally Mr. Douglas said, 'Mr. Lincoln, what do you think will be the outcome of these issues if they become laws.' Mr. Lincoln answered loudly; 'War! The most dreaded war in American history, for it will be son against father, and brother against brother, for the people of the North do not want any more slave states.'

"Again Mr. Douglas said, 'Mr. Lincoln what are your views on emancipation?' He answered and said 'When a boy or girl in slavery works for the Master a certain number of years set by law, they should be made free. This is my thought of gradual emancipation.'

"Mr. Lincoln loved to joke. The one that Douglas disliked most was when Lincoln arose on his tiptoes and pointing would quote Douglas' last remark and say that little man over there says so and so."

Seattle Wash, July 27 1928

Dear Sir

Find enclosed the page for your Book as you request. My rememberance of our beloved President. Had you sent me another sheet of paper I might have done a better job of writing as I am aged. My hand cramps and gets shaking and some way can not comand it as well as pencil. If you send me another will try to do better —

I send you a slip I wrote to National Tribune. You see they do not give cradence for his Speaking at Urban Decator or Clinton Ill. Write to Mr Charles Van-Doren 733 East 51 Grinnel Iowa he hurd him a Clinton Ill,

Yours &c
Mrs A A Glasco
4132 Ada St S.
Seattle
Wash.

1858   I first saw Abraham Lincoln in when he and S. A. Duglass held there famous Debate at Urbana Illinois I stood beside My Father in Spring of 1858 when mutual friend introduced them to Mr Lincoln I saw him many times on the Streets of Urban as he often attended Court there with Judge Davis of Springfield I heard Lincoln and Duglas debate on the fugitive Slave Law and Squatters Rights Clause I listened Closley as I dispised Slavrey. Finely Mr Duglas said, Mr Lincoln what do you think will be the outcome if theas issues become laws. Mr Lincoln answerd loudly War the most dier War in the American History for it will a gens Father and Brother agant Brother. for the People of the North do not want any more Slave States. Again Mr Duglas said Mr Lincoln what are your veiws on Emacipation he answered and said when a Boy or Girl borne in Slavrey works for the Master a cirten number of Years "Set by Law" they should be made Free this My thought of Gradual Emancipation Mr Lincoln loved to joke the one that Duglas disliked most was when Lincoln arose on his tip toes and pointing would quoat Duglas last remark would Say that little Man over there says So & So

Yours truly
Mrs A. A. Glasscoe
4182 Ida St S
Seattle
Washington

The Last of the Great Debates

G.W. BEAMAN

There was a debate in Ottawa in August, and though it was held to awaken the citizens of Illinois to the merits of Stephen A. Douglas and Abraham Lincoln for the office of the United States Senator, the reports of the speeches awakened interest throughout the whole country. The candidates were the best known men in the State, and a great majority of the people took a decided stand for the Little Giant, or for Honest Abe. One wished to have slavery in the territories if a majority in that new land wanted it, was in favor of Fugitive Slave Law; to allow owners to bring slaves in Free States, favoring the Dred Scott Decision, willing to give the Slave States every right to their property as stated in the constitution, and many other advantages they declared were rights.

The other side was as strongly opposed to the spread of the curse, opposed to the Supreme Court's decision, opposed to giving the slave owner the right to bring Dred Scott to Illinois, was willing to overlook the breaking of the fugitive and every other law that protected the evil, and was anxious to see slavery disappear, Lincoln saying at the time, "A house divided against itself cannot stand. I believe this government cannot endure the permanently half slave and half free. I do not expect the house to fall-but I do expect it will cease to be divided."

One was fighting for the principles of the new Republican party, which wanted to drop the old order and change many laws they believed to be unsound. They were progressive, or radical party, while the other maintained the Democrats were following in the footsteps of the fathers of the Republic and change would ruin the nation.

Their views were so clearly stated the news papers published long reports of the debate and when they met at Freeport nearly a week later, newspaper men from out of the state stood near the platform to get the speeches at first hand.

That debate aroused the country and gave Lincoln much credit because of his ability to combat the oratory of the famous Senator and leader of the Democratic Party. The debates at Jonesboro, Charleston, Galesburg and Quincy, which followed at periods of a week or more apart, created so much interest throughout the country, that when the last was to take place at Alton on October 15th, large numbers came from other states to hear the speakers.

The interest was intense. Lincoln became the champion of the Republicans, while Douglas, though he would win the election, had lost nearly all his friends in the South. The tremendous ability of Lincoln as a debater was clearly brought out and he drew from his opponent many statements that made the Southern leaders detest him, resulting two years later in splitting the Democratic Party, thereby assuring a Republican President when the votes were counted in the fall of 1860.

G.W. Beaman lived in that center of culture near Harvard College and heard many noted speakers. He journeyed west in 1858 and stopped at Alton to hear the last debate. Admiral Beaman was born on May 7, 1837, was a first voter, was deeply interested in politics and was much impressed with the debate.

The young man entered the Navy in the Civil War, and stayed until retired because of age, as a Rear-Admiral. He died at Cambridge, Mass., on May 31, 1917.

Dear Sir:

In response to your enquiry I may say that it is somewhat singular, (for during the Civil War I was quite frequently in Washington,) I never saw President Lincoln. I have, however, a very vivid remembrance of a pleasant Autumnal afternoon, in October 1858, when I had the pleasure of listening to the joint debate between Lincoln and Douglass, at Alton, Illinois. These debates were extended to all parts of the State, and as is well known, did much to call the attention of the Country to Mr. Lincoln's great ability as a public speaker. The fact that his antagonist was Senator Douglass, the author of the bill repealing the Missouri Compromise, and perhaps its most powerful advocate, served to excite great interest in the canvas for the Illinois Senatorship throughout the entire Country, north and south.

En route from Boston to St. Louis, I had stopped over a day at Alton for the sole purpose of listening to this debate. It was my first visit to the West. For a young man I was quite familiar with the public speakers of New England and New York, with the result that, not unnaturally, I had looked forward to seeing men more or less of the eastern type, come forward on that rude platform. The characteristics of a typical western audience might have sufficed to advise me to the contrary before the speakers appeared, but it had not. I looked for men of the type of Wendell Phillips, Charles Sumner, Geo. W. Curtis, Edward Everett, clad in the conventional broadcloth of their day. Through the favor of a friendly newspaper man I had a seat on the speakers' platform. When, after some little delay, the two speakers appeared young Boston received a shock that

for the moment was almost overpowering. The great
Lincoln, tall, gaunt, his rugged face exhibiting
slight traces of tonsorial care for some time previously, and wearing a long linen duster, which had
evidently been on the circuit for a prolonged period,
served to increase the wearer's height to seven feet,
at least. But what served to impress me most were
his wonderful eyes, which at rest seemed to have a
far-away, dreamy, almost sad expression. As
from time to time he recognised some old acquaintance
among the audience, they lighted up with a most kindly
expression, and when, with a genuine western cordiality,
he responded to their salutations. But the honorable
senator ! A man in more striking contrast to Lincoln could with difficulty be found. He was as
short and fat as Lincoln was long and gaunt. The
little giant was arrayed in evening dress, if one can
so term a costume with a blue "swallow tail" coat
with brass buttons. The large expanse of shirt-
bosom was so liberally bespattered with tobacco juice
as to be simply disgusting and his entire costume
was in keeping. The general appearance of the
Senator was that of a man brought before a police-
court the morning after.

Of the debate it is not necessary to speak. It
is now a matter of history. It and Lincoln's discussions were all more or less reported, and are
available in all good libraries.

Very truly yours,

[signature]
Pay Director USN
(Retired)

Cambridge, Mass.
January 20, 1915.

A Debate at Macomb

THOMAS GILMORE

In the old days opponents stood face to face on the same platform, each hearing the arguments of the other and answering them. Lincoln was a candidate for the United States Senate; so was Douglas, and they held several nationally interesting debates from August to October 1858, but nearly two weeks after the last debate at Alton, they met at Macomb on October 26th, where they again addressed a big crowd, speaking for the principles of the side each represented.

Writing of that day many years after, Thomas Gilmore, still a resident of Macomb, said,–"I heard a great deal about Lincoln before I had seen him, because our representatives to the legislature at Springfield always brought home some new joke he had used in his speeches in that body.

"His speeches as I heard them were along the lines of cool common sense and sound reasoning. It was in October, 1858 that I first heard him, he being the republican candidate for the senate of the U.S. against Stephan A. Douglas, who was at that time the foremost man in the State of Illinois. Lincoln's education was very limited, as is now well known, but he always had a thirst for the truth and sound information. When he and Douglas were speaking from the same stand, Douglas hated to hear himself picked up in his inconsistencies, he would keep looking at his watch, and the moment Lincoln's time was up he would yell 'you're time is up Lincoln.'

"At the end of those debates, he said to the men who were with him, 'I shall tomorrow ask Douglas this question; Who should determine whether a State should be slave or free.' They told him if he did that Douglas would answer it in such a way that it would beat him. 'Then,' said Lincoln, 'I will beat him for the Presidency.'

"I am often asked if I thought Lincoln great. A man is not great in his appearance but in what he has the capability and does it. Lincoln put through to a successful conclusion one of the worst civil wars that ever occurred. He stood firmly on the proposition that government of the people, by the people should live. I now only shook hands with him, but was with him two days of his speech making. While he loved and enjoyed a joke, he was serious about serious things, yet could explain a serious matter with a story when anyone was trying to move him from his position. He was a kindhearted man and had a deep interest in the well being of others. Please excuse blots and errors, my eyesight is poor, not so firm at 102 years of age."

I heard a great deal about Abraham Lincoln before I saw him, because our Representative in the Legislature at Springfield always brought home a new joke of his. His speeches as I heard them were along the lines of cool common sense and sound reasoning. It was in October, 1858 that I first heard him when he was the Republican candidate for the U. S. Senate against Stephen A. Douglas.

When he and Douglas were speaking from the same stand, the time of each was limited, and Douglas hated to hear himself picked up in his incomsistencies. He would take out his watch, and the moment Lincoln's time was up he would yell, "Your time is up Lincoln."

I not only shook hands with him, but was with him for two days of his speech making. While he loved fun and enjoyed a joke, he was serious about serious things, yet he would explain a serious matter with a story when any one was trying to move him from his position.

Lincoln was a very kind hearted man and had a deep interest in the well being of others.

Lincoln & Douglas had agreed to speak from the same stand at seven different in Illinois on the same day. One day Lincoln said the men that were with him, "Tomorrow I shall ask Douglas this question; "Who should have the right to say whether a state coming into the union should be slave or free"? They told if he did that Douglas would answer it in such a way it would beat him for the senate It may Lincoln but it will beat him for the Presidency.

Yours truly
Thomas Gilmore
Macomb Illinois
November 12 A.D. 1932,

Macomb Ills
Nov. 12/32

Mr John E. Boos.

Yours of 6th received. Do not know whether is just what you wanted. You can of course make any use of this that you see fit.

Yours truly,
Thos Gilmore
Macomb
Ills.

P.S. Think my father wrote to you in a former letter that A. Lincoln spoke in Macomb, Ill. Oct. 25th, 1858. I find on the the memorial on our Court House where A. Lincoln stood when he spoke here that it was October 26th, 1858, which is no doubt correct. He spoke in Augusta, Ill. the following day, Oct. 27, 1858. Thought you might like to have the exact date.

Belle Gilmore
(daughter of Thos. Gilmore)

Mr John Bros

Dear Sir you letter of Oct 12 rec'd and I shall endeavor to give to you the best of my recollection of Abraham Lincoln. I heard a great deal about him before I had seen him, for our representatives to the legislature at Springfield always brought home some some new joke. His speeches as I heard them were along the lines of cool common sense and sound reasoning. I was in October 1858 that I first heard him when he was the Republican candidate for the senate of the U.S senate, of this state against Stephen A. Douglas who was at that time the famoust man in the U.S senate

limited as now well known but he alway had a thirst for truthful an sound information. When he and Douglas were speaking from the same stand each were limited, and Douglas hated so hear himself picked up in his incosistencies that he would take out his watch and the moment Lincolns time was up he would get our your time is up Lincoln. At the time of those debates he said to the men who were with him "I shall to morrow ask Douglas this question, Who shoud determine whither a slave should slave or free." They told him if did that Douglass would answer it in such a way that it would beat him fo the senate Says Lincoln I will beat him for the Presidency. I did

...great man is not great in his appearance but in what [is] the capability does it. Lincoln successfully put through to a successful conclusion one of the most far reaching and deeper to civil wars that ever occurred on the earth. He stood firmly on the position that "government of the people, by the people" should live and die.

I not only shook hands with him but was with him for two days of his speech making.

While [he] loved fun and enjoyed a joke, he was desirous about serious things, [and] would explain a serious matter with a story when any one was trying to move him from his position.

...was a very kindly natured man and had a deep interest in the well being of others. Though born and raised in a slave state he always hated slavery, but was in favor of the slave states handling their condition themselves. But opposed to any free territory being made a slave state.

Yours truly
Thomas Gilmore

P.S. Please excuse blots and errors, my eyesight is poor, not uncommon when 102 years of age.

Part Three: Lincoln's Farewell Address

"'My friends, no one in my position can appreciate the sadness I feel at this parting. To this people I owe all that I am. Here I have lived more than a quarter of a century. Here my children were born, and here one of them lies buried. I know not how soon I shall see you again. A duty devolves upon me which is greater, perhaps, than that which has devolved upon any other man since the days of Washington. He never would have succeeded except for the aid of Divine Providence, upon which he at all times relied. I feel that I cannot succeed without the same divine aid which sustained him, and on the same Almighty Being I place my reliance for support, and I hope you, my friends, will pray that I may receive that divine assistance without which I cannot succeed, but with which success is certain. Again, I bid you all an affectionate farewell.'

"There was a slight sprinkle of rain; the breeze was raw and damp, but the crowd stood with heads uncovered until the train was out of sight, Mr. Lincoln still standing on the rear platform with head bowed in sadness. That was the last time I looked into the face of my sincere friend and neighbor."

Dr. Preston Bailhache

I had the good fortune in 1914 to become acquainted with Dr. Preston Bailhache, who had been the Lincoln family physician for a short time before the President-elect left Springfield for Washington, he having been a close friend and ardent anti-slavery man since his arrival in the city in 1856. His brother was the editor of the leading paper, and shortly after Lincoln's defeat for the Senate in 1858, the brother ran a line on the front page of every issue reading "Lincoln for President."

Dr. Bailhache entered the army as an assistant surgeon in the 19th Illinois Volunteers as soon as war was declared, and later in the war became Surgeon of the 14 Illinois Calvary. After the surrender at Appomattox he entered the Public Health and Marine Hospital service and after his retirement lived in Stapleton, Long Island, where he died on October 28, 1919.

The Kaiser's armies were driving everything before them when I visited him one sunny afternoon, and the fine old warrior was very much wrought up at the way the Allies were fighting, and he was sure Grant or Uncle Billy Sherman or Old Pop Thomas could show them the tricks of the trade, and they would wipe the Huns off the map in jig-shape. Modern equipment and new engines of war meant nothing to him, and he insisted it was brains and strategy and intelligent moving of large bodies of men that counted more than tanks, flying machines and big guns. Abraham Lincoln was his ideal leader, and U.S. Grant his matchless soldier.

The mention of Lincoln afforded the opportunity I had been waiting for and I made the suggestion that the "Wide Awakes" in the 1860 campaign must have been a conquering army, because they had done more with their torch lights and oil-cloth capes than any other agency used to elect the Railsplitter to the Presidency.

"I, too, think they did," he answered; "they created a furor among old and young that could not be resisted, and what started as a Marching Club soon became the largest and most soul-inspiring organization the country had ever seen. Miles of 'Wide Awakes' with their lighted torches carried by thousands of uniformed men and boys clad in glazed capes and caps with spread eagle badges made sight to stir the blood in every patriotic heart.

"There was no building in Springfield large enough to hold the immense crowds that wished to hear the speeches made by the friends of Mr. Lincoln during the campaign, so a large tent was erected. It as named 'The Wigwam,' and here the most enthusiastic audiences were gathered. The 'Wide Awakes' made things lively for the boys, and the Glee Clubs sang patriotic songs, while the drums and fifes added not a little to the general excitement and fun, so that 'The Wigwam' cam in for one of the most sought and popular resorts day and night.

"Of course, Springfield was the Mecca of Central Illinois on that night of all nights when the news flashed over the wires that Abraham Lincoln was elected President of the United States.

"In the meantime, early in the evening, a large number of ladies and gentlemen gathered in Ben Watson's Ice Cream Saloon to watch the parade and hear the dispatches read. While waiting for the news, campaign songs were sung. Later, coffee and oysters were served and we were all having a good time when the dispatches began to come in to liven up things still more. My Lincoln, with a few friends, was at the telegraph office near by, and toward midnight he and the others joined the gay crowd. At last a dispatch was handed him at midnight stating that New York City had given him a 28,000 majority, and the State a 50,000.

"I dare not even try to describe the scene that followed, where men fell into each other's arms shouting and crying, yelling like mad, jumping up and down-pandemonium, in fact-but Mr. Lincoln slipped out quietly, looking grave and anxious.

"I saw very little of him after that, being away from Springfield most of the time, but I was present when he left for Washington in the early morning of February 11th, and watched him closely while he looked into the sad faces of his neighbors, tears glistening in his eyes, and said."

Part Four: Gen. Thomas

George H. Thomas

Thomas is a Virginian from near Norfolk and say what we may he must feel unpleasantly at leading an invading army. But if he says he will do it, I know he will do it well. He was never brilliant but always cool, reliable and steady, maybe a little slow.

From a letter of

Gen. William T. Sherman

To his brother John, June 8, 1861

And now we place these garlands
    Above your silent dust,
And crave from Him a blessing
    In whom we ever trust;
Strong hands shall bear the standard
    You nobly sought to save,
In triumph it shall ever
    Above you proudly wave,

To
HENRY HIRSCHFELD.

A Judge who would much rather judge men for their good traits rather than their bad.

Henry Hirschfeld
July 20, 1931

Memorial Services

Sunday, May 28th
2.30 p. m.

Held at the Sepulcher of Major General George H. Thomas, in Oakwood Cemetery

Major General George H. Thomas

Services held under the auspices of

The Rensselaer County Patriotic League

Program

1. Assembly .... By George F. Doring

2. Invocation .... Rev. Mitchell Bronk, D. D.

3. "Onward Christian Soldiers" .... Doring's Orchestra

4. Opening .... Comrade B. B. Martis
   President of the Rensselaer County Patriotic League

5. Quartet—"American Hymn" .... Kellers
   Miss Gertrude Shacklady, soprano; Mrs. Edna Herrick Peck, contralto; Mr. Ernest Ruether, tenor; Mr. Herbert Vanderpool, basso.

6. Recitation—"The Nation's Dead" .... Harold Webb
   Troy High School Cadets

7. Solo—"Abide With Me" .... Mr. Fred C. Comstock

8. Roll call of States and placing of flowers by members of League.
   Mr. John Tallmadge, Geo. H. Thomas Post, 5, Chicago, Ill.
   Mrs. Eva Cipperly, Geo. H. Thomas Post, 14, Benton Harbor, Michigan.
   Mrs. John Beal, Geo. H. Thomas Post, 84, Lancaster, Pa.
   Mrs. Katie Davis, Geo. H. Thomas Post, 17, Indianapolis, Indiana.
   Geo. H. Thomas Post, 18, Ottawa, Kan.
   Mrs. Minnie Horton, Geo. H. Thomas Post, 131, Leicester, Mass.
   League, Comrade Hiram N. Wager.

Program

9. Idyl—"Farewell to Thee" .... Logan
   Doring's Orchestra

10. Quartet—"Tenting Tonight" .... Smith

11. Address .... Hon. Frederick C. Filley

12. Solo—"A Perfect Day" .... Bond
    Mr. Fred C. Comstock

13. Address .... By Rev. Milton Butler Pratt, D. D.

14. Reverie—"Twilight" .... Bendix
    Doring's Orchestra

15. Quartet—"The Vacant Chair" .... Root

16. "America" .... Sung by the Assemblage

17. Benediction .... By Rev. Mitchell Bronk, D. D.

18. Taps .... George F. Doring

High School cadets will act as orderlies, those serving being: Fred Mahoney, captain of Company A; George Caswell, first Lieut. Company A; Guy Potter, second Lieut. Company A; George O'Connor, captain Company B; Alexander Roberts, first Lieut. Company B; John Barnes, 2d Lieut. Company B; William Boughton, captain Co. C; Ross Diggs, first Lieut. Company C; John Farrell, 2d Lieut. Company C.

And now we place these garlands
    Above your silent dust,
And crave from Him a blessing
    In whom we ever trust;
Strong hands shall bear the standard
    You nobly sought to save,
In triumph it shall ever
    Above you proudly wave.

Rensselaer County Patriotic League
Organized September 1, 1914

Nashville, Tenn.
June 23, 1866

Sir:

Your favor of the 21st was received this morning.

*I remember very well that * in answer to Chaplain * Van Horns inquiry of me * whether or not he should * have the dead buried by states * I answered that I wanted * them buried in such a manner as to create the * impression of National care, not sectional or * State, as we had had * enough of States Rights. * It is probable that * Mr. Van Horn has * quoted me correctly * and those being my * sentiments, I have no * objection to your quoting * them in your article * on the National Cemetery * at Chattanooga.*

Very Respectfully,

Gen. H. Thomas
Maj. Gen. U.S.A.

Nashville Tenn
June 23. 1866

Sir:

Your favor of the 21st was received this morning. I remember very well that in answer to Chaplain Van Horn's inquiry of me whether or not he should have the dead buried by states I answered that I wanted them buried in such a manner as to create the impression of National Care, not sectional or State, as we had had enough of States Rights. It is probable that Mr Van Horn has quoted me correctly, and those being my

[handwritten letter:]

...tentments, I have no objection to your quoting them in your article on the National Cemetery at Chattanooga.

Very Respectfully,
yr obt st
Geo H Thomas
Maj Genl

J. S. Wiltse
Harrison Ind.

Few in New York State realize that "Pap" Thomas, as his soldiers lovingly called him, lies buried in Oakwood Cemetery, Troy. Few would believe that one born a Virginian, an officer of the Army in many States; a soldier in Mexico and in Kentucky, Georgia and Tennessee; a military commander in the South and on the Pacific Coast should find his last resting place so far north an east as the "Collar City."

Born and bred a Southerner, he put country above state and family when Fort Sumter was fired on, and his loyalty to the Union costs him the love of kindred and the enmity of his Virginia neighbors and friends. Having been married to a northern girl on November 7, 1852, he was buried in the plot of her family, she being Frances L. Kellogg, daughter of a prominent Troy manufacturer.

His biographer says,–"He was second to none in representing all that is best and noblest in the life of the freest and greatest nation on the globe."

He proved his worth as an American at Monterey and Buena Vista, where he was promoted for distinguished bravery; he showed his great courage when he parted from friends and family and offered his services to President Lincoln in 1861, and his loyalty to the Union was proven at Mill Springs, at Peach Tree Creek and at Nashville. To his soldiers, he was "Old Pap"; to his superiors, he was "Old Slowfoot;" and to the nation he was "The Rock of Chickamauga."

He only moved when he was sure; he only struck when prepared; but when he did move or did strike, the whole South could not stop him. His monument reads,—

> "George H. Thomas
> Major General U.S. Army
> Born South Hampton County, Va., July 31, 1816
> Died San Francisco, Cal., March 28, 1870"

It ought to read; Here lies the man who won the first decisive victory of the Civil War; upon whose shoulders rests the honor of completely routing an army; who held the enemy at bay near Chattanooga, when defeat seemed certain, and whose name shall go down in history as the "The Rock of Chickamauga."

Then all who come near, will see at a glance that illustrious dust lies beneath the monument, and will pay tribute to him who deserves much. On Memorial Day, 1916, the one hundredth anniversary of his birth, distant States remembered his services to the Union, and wreaths were sent from Indiana, Illinois, Kansas, Michigan, Massachusetts, Pennsylvania and Washington, D.C.

Gen. Thomas was born in Virginia on the 31st day of July, 1816. He received his education in Southampton Academy, and then took up the study of law in the office of an uncle. One day the member of Congress from his district, Hon. John Y. Mason, came into the office, and during the conversation, turned to Young

Thomas and asked him how he would like to enter West Point. The future General answered he would gladly accept a chance if offered and in a few days he was notified to prepare for the entering examination, which in due time he passed, and was enrolled as a member of the class of 1840.

He paid close attention to his duties, studied hard, and upon graduation day, ranked twelve in a class of forty-two, Gen. W.T. Sherman standing sixth. July 1st, of the same year he received the appointment of 2nd Lieutenant in the 3rd U.S. Artillery.

In 1841, he was sent to Florida, and took part in the Seminole War, receiving on the 6th of November, a brevet of 1st Lieutenant, "for gallantry and good conduct in the war against the Florida Indians." He held this commission until April 30, 1844, when he was promoted to 1st Lieutenant of his company. For more than a year he did routine work, improving his leisure hours in study, and on June 26, 1845, received orders to proceed immediately to New Orleans and report to Gen. Zachary Taylor. Upon his arrival in the city, he lost no time in getting ready to proceed to Texas, and sailed for that frontier, July 24th.

In August, his regiment, with the 4th United States, entrenched at Corpus Christi, they being the first troops to occupy the State. Here the regiment stayed until March, 1846, when Thomas' company advanced with other troops to the Rio Grande. With the 7th Infantry and Company I, 2nd Artillery, they were ordered to garrison a fort opposite Metamoros, where they were subject to a bombardment from the 3rd to the 9th of May. During June and July, Lieutenant Thomas was detached with a section of his battery, marching in the vanguard during the advance to Reynosa and Camargo. Rejoining his company, they took part in the battles around Monterey, September 21 to 23, and his soldiership and gallantry so impressed his superiors, that Gen. J.P. Henderson, commanding the Texan Volunteers, wrote in his report,–"I beg leave also, under the authority of Gen. Lamar, to compliment Lieut. Thomas of the Artillery and his brave men for the bold advance and efficient management of the force under his charge. When ordered to retire, he reloaded his piece, fired a farewell shot at the foe and returned under a shower of bullets."

From Nov. 21, 1864 to Feb. 4, 1847, Lieut. Thomas commanded the company, the Senior Lieut. Braxton Bragg, afterward Confederate General, having been promoted to a Captaincy.

In the battle of Buena Vista, which was fought February 22, and 23, 1847, Lieut. Thomas again showed his great qualities as a soldier and leader, and later received a brevet of Major, "for gallant and meritorious conduct." Capt. T.W. Sherman, writing of the battle said; "I was directed to take my battery back to the plateau, where I joined Lieut. Thomas, who had been constantly engaged during the forenoon in the preservation of that important position, and whom I found closely engaged with the enemy, and that, too, in a very advanced position. ***Lieut. Thomas more than sustained the reputation he had long enjoyed in his regiment as an accurate and scientific artillerist." Gen. Wool also mentioned Thomas' name among others in his report, "whose services on every part of the field, I think it but justice to say we are mainly indebted for the great victory so successfully achieved by our arms over the great force opposed to us."

At a meeting of citizens of Southampton Co., Va., held July 19, 1847, it was resolved to purchase a sword, upon which was to be engraved an appropriate inscription, and which was to be presented to Lieut. Thomas as a token of the respect in which he was held by his friends and neighbors.

At the close of the Mexican War, he was placed in charge of the commissary depot at Brazos, Santiago, and remained there until February 1st, 1849, when he was given a six months leave of absence. On August 1st, he rejoined his company, and on the 6th was transferred to Co. B, leaving with his company for Florida in September to take part in an expedition against the Florida Indians, who had again become restless and were on the war path. He remained in the State until December, 1850, when he was assigned to duty at Fort Independence, Boston Harbor, and in March, 1851, left that post to become instructor of artillery and cavalry at West Point.

On December 24, 1853, he was promoted a Captain in the 3rd Artillery, and when relieved from the duty at West Point, was placed in command of a battalion of artillery which was sent to California by way of Panama. Arriving at San Francisco, July 1, 1854, he was ordered to take command of Fort Yuma in lower California, where he remained until July 21, 1855. On May 12, of that year, he was promoted Major of the 2nd U.S. Cavalry and joined his regiment at Jefferson Barracks, Mo., in the following September. The Colonel of the regiment was Albert Sidney Johnson, the Lieut.-Col. Robert E. Lee and the Senior Major, W.J. Hardee, all of whom afterward held high rank in the Confederate Army. The Junior Major, though a Southerner by birth, was a different caliber, and when was inaugurated, he refused to join his brother officers in the rebel cause and remained loyal to the Union, in which he firmly believed. He remained with the regiment until 1859, when he went to the headwaters of the Canadian and Red Rivers, which he explored. A similar expedition was undertaken by him in the summer of 1860, embracing the sources of the Conejo and Colorado Rivers. While on this expedition, his party fell in with a war party of Indians, and during the skirmish, Major Thomas was struck in the chin by an arrow, which also penetrated his breast. Though not dangerous, the injury was very painful. Exposed to danger innumerable times and under fire of the many battles, this was the only time he was ever wounded.

In Nov. 1860, while returning home on a leave of absence, Major Thomas' spine was injured in a railway accident. He never fully recovered, and the lameness of his spine had a good deal to do with his deliberate personal movements and slow, halting step.

His biographer, Van Horne, in speaking of him about this time, says, "He was about six feet in height, with proportions large and symmetrical. His thick hair and heavy beard were light brown, slightly tinged with red and sprinkled with gray. His head was large, forehead broad, eyes blue, features not entirely regular, but harmonious and strong. His presence was commanding and his manners winning. His expression was usually exceedingly mild, but yet there was in the easily compressed lips and change of cast in the soft, blue eyes, the plainest indication of an iron will. His person impressed strangers, and few men would look upon him for the first time without discerning his power and the certainty of its beneficent exertion. He was the embodiment of strength, and yet his power transcended all outward seeming. Beyond his sober bearing and quiet dignity, the usual exponents of conscious strength, there was in the frequent introspective look an indication of the reserve power which was to be the source of safety to great armies."

April 25, 1861, the Virginia Convention passed an ordinance adopting and ratifying the Constitution of the Confederate States, and every citizen of the State was invited to take up arms against the government. Nearly all her sons in the Army and Navy answered the call; but at least three stood firm for the old flag, all of whom soon earned the undying gratitude of their countrymen,–Winfield Scott, David Farragut and George H. Thomas.

May 3rd, Thomas was appointed Colonel of the 2nd Cavalry in place of Albert Sidney Johnson, and on June 3rd became the commander of the First Brigade of the Army of Pennsylvania, and marched his troops across Maryland, taking part in the engagement at Falling Waters, Va., on July 2nd.

August 24, 1861, Thomas received a commission of Brigade-General of Volunteers, and two days later was ordered to report to Gen. Robert Anderson at Louisville, Ky., where he was assigned to command the troops then concentrating and drilling at Camp Dick Robinson. The troops were nearly all raw, poorly equipped and disciplined, but Thomas went immediately to work, and with untiring zeal and labor molded them into a fighting body by the first of January.

On the 19th of that month, 1862, he met the enemy at Mill Springs, Va., and badly defeated them, Gen. Zollicoffere, one of the leaders being killed. Opposed to the forces of the Union were 10 regiments of infantry, one battery and a part of a regiment of cavalry. The enemy advanced with cheers, confidently expecting to overwhelm Thomas at the first onslaught, but after a hard all night battle, "Old Pap," was still holding his own, while the Confederates retired to their entrenchments. When day dawned, the enemy had disappeared, "leaving all his badly wounded, 12 pieces of artillery, a large amount of ammunition, a large number of small arms, 150 wagons, more than 1,000 horses and mules, and abundant quartermaster's and commissary stores."

"The victory at Mill Springs was the first decisive one that crowned the national arms, and it gave joy and hope to the loyal everywhere. The President issued a congratulatory order, and the General-in-Chief charged Gen. Buell to convey his thanks to Gen. Thomas and his troops for his brilliant victory."

April 25, 1862, Gen. Thomas was appointed a Major-General of Volunteers, and assigned to the command of the Right Wing of the Army of the Tennessee, under Gen. H.W. Halleck. His division did not take part in the battle of Shiloh, being too far in the rear. When the enemy retreated from Corinth, Thomas was placed in command of the place on June 5th, and plans were immediately made for an attempt to drive the enemy out of Chattanooga, East Tennessee and Northern Georgia. Gen. D.C. Buell, who was at the head of the Army of the Ohio, had carefully made his disposition and plans of attack, when, to the great surprise of Thomas, he was ordered to relieve Gen. Buell and lead the army in his stead. Believing it to be rank injustice and unmerited treatment of his superior, he asked to be allowed to keep his place at the head of his division, which request was granted.

On October 8, 1862, the battle of Perryville was fought by Gen. Buell's troops, which resulted in a victory over the Confederates under Gen. B. Bragg, and Thomas did a large share in winning the battle. The officials at Washington became very much dissatisfied with Buell's manner of conducting the campaign, and he was relived, Gen. Rosecrans taking his place. Gen. Thomas was very indignant over the appointment and protested to Gen. Halleck, claiming he ought to have the place, as he had been second in command and had proved his worth in every engagement of the army. His protest went unheeded, and from then on, to the end of the war, he never made a request to his superiors for preferment.

Rosecrans placed Thomas in charge of the work of concentrating supplies and equipment at Nashville and to repair the railroads so that the army could move south as soon as possible. December 28, the army marched from Nashville by different roads, and on December 31, 1862, the battle of Stone River was fought. When night came, the contest looked so near like a defeat, that Rosecrans proposed a retreat, but after a long conference of the division commanders, the idea was abandoned, and during the night of the 3rd of January, the confederate troops retreated.

In 1863, the army remained for a long time inactive, but when they did move forward, the enemy abandoned Chattanooga and moved south. The Union troops occupied the place and Thomas advised holding it, fearing that pursuit would lead them into a trap. Gen. Rosecrans felt differently, and gave the order to pursue with all haste.

Concentrating at Chickamauga, Bragg hurled his forces at the Union advance, while recoiled and were being beaten back when reinforcements came up, and the line was held. All day the battle raged, each side advancing a little, then falling back; the lines of both being penetrated, then close again, and during all this time Thomas directed the movements of the troops and saved them from defeat. The next day, the battled raged even harder; Rosecrans ordered part of the army to retreat, but Thomas stood firm and when he was told to withdraw the army at his discretion, replied; "It will ruin the army to withdraw it now. This position must be held till night." He did hold his ground and saved the army after half of it had retreated, and after the commanding General, Rosecrans, had gone to Chattanooga. His clear judgment and great ability to get troops to the vital points of attack, saved the day, and his heroic stand earned him the title of "Rock of Chickamauga."

On September 30th, Stanton, in writing to Charles A. Dana, said,–"If Hooker's command gets safely through, all the Army of the Cumberland can need will be a competent commander. The merits of Gen. Thomas and the debt of gratitude the nation owes to his valor and skill, are fully appreciated here; and I wish you to tell him so. It is not my fault that he was not in chief command months ago."

October 16, 1863, Thomas succeeded Rosecrans in command of the Army of the Cumberland, which was then fortified at Chattanooga. Grant was afraid he would retreat and telegraphed on the 19th to "Hold Chattanooga at all hazards."

"We will hold the town till we starve, "flashed back over the wires, and the town was not alone held, but when he was ready, his men crushingly defeated the enemy in the "Battle of the Clouds."

The soldiers climbed up the almost perpendicular face of Lookout Mountain, and fresh laurels were added to their credit in what has gone down in history as the Battle above the Clouds."

Next day Missionary Ridge was fought, and Grant wrote to Sherman,–"No doubt you witnessed the handsome manner in which Thomas' troops carried Missionary Ridge this afternoon, and can feel a just pride, too, in the part taken by forces under your command, in taking, first so much of the same range of hills, and then in attracting the attention of so many of the enemy as to make Thomas' part certain of success."

In the advance on Atlanta, Ga., in July, 1864, the Army of the Cumberland was attacked by Gen. J.B. Hood's whole army at Peach Tree Creek, and after a hard battle the Confederates were compelled to fall back. At one time, it looked as though the army was lost, the Confederates having gained the left and rear. Thomas immediately rode to that point and personally directed the troops, who pushed back the enemy and saved the whole line. The dead and dying were thickly strewn over the ground; grim reminders of the terrible conflict which added another star to Thomas' crown, and a victory for the Union.

September 29, 1864, Gen. Thomas was detached from Sherman's main army and sent into Tennessee. On October 26, he was placed at the head of the Department of the Cumberland and charged with the duty to keep Hood's army out of Tennessee and Kentucky and if possible to bring on a battle and crush him.

In November, Hood commanded his advance, and on the 29th and 30th, the battles at Spring Hill and Franklin were fought, the Union troops being forced back to Nashville, which was strongly fortified, and which Hood intended to siege and capture.

Grant, Sherman, and officials at Washington now began to urge Thomas to attack the enemy, but he refused until his forces were adequately equipped and prepared. Urging turned to positive orders and threats of dismissal, but still he did not move. At last, Gen. John A. Logan was sent to take his place, but before he arrived at Nashville, Thomas was ready and the battle opened on the morning of December 15, 1864, continued that day and all of the 16th, the result being, the Confederate Army was scattered to the four winds. Hood's army was crushed, the troops rushing in a riotous mass toward the South, it being the only time during the war that an army was so badly defeated. Censure now turned to praise. The whole country was overjoyed when news of the victory flashed over the wires, and everybody, including those who criticized strongest of War sent the following message the next week,-

"War Department, D.C.
December 24, 1864
Major-General George H. Thomas,
Headquarters Dep't Cumberland
Via Nashville, Tenn.

With great pleasure I inform you, that for your skill, courage and conduct in the recent brilliant military operations under your command, the President has directed your nomination to be sent to the Senate as a major-general in the United States Army, to fill the only vacancy in that grade. No official duty has been performed by me with more satisfaction, and no commander has more justly earned promotion by devoted disinterested and valuable services to his country.

Edwin M. Stanton

Secretary of War"

When he received this dispatch, he slowly read it, then stood lost in thought for a minute or two, and turning to Dr. George E. Cooper, medical director of his department, said, "What do you think of that ? handing him the paper. "it is better late than never," answered the Doctor. "I suppose it is better late than never, but it is too late to be appreciated; I earned this at Chickamauga." He spoke with strong emotion, plainly showing how deeply he felt the unjust way his superiors had treated him throughout the war, and the humanitarian of being disturbed because of his Southern birth.

Thomas did little real fighting during the Winter, but he prepared Gen. Wilson's cavalry for a raid through Alabama. When they started, they swept everything before them, badly defeating Forrest's Cavalry, later capturing Capt. Wirs, the Andersonville Prison keeper and the Confederate, Jefferson Davis.

The war was near an end; the great fighting was going on before Grant at Petersburg, and Sherman in his march through the Carolinas, while Thomas commenced this work of ridding, the country under his command of all enemies of the government.

June 7, 1865, Gen. Thomas was placed at the head of the Department of Tennessee, which compromised the States of Kentucky, Tennessee, Georgia, Alabama, and Florida, and his headquarters were to be at Nashville. On December 16, 1866, the citizens of the State presented him with a gold medal in recognition of his services in saving the city and defeating Hood's army two years before. In his speech accepting the medal, he said of the battle of Nashville,–

"Gen. Steedman commenced the battle on the left and so occupied the attention of the enemy, that he appeared entirely to forget the other portions of his line, and concentrated heavily at that point, evidently expecting a battle there. This was expected in my programs, and after Gen. Steedman had opened the battle and been engaged about half an hour, the troops were moved on their respective positions, and, almost like men in review, took post, and drove the enemy to the hills.

"The next day, by the skillful maneuver of the cavalry commander, the enemy's left was entirely turned; and then, by one of the most gallant assaults I have ever witnessed, the entire line of the enemy was swept from left to right, and so ended one of the strongest and most daring armies the enemy ever equipped.

March 11, 1867, Pres. Johnson sent Gen. Thomas' name to the Senate, asking that body to confirm him as a Brevet Lieutenant-General and General in the U.S. Army. Reading in the news-paper the next morning of what the President had done, the General immediately forwarded the following dispatch,–

"*Louisville, February 22, 1868, 2:30 P.M.*

Hon. B.F. Fade

President of the United States Senate:
The morning papers of Louisville announced officially that my name was yesterday sent to the Senate for confirmation as brevet lieutenant-general and brevet general.
"For the battle of Nashville I was appointed a major-general in the United States Army. My services since the war do not merit so high a compliment, and it is now too late to be regarded as a compliment, if conferred for services during the war. I therefore earnestly request that the Senate will not confirm the nomination.

Gen. H. Thomas
Major-General."

The nomination was withdrawn, but the General was not allowed to remain quietly in his position very long. Soon after this incident, his name was suggested for the nomination for President, and the agitation became so strong, that he was compelled to write again, advising his friends that he would, under no circumstances, accept the subject, and am extremely adverse to permitting such a disposition to be made of me. I am also afraid that the military arm, it becoming more or less infected with politics; let us by all means keep that branch of the public service free from the taint of intrigue and party strife."

June 1, 1869, Gen. Thomas took command of the Military Division of the Pacific, and remained there until his death, March 26, 1870. He appeared in the best of health during the morning, and kept busy at his desk until nearly 1:30 p.m., when he was stricken and fell to the floor. He soon rallied, and appeared to be gaining until early evening, when he rapidly sank, soon becoming unconscious, and died at 7:25 p.m.

In the evening, Gen Stewart L. Woodford delivered an eloquent address on the life and services of Gen. Thomas in the First Baptist Church.

Though one of the best generals in the war, he was not given the rank he deserved, and influences at Washington kept him back as much as possible where they dared, and criticized him in the severest terms for ever supposed wrong. Others were placed over him, an independent command was kept from him as long as possible, and his battles were sometimes fought with little aid from those higher in command. He said nothing through the war, but when that struggle ended, he demanded justice, and it was grudgingly given him.

His biographer says he "discerned all that is pure, noble and spiritual in human life. Few men have had as lofty ideals of public and private conduct, and seldom have men approximated more nearly to subjective standards, or conformed more outwardly life more fully to convictions of duty.

"One of his most prominent characteristics was his breath of sympathy with all the rightful interests of men. His country,–its integrity and destiny,–commanded extreme devotion. At the beginning of the war, against his family with all its wealth of affection, his State with her traditions of leadership and power, his section with time-honored institutions and chivalrous sentiment, and against a degree of personal sympathy, he was victorious in the struggle between sentiment and duty, and gave himself to his country in the great Civil War, with the most unselfish and most ardent patriotism."

When the time came for Gen. Robert E. Lee to make a choice, he pondered long and chose his State; but George H. Thomas never thought of making a choice, because the Nation was everything to a free people and he stood by that Nation with the same fidelity in war as he did in peace, and the path he took to defend his flag was sacred, above state, friends, and family.

The City of Troy can feel justly proud the last resting place of George H. Thomas is within its bounds.

JAMES C. BLAINE

After his death, James C. Blaine said,—"Peculiar circumstances surrounded the career of Thomas, imparting great interest and enlisting on his behalf a strong affection among the loyal people of the nation. The popular regret that he had not been appropriately recognized by the National Government for his great services, was deepened by his untimely death. The regard usually felt by soldiers for their successful leader was exceptionally strong in his case, and manifested itself in the many acts of personal devotion. He was commended to popular favor by his steadfast loyalty to the Union when he was subjected to all the temptations and all the inducements which had led Lee and Johnston into the Rebellion. He, like them, was born in Virginia, was reared in Virginia, was appointed to the army from Virginia; but in the hour of peril to the government he remembered that he was a citizen and soldier of the United States, and had sworn to uphold the Constitution. How well he maintained his faith to his country is written in the history of the great battles and great victories."

J. E. Mason Regt Merrill Horse Co H Saw Gen Thomas at Chattanoga Ten in 1864

*William A. Boyd
Chairman Memorial Committee
County of New York,
71st Regiment N.Y.S.M.
62nd Regiment N.Y.S. Vols.*

Philip G. Woodward
Capt Co C 36th Mass Vol
Infty
Executive Committee
National Council
Past Dept Commander
Dept of Minnesota GAR

John J. McAleer,
Cambridge Mass.,
Private of Marines,
U.S.S. Kearsarge.
Secretary Kearsarge Survivors

Geo. B. Wright   Wisconsin
Co. G. 48th Regiment. Vol. Infty

Adam Schaible
46 - N.y. V.L.
never saw Lincoln

Troy, Aug. 27, 1912.

H. G. Waite
13" N.Y. H. Arty
I never had the honor to
meet President Lincoln

May 30, 1912.

Henry H Hulbert of Norwich, N.Y.
Co A 43 N.y

Asa B. Baker
Rear Admiral
U.S. Navy

Lenzero Durand

Enlisted in Co. B. Thirteenth Mich Infantry at Monterey, Allegan, Co.

I was with the Western army and was taken prisoner in Salisbury and Libby prisons. I never saw Abraham Lincoln.

Edward W. Castell
52d Regt N.Y.V.

> Portland 12-28-1918
>
> I never had the pleasure of seeing Mr. Lincoln, much as I desired. I regard him as the greatest of all Americans. He was undoubtedly a man ordained for a special work and did it as only Lincoln could. The farther we get away from his time, and deeds, the more brilliant shines his star of destiny.
>
> Respectfully in F. C. & L.
>
> Co. D.
> 40 Reg. Ind. Vols.
>
> J. G. Chambers
> Senior Vice Commander in Chief
> G. A. R.

Haerbert J. Hyde
(HERBERT J. HYDE)

Seventh Michigan Light Artillery
(Never saw Abraham Lincoln)

Lester J. Haughton

Co. H. 171st O. M. G.
Co. H. 184th O. N. G.

Never saw Abram. Lincoln

Lester J. Haughton
Phalanx Station O.

James $\overset{his}{\times}$ Joyner
Mark
Goodlettsville Tenn.
Severed in
13th Colored Infantry.

Wm Stubblebine
53 Reg Penn Vol
[illegible] saw Lincoln

Alvin L Hemstreet [illegible]
44th N.Y. Vol [illegible]
Troy, Aug. 29, 1912.

JOHN L. STAHL

On September 19, 1863, Gen. Bragg commenced the battles to recapture Chattanooga, from which he had been driven a short time before. He had an army of experienced fighters with able leaders, almost equal in numbers to the Union forces, and every indication pointed to success. Rosecrans' forces had been divided in a game of hide and seek to battle the enemy, and Bragg, realizing this, suddenly threw his whole army on the Union flanks. The battle raged all day, darkness only stopping the fighting, with the gains in favor of the Confederates, who were now elated at their successes and anxious to renew the content.

In the night, Rosecrans changed his positions to meet the onset, the troops getting very little rest and practically no food or water. They had only time to throw up slight breastworks, when at daylight the famous Rebel yell sounded over the fields and through the woods. The roar of cannons opened the Sabbath day, the charging columns broke round of shot into them, line following line breaking while others moved up to crush the gallant men. Rosecrans, who was directing the battle, could not send support, as every part of the line was engaged, the enemy constantly making attempts to flank the troops and gain the rear. At noon, Gen. Bragg was ordered to leave his place and support a part which locked as though it would break, the enemy immediately grasping the advantage, rushed in, gaining the open space between the lines and rolled up the Federals on either side. The battle was lost and soon became an almost rout, but Gen. Thomas quickly fell back to a position between Missionary Ridge and another place of higher ground, arranging his forces to withstand the new shock soon to reach him. When it did come, Gen. Rosecrans was gone, having retreated toward Chattanooga, and Thomas, acting independently, riding back and forth, sanding new troops here, re-organizing others there and moving them to better meet the assaults, held the line until darkness set in. At night the troops fell back to Roseville, where they hurriedly threw up breastworks. The battle was not renewed when day dawned, Chattanooga was saved to the Union and Thomas became known as The Rock of Chickamauga. It had been terrible punishment,–one-third of an army of more than 50,000 men having been reported, dead, wounded and missing, September 20, 1863, being a day long remembered for terrific fighting and also for the superb heroism on both sides.

One of the men who fought through all the battles of the Army of the Cumberland was John L. Stahl a private in the 104th Ohio Vols. "I followed my regiment through all the battles of the Western Army to Franklin, Tenn., where I was taken prisoner and sent to Meridian, Miss., and spent my Christmas there, a sad day; and though we longed for, we did not receive any neatly wrapped packages tied with the red ribbon. We were transferred to Andersonville, Ga., Jan. 4, 1865, where I spent my 24th birthday on Easter Sunday, April 20th. We were turned loose on April 28th, and had to find our way as best we could to Jacksonville, Fla., where we were sent home and were discharged June 13th. I am not living at Glouster, Ohio, Mar. 1928, am 87, blind, but otherwise strong and happy."

Glouster Ohio. March 5th 1928 Page No I
Mr John E. Boos Dear Sir. you Ask for My Autograph of My Life as an Merican I am A. Fullblooded German My Parents came to Ohio. from Bavaria Germany in 1840 and landed at New Berlin now North Canton where I was Borne on the 20th day of April 1841 I was Raised in Stark Co. Ohio. untill I was 21 years old and was Able to Build Houses and Barns as A. Carpenter in 1862 I Enlisted in Co. B. 104th Regt. O. V. I. we were sent to Camp Massillon Stark Co. Ohio. where we were Equiped with old Austrin Riffles and sent from there to Fort Michell Ky. where we were put in the front line as Skirishers where we lost one Man killed and two Wounded and we drove Kirby Smith clear out of Ky. I Follow ed My Regt. through all the Battles Fought in the Western Army under Grant Burnside and SherMan to the Battle of Franklin Tenn. where I was taken Prisner in the front line of Battle it was Fought By Schofield Cox and Stanley we Fought Mostly in the 23nd Corps first Brigade third Div. then Called the Army of the Ohio. Now as Prisner I was taken to Maridian Miss. where I Spent My Christmas and got No Presents A Sad day

Page No 2

we were taken from Miss. Andersonville Georgey on the 4th day of Jan. 1865 where I spent My 24th Birthday on Easter Sunday April 20th on April 28th they took us out of Prison and March us to Tomassille Georgey where they turned us loose and we Grouped our way to Jacksonville Fla. they sent us around the Coast to Indianapolis Md. we were sent from there to our own State Columbus where I was DisCharged on the 13 day of June 1865 where I Married on the 4th day of Jan. 1866 My Wife Father and only Brother was in the Army with Me in 1867 I was Mustere in the 3nd Post Organized in Ohio. at Alliance Stark Co. Ohio, when John A. Logan was Com. inchief in the G. A. R. Now I want to tell how far back I can remember when My Father had his first Vote for President when I was 7 years old James K. Polk was Nominated for Presiden My Father said he would not Vote for that Slave holder and from that time on he Voted the other way and he was glad to Vote for J. C. FreeMont and Abraham Licolin and I was only 20 years old then so I couldent Vote but I Vote for him at Nashville Tenn. and I neaver saw him before or since. Ian Blind and soon will be 87 years old and I wich you God Speed hope this will do
Allen

WILLIAM J. KAY

In January 1862, Gen. Zollicoffer held a strongly entrenched position on the Cumberland River in Kentucky near Mill Spring. About the first of the month, Gen. Crittanden arrived and took charge of the Rebel camp. Moving over the mountains toward him came Gen. Buell from one direction and Gen. Thomas from another, the two commands expecting to combine and march on Bowling Green, Ky.

Crittenden, having received news of Gen. Thomas' advance, determined to attack him before Buell could join forces with him. The Confederates advanced early on Sunday the 19th, and tried to surprise Union forces in their camp at Logan Crossroads. The first news of the nearness of the Rebs was the firing of the pickets that had been placed some distance in advance. The long roll was sounded, and when the skirmish retired, Thomas had his forces in line to meet the attack. The 10th Indiana met the oncoming Johnnies, and held their ground for nearly an hour before the 4th Kentucky regiment came to their support. The ammunition was almost exhausted when the 9th Ohio and the 2nd Minnesota arrived and took position. The ground was heavily wooded, and when chance offered, the Union troops charged bodies of the enemy, driving them to cover, until the 9th Ohio, led by the gallant Col. McCook charged the center of the line, breaking it, and the whole Confederate force retreated back to their works at Mill Spring, closely followed by Gen. Thomas and his men.

William J. Kay was in many battles under Thomas and he said, "I enlisted in my 19th year at Plattsville, Wis. I was sworn as a private at Milwaukee in the 10th Wisconsin Volunteers. In Nov. 1861, was at Louisville, Ky; at Bowling Green in Feb. 1862, then marched to Memphis, Tenn., and Huntsville, Ala,; retreated under Buell back to Louisville, Ky., and then forward again to the Battle of Perryville. Later took part in the campaign to Atlanta, Ga., and from there was sent back to Tennessee with Thomas, being discharged Nov. 18, 1864."

William J Kays born 1842. lived on farm untill 1861 & enlisted in my 19 years at Plotteville Wisconsin in Sep 14 "61 was sworn into U.S. service as a private at Millwaukee was asigned to Company D 10th Reg't wis. vol inf'y we left the state Nov 14. arived at Louisvill Ky was asigned to O M Mitchells Command. the first of Feb 1862. we left for Bowlingreen where we was placed in deribners brigade O M mitchells command. in march we took the memphis and Charlston. R R at Huntsvill ala the next was the Buell retreat back to Louisville then the battle of Perryvill the Regimen in Campain of 1863 & 64 ending a Atlanta we were relained from duty when Sherman started for Savanna and Thomas for the Cumberland river arriveing at home and discharged may 13 1864

it is now nearly 78 year since the ended what do we see what has become of that great army of 1861 to 65. the most of them have followed their immortal leader Abraham Lincoln whom I never saw. there the. G A R the order that taught F C L to the Nation we live in and made this Nation the greatest Nation on earth. but alas they are passing on to the reword of the faithfull. and we will only be remember for it did

W $ Hays

38

SIDNEY W. DAY

Near the end of 1861, Gen. Thomas was sent by Gen. Beuell to take command in the Cumberland, and had reached Logan's Cross Roads where Gen. G.B. Crittenden, attacked his army in the night with eight regiments of infantry, six cannon and two battalions of cavalry. Thomas had kept pickets, both infantry and cavalry on guard a distance from his camp, so the surprises was a failure, the Union troops being prepared for them when the Rebel soldiers charged. The battle raged for two hours, but the enemy was put to flight just after daylight by charge of the 9th Ohio Volunteers, and they were rushed through the rain to their camp at Beach Grove. The entrenchments were immediately shelled, but at dark both sides rested until daylight. During the night the enemy crossed the Cumberland River, and when day dawned, the Union troops took possession, finding 10 cannon, many muskets, about 1200 horses and mules with much other war material.

Sidney W. Davy enlisted Jan. 22, 1864 in the 22nd in the Michigan Volunteers, a part of Thomas' army and in a letter written many years later he said; "I went from Mich. to Chattanooga, Tenn., was at the taking of Kenneshaw Mountain, as my regiment was Gen. Thomas' headquarters guard. The Rebs left the mountain the night of July 3, '64 and I marched in and through Marrietta, Ga., on the 4th of July, and from there on to the siege and taking of Atlanta. I was transferred to the 29th Mich., June 26th, 1865 and mustered out Sept. 20 at Murfreesboro, Tenn."

Clarion RFD #1 Mich,
Sep, 20 1928
Mr John Boos Albany N.Y.

Dear Sir,

I was a member of Co. B. 22ond Mich. Inf. Was enrowled in the U.S. Service on the 22ond day of Jan, 1864 was in the Cumberland army. Went from such to Chattanooga Tenn. Was at the taking of Kennesaw Mount, as my reg, was general Thomas's Head quarters guard. The rebs left the mountain the nite of July 3d and I marched with my Company and reg, in and thru ~~marri~~ ~~eth~~ Marrietta Ga, on the 4th of July 1864, Then on to the siege and taking of Atlanta Ga., I never saw ABRAHAM Lincoln as he did not visit the army of the Cumberlanch during my Millitary Service. I was transfered to the 29th reg. Mich Inft, June 26 1865 and mustered out Sep. 20 at Murfreesboro Tenn, 1865. I will be 84 the 12 of Nov. next

  Sidney W. Davy

I see you have my name miss spelt its not Darry.

General Gordon Granger

1925 Tory Hospital

Gen. Gordon Granger was posted at Roseville, Ga., on September 18, 1863, holding the roads in every direction, and from the reports of his generals and scouts he was sure Gen. Bragg was engaging Thomas in battle. He sent troops to aid, but at daylight of the 20th, hearing the roar of guns about 3 miles distant, he moved without orders and reached the battlefield at about 3 p.m. His men arrived at a critical moment, going immediately into the fight. The right flank and rear was threatened by the Confederates under Gen. Hindman. Two of Granger's brigades charged the brigades charged the foe. Col. Steedman seized the flag of one of the regiments, and waving it, and cheering the brave man on, and though the loss was heavy, the flank was held intact and the enemy forced back Col. Steedman's horse was killed and though the intrepid leader was injured, he stayed on the field until the firing ceased at dark.

After the battle, one of Granger's men wrote;

"The contest continued until dark, and all the time we held the ridge. Sometimes a regiment or more would fall back beyond the ridge, but enough always remained to hold it. At, last, Gen. Thomas gave the order to retire; but it failed to reach a portion of the 96th Illinois, and a remnant of the 131st Ohio, who at the time occupied a position on the right, somewhat advanced beyond the line; and there for a considerable time they continued to fight with unabated vigor. The order to retire was at last give to this devoted band, who reluctantly left their position. That closed the fighting for the day. We retired from the field, not knowing that the enemy was also retreating, baffled and discouraged.

"The bloody field was left unoccupied that night. Not wholly unoccupied, for James T. Gruppy, a private of Co. E, 96th Illinois, not knowing that our troops had fallen back, slept upon the battlefield, and next morning, as he awoke, found a Rebel surgeon hear him, looking for the rebel dead, who advised him, if he ever wished to see his regiment again, to hurry on to Chattanooga."

James W. White

James W. White enlisted in the 15th Ohio Volunteers and fought under Thomas at Franklin and Nashville. He was a member of Company A, and when the regiment was allowed to vote in the fall of 1864, the result showed 129 for Lincoln and 9 votes for McClellan, and "many of these voters were afterward killed at the battles of Franklin and Nashville." Mr. White was not mustered out until the end of the war, when he returned to his home at New Concord, Ohio, where he lived until his death.

New Concord Ohio July 17.
The vote for A. Lincoln & Johnson. at Pulaska S.W. Tenn. was 129. Lincoln, and 9 for McClelland — Many of the boys were not old enough to vote. I was 3 days over 21. Many of the voters were killed at the battles of Franklin Nov 30. 1864. and Nashville " Dec-15 and 16" our Captain (Leo A) was the only man killed in the company. The rebels said the battle of Franklin was "but —" Gen Speedy he was in the proper place at the right time with his briga— with bayonets fixed and loaded guns helpt to win the victory after our line was broken, rebel loss over 600. our loss 2300 a large field was used as a rebel cemetery report said 2800 of the rebels interred there.

on the Atlanta Campaign May to Sept. 1864. 4 months of a Campaign Marching thro-Ga. Rebels talked about destroying the tunnel report said one Johnnie replied What? "Gee Old Sherman" carries duplicate tunnels. Our engines with trains come up very close to our front lines with supplies, and the troops of both armies let out a yell could be heard for a mile. Yank. called across the river to Johnnie how many men have you over there. Answer about enough for another killing. who commands your army. Sherman. how is that whenever Yuns move, we'ns move. a cessation of firing. Yank. would march part way over. Johnnie met him with a good supply of "Tobacco" and trade for "Coffee". Sincerely James W. White Company A, 15th. Ohio Veteran Volunteer Infantry.

A.D. French

Chickamauga had been fought. Thomas, after holding back the Confederate Army retreated to Chattanooga. Gen. Bragg and his rebels fortified all but one road to the city, almost bottling up the Union troops. Gen. W.S. Rosecrans was in command of the Department of the Cumberland, and on Oct. 19th, 1863 almost a month after the terrific fighting at Chickamauga, he received an order to turn over the command of his department to Gen. Thomas and proceed north. Immediately after the receipt of the news of his promotion, Thomas received a telegram from Grant who was at Louisville, Ky., ordering him to hold on at all hazards.

"I will hold on till we starve," answered Thomas. The nation believed him, and renewed confidence gripped the loyal people.

While these events were happening, A.D. French lay wounded in the military hospital, having been hit during the severe fighting the afternoon of the 19th of September, and was unable to take part in the battles later fought to drive the Confederates out of that region. Mr. French was born in Williamsville, Mass., Jan 13, 1842, moved to Illinois in 1858 and enlisted in Chicago, August 14, 1862 in the 89th Illinois Infantry. He took part in the battles of Stone River, Liberty Gap, and when wounded, lay on the Chickamauga battlefield about 20 hours before his wound was bandaged, and he was put in a wagon and taken to a hospital. During his last years he lived in Glenwood, Iowa.

I was born in Wmsville West Stockbridge Twp - Berkshire Co., Mass. Jan. 13-1842; moved to Illinois in 1858. Enlisted in Chicago Aug 14-1862 in Co. "A" 89th Ill. Infy; also known as "The Railroad Regiment"; Assigned to August Willich's Brigade. Johnsons Division, McCooks Corps. Army of the Cumberland. Participated in Battle of Stone River Dec. 31-1862 & Jan 1. & 2=1863. Liberty Gap. June 24 & 25-1863. and Chicamaugua Sept 19 & 20 1863. Was wounded at 3 P.M. Sept 19th 1863. and lay on the Battlefield until 10 AM. next day. Discharged May 24-1865.

My Pension Certificate is No. 49.499 -

A. D. French

Glenwood - Iowa.

= Aug 10 - 1929 =

M.B. WILLIS

In March, 1864 Gen. Grant placed Gen. Sherman in command of the Military Division of the Mississippi, taking in four great departments, namely the Ohio, the Cumberland, the Tennessee and the Arkansas. May 6th, he commenced his march to Atlanta, fighting flanking and maneuvering the enemy out of position after position until that city was occupied on September 1st.

Sherman marched from Chattanooga for Dalton, but was stopped at Rocky Face Ridge, the pass being called Buzzards Roost Gap. When Thomas assailed the front of the enemy, McPherson moved on the flank, the rebel General Joe. E. Johnson being compelled to fall back through Dalton to Resaca, where a hard fight took place May 15th. Thomas pushed Hardee's troops through Resaca, fighting and skirmishing to Adairsville and to Rome. There was fighting through Dallas, New Hope Church, Allatoona Pass; Pine, Lost, and Kenesaw mountains, to Marietta. Then across the Chattahoochee to Peach Tree Creek, where another hard fight took place. Then came the dogged battering near Atlanta, the Federals steadily advancing, until on the morning of September 1st, at daylight, the sounds, first heavy, then lighter, from the north, indicated to Sherman that something momentous was occurring in Atlanta 20 miles distant. They might have proceeded from an attack on that stronghold by Slocum, but the more probable supposition pointed, that Hood, completely outgeneraled, and at his wit's end, was blowing up his magazines, burning his stores and escaping with as little he could, deprived of railroads, carrying off in his flight."

Atlanta was fallen, and on September 23, Gen. Thomas was sent back to Nashville, where immediately set to work, fortifying and organizing the troops in the region, while Sherman, cutting all communications commenced his famous "March to the Sea."

M.B. Willis was a sergeant in the 44th Indiana Volunteers for nearly three years, receiving the promotion to Captain of his company on January 16, 1855. He was wounded in the right hand at Shiloh, fought at Corinth, Stone River, Chickamauga and Missionary Ridge. He lived at Auburn, Ind., until his death, and never tired talking of the Old Pap Thomas.

Auburn Indiana
May 18" 1915

Mr. J. E. Boos.
Albany New York.

Dear Sir. Your request was received a few weeks ago, but I have been too busy until now to comply with same. I was a Sergt in Co "K" of the 44th Regt Ind. Infy Vet Vols for nearly three years, was then promoted to 1st or orderly Sgt until Jan 16" 1865 when I was made Captain of my company until muster out in Nov 1865. I was engaged in the battles of Shiloh, Corinth, Stones River, Chickamanga, Mission Ridge and many skirmishes, wounded in right hand 2nd day at Shiloh. Never was a day or night in Hospital. Am in my 76" year, but never had the pleasure of meeting our beloved Lincoln,
Resptfly Capt N.B.Willis
Auburn Indiana

Hooker had captured Lookout Mountain, and Grant, who had arrived at Chattanooga, very carefully planned the battle of Missionary Ridge, but the troops went far beyond his plans by climbing the steep side of the mountain, driving the Rebels from their trenches and sending them southward in an almost rout. Gen. Bragg, with such able assistants as Generals Hardes, Cleburne and Breckenridge, did all that experienced leaders could to rally the men, but the jubilant Yankees charged every line and drove it back as fast as it was formed, capturing many guns, much equipment and a large number of prisoners.

Hooker had advanced on the right, Thomas sent his forces at the front in the face of the enemy, and those long last days of November battles in 1863 were over at nightfall of the 25th, the siege of Chattanooga was raised, the dead at Chickamauga were avenged, and the miles of lost ground over which Thomas had fought so hard and disastrously a little more than a month before was again in possession of the forces of the Union.

In his report, Thomas said,–"Our troops advancing steadily in a continuous line, the enemy, seized with panic, abandoned the works at the foot of the hill and retreated precipitately to the crests whither they were closely followed by our troops, who, apparently inspired by the impulse of victory, carried the hill simultaneously at six different points, and so closely upon the heels of the enemy, that many of them were taken prisoners in the trenches. We captured all their cannon and ammunition, before they could be removed or destroyed. After halting a few moments to reorganize the troops who had become somewhat scattered in the assault on the hill, Gen. Sherman pushed forward in pursuit, and drove those in his front, who escaped capture, across Chickamauga creek. Gens. Wood and Baird, being obstinately resisted by re-enforcements from the enemy's extreme right, continued fighting until darkness set in; slowly but steadily driving the enemy before them. In moving upon Roseville, Gen. Hooker encountered Stewart's division and other troops; finding his left flank threatened. Stewart attempted to escape by retreating toward Greyaville; but some his force, finding their retreat threatened in that quarter, retired in disorder toward their right along the crest of the ridge; where they were met by another portion of Gen. Hooker's command, and were driven by these troops and nearly all made prisoners."

CHARLES W. BENNETT

"Missionary Ridge was one of the most spectacular battles of the Civil War," said Charles W. Bennett of Coldwater, Mich., on July 9, 1912, and he ought to know, because he was one of the fighters on the side of the Union that day.

"I enlisted as a private in Co. G, 9th Mich. Infantry, August 5, 1861. Was promoted through the grades to 2nd Lieutenant, and later transferred to the 13th U.S. Colored Infantry as Captain. Left the regiment January 10, 1866 with the brevet of Major."

Mr. J. E. Boos,
  Albany, N.Y.

Comrade:— I did not have the good fortune to see Abraham Lincoln. My whole four years and five months were spent in Ky. and Tenn.— largely under Rosecrans and Thomas.

I enlisted as a private in Co. G, 9th Mich. Infty, Aug. 15, 1861. Was promoted to Sergeant, First Sergeant and 2nd Lieut. of that regiment; then to Captain of Co. F, 13th U.S. Colored Infty, and was Brevetted "Major" for meritorious services in that regiment, and discharged Jan. 10, 1866. Was in the battles of Stone River, Chickamauga and Nashville.

Yours very truly,
C. W. Bennett,
Coldwater, Mich.
July 9, 1912.

Charles Wilkes Bennett.
  74 years old.

Samuel L. Harman

Samuel L. Harman was a business man in Lancaster, Pa., and in 1911, thinking over the days he was in the army he wrote out a few thoughts of Gen. Thomas, saying,—"I never had the pleasure and satisfaction of seeing either Thomas or Rosecrans conducting battle. At the battle of Stone River, Thomas commanded the 14th corps of the army of the Cumberland, the center of Rosecrans Army. My regiment, the 79th Penn. Was attached to that corps, I being seriously ill at Nashville, Tenn., with Typhus Fever. At the time of this battle I was absent from my regiment serving on detached duty as aid-de-camp on the division staff of Major-General Lovell H. Rousseau of the 14th corps. I was with Gen. Rousseau in the previous battle at Perryville, Ky., in the capacity of aid-de-camp, Gen. D.C. Buell being commander. Gen. Rousseau's bearing at all times was very enthusiastic and attractive, would be cheered by soldiers of other commands, not his own. He had a very martial bearing and had the power of inspiring soldiers to deeds of valor in battle. Gen. Thomas when in repose had the appearance of a man of great firmness, his personal address was uniformly a man of few words, kind and gentle to every one's approach; careful and considerate, large physically, weighing over 200 pounds, deliberate and accurate in judgment adhering to it with great tenacity, slow in action, with a hold on and hold out spirit. Gen. Rosecrans has been described as very alert on the field of battle, skillful in planning battle. A man of quick perception, ready conclusion and action, of demeanor and courteous address, a civil engineer of high order. I heard Gen. O.O. Howard say a short time before his death, he having served under both Generals McClellan and Rosecrans, that he though Rosecrans the best engineer of the two. This accomplishment enabled him to achieve the great flanking movements against Gen. Bragg, that he did in the march from Murfreesboro, Tenn., to Chattanooga. Neither Generals had the traits of a Martinet in their makeups. I think that Gen. Rosecrans had the greatest obstacles to encounter in his search from Bowling Green, Ky., than any other General in the Union Army, having but a single track of railroad with which to bring supplies to his army, accomplished his task with the loss of less men in killed, wounded and missing than any other commander did in marching over a similar number of miles, which a study of records will develop."

F.J. Young

Another fighter under Gen. Thomas was F.J. Young, who until his retirement, was a clerk in the Treasury Department for 42 years. He enlisted Jan. 4, 1864 in the 2nd Illinois Light Battery at the age of 18 and took part in the battle of Nashville. His battery was later sent south and he was in the siege of Mobile in April, 1865, being mustered out of the service on the following Sept. 4th.

"I never saw the great Lincoln," he wrote, "but I have seen every President since, including Herbert Hoover."

W.W. ROBERTS

Gen. Hood, confident of driving the Federals out of Tennessee had pushed them back to Nashville, although he had been severely punished a number of times while doing so. His army was entrenched in front of the city on the early morning of December 15, 1864, is men having suffered a great deal from cold and bad weather, and, they were, no doubt, not in a very good humor to give battle. The weather had warmed when day dawned. It was much milder than it had been for days, although a heavy fog hung over the country until noon. Gen. Thomas was fully prepared for battle, having been impatiently waiting for the ice, which covered roads and fields, to soften a little so that his infantry and cavalry could move more freely. Gen. A.J. Smith's cavalry started before daybreak, with Wilson's cavalry on his sight and before the Rebels realized it, the battle had opened and the troopers were in the enemy entrenchments driving everything before them. The Confederates were attacked at every point, and in the afternoon Hon's entire line fell back. They were pushed further before dark, leaving 16 guns, 40 wagons and more than 1200 prisoners as the spoils of the fight. "Never had men fought with more alacrity or greater steadiness than those who now lay down on their arms, prepared to finish work on the morrow," wrote the editor of the New York Tribune.

Gen. Thomas determined to give the enemy no rest, and at dawn, Gen. Wood advanced, pushed back the skirmishes and was soon in front of the main works at Overton Hill. Before dark, the Union troops valiantly forced the enemy from their trenches after hours of terrific battle, and then began a pursuit that scattered a Confederate army of nearly 40,000 men to the four winds. More than 4,000 prisoners were captured, 287 of which were officers.

Old Slowfoot had cleared Tennessee of the enemy, and Andrew Johnson's state was now surely and safely in the Union. On January 23, 1865, because of his terrific defeat by Thomas, Gen. hood was relieved from active duty at his own request.

W.W. Roberts of Flat Ridge, Va., was one of Gen. Thomas's fighting men, and in a letter written on his 88th birthday, he said, "I was a member of the 13th Tennessee Cavalry and fought in the Army of the Cumberland. I was wounded when we drove Hood out of Tennessee and while laying in a Nashville Hospital had the honor to talk with Clara Barton. She laid her hand on my head and said many kind words to me. When I saw the account of her death it brought tears to my eyes. May she ever be remembered as one of the greatest of her sex. I had three brothers in the army, two of them being killed in the service."

Flat Ridge Va. April. 20. 1925
yours of the 13· Received John E Boos
I belong to Company. D. 13. Tenn
Cavelary Army of the
Comberland, I never meat
Abraham Lincon. I was
in hospitel at Nathvill Tenn
and saw Miss Cleare Barton
she laid her hond on my
brow and said meny kind
words to me. and when I saw
the acount of her death
it brought tears to my eyes.
O may she ever be remembrd
as one of the gratest of her
seck. I had three Brothers
in the U.S. army 2 of them
was kiled in the survis
I was boarn in Virginia and
rustt in Grayson County and
I am in my 86 year.
yours Respfuley
    W. W. Roberts

R.R. GRAHAM

March 4, 1865, Gen. Thomas was at Eastport, Miss., aiding one of his subordinates, James H. Wilson to organize his cavalry for a raid through a part of Alabama and Georgia. When Gen. Wilson started on March 18th, he had 13,000 mounted men under his command, with 6 batteries of artillery, a wagon train and a light pontoon of 30 boats. There was skirmishing every day of the advance, and the first real fight took place near Plantersville, Ala., where Gen. Forrest was strongly entrenched, but Wilson soon had him flying, pursuing him to Selma. April 3rd, the works at Selma were charged and the victorious Yanks drove the much heralded invincible Rebel out of the city, although some of the fighting took place after dark, which gave Forrest and 3,000 of his men a chance to escape. The next morning everything contraband was burned or destroyed, including the arsenal, foundries, factories and warehouses. Beating a few days while the bridge over the Alabama River was reconstructed, the command moved forward, reached Montgomery on the 12th and discovered the enemy had burned about 125,000 bales of cotton.

April 8, 1865, Columbus Ga., was attacked, and shortly after dark the city was captured "with 1,200 prisoners, 58 field guns and large quantities of small arms and stores. The rebel hold was destroyed, 15 locomotives, 250 cars and 115,000 bales of cotton. "On the same day West Point was captured, and the next day, when nearing Mason, Ga., the Confederate General, Howell Cobb, assured Gen. Wilson the war was almost over and the fighting ended."

Richard B. Graham of Madisonville, Wis., one of the survivors of Thomas's Army wrote in his 83rd year that he "Was in the 27th Kentucky Infantry, left Atlanta in October, '64 when Hood stole the march on Sherman at Kensehaw Mountain. My regiment was in camp near Gen. Sherman's headquarters. I and one more boy was near the General's tent. He was sitting in a chair. He asked us if we could see the Johnnys in the distance. We answered we could only see smoke. 'Come close to me,' he said; "I can see one frying meat and another making coffee. If they will only stay there a little while we will go after them.'

"When the army was divided near Atlanta, we were left under Gen. Thomas, that grand old hero of Chickamauga. We were sent by rail from Chattanooga to Huntsville Ala., marched to Pulaski, Tenn., forded Elk River in icy water and then fought our way from Columbia, through Spring Hill and Franklin to Nashville. My regiment fought at the right of the cotton gin and the Carter house in the fighting Nashville that drove Hood's Army out of Tennessee."

153

Madisonville Ky- Mar-29, 1929
I served during the civil war in Co. E 27' Ky Inft 2' Brig. 1' Div. 4 army Corps am 83 years old my serves was short but had all the experiences of a soldier left Atlanta Ga: in October 64. When Hood stole the march on Sherman at Kenesaw Moun- my Reg- wer in camp near Gen- Sherman's hed quarters I and one more boy wer near the genrs tent he was seting in a chaire he remarked boys con you see the Johneys we says no nothing but smoke come here closer to me I can see them one is frieing meat and another is making coffee he says if they would just stay there we would go after them I never had the honer to meet the immortal Lincoln

Wel from Kenesaw Mt. we hiked for Altoony Pass we wer near anof to here the cannon when the Johneys wer trying to take fort we doubled quicked for about a mile when we got there the Johneys had puled out and left Gen- Corsey victors we wer under Gen Sherman until we reached near Gailsville Ala- then the army wer divided Sherman taken one part & turned back for Atlanta & the sea we the 4th & 23' corps wer left under Gen Thomas that grand old hero of Chickamauga after our hard march we wer sent by rail from Chatnooga to Huntsville ala- from ther marched to Pulaska then forded Elk River in very works like horses Hoods arny pressing us from there to Columby then to Zeranklin Tn had some experance at Spring hill Johneys liked to cut us off but sliped by without much loss so on the 30" of November 64 the battle was faught my Reg- was at the right of the Cotton find & Carter house 15" & 16 December wer in South at Nashville follode Hood to the Tenn River

wer in Huntsville ala- for rest of winter in march wer sent by rail to east Tenn to Strawbery plains from ther marched 50 miles beyond Boots gap when Lee surenderd sent back to Nashville there I was discharged under an order from war Dept the Commad wer sent from ther to Galveston Tex- the 21' Ky wer discharged in Tex.

Richard R. Graham

W.A. MARIETTA

Gen. Thomas had been placed in command of the Army of Cumberland after the heroic stand at Chickauaupa and Grant had come over the only road now held by the Union troops to study the situation and aid Thomas. A surprise attack was planned on Brown's Ferry 3 miles below Chattanooga, the troops moving in the darkness, and when the charge was made at daylight, it proved a complete success, the surprise attack finding the Confederates unprepared to meet it. The Federals now controlled another avenue to convey supplies in the beleaguered town. Gen. Howard's Corps pitched camp about a mile from Brown's ferry. Gen. Geary moved his troops to Mauhatchie and were encamped there when they were attacked in the night, the tactics of Thomas being adopted by Gen. Bragg. Gen. Schurz's troops were immediately sent to help Geary, followed by Tyedale, and later by Steinwehr, but the Confederates had moved along the heights beside the road and kept up a severe fire of musketry which was very destructive to the advancing troops. Orders were given to charge heights nearly 200 feet high and dislodge the enemy. The men climbed and scrambled up the steep hills, not a company wavering, and at the top, without firing a shot, charged with fixed bayonets and pursued the enemy until after daylight. Other troops had moved forward along the road, the enemy in front of Gen. Geary was repulsed, and Lookout Valley was again safe for the forces of the Union.

Gen. Thomas said of the fighting on the ridge; "The bayonet charge of Howard's troops, made up the side of a steep and difficult hill over two hundred feet high, completely routing the enemy from his barricades on the top, will rank among the most distinguished feats of arms of this war."

W.A. Marietta of the 11th Ohio Volunteers was one of the brave men who fought in the moonlight at Wauhatchie and though exhausted after the fight, was always proud of his share in it. Writing in 1928 from his home in Dayton, O., he said he "Was in the Civil War 3 years. First in the West Virginia, then sent east and was with the Kanawha Division in Second Bull Run, Frederick City, South Mountain and Antietam. Then sent west, and fought at Chickamauga, Missionary Ridge, Buzzards Roost and Resaca, being mustered our in 1864."

Dayton Ohio,
February 20. 1928.

Jno E. Boos,
Albany. N.Y.

Dear Sir — Replying to your letter of inquiry the 8th have this for your information:
Was in the Civil War three years. Was first West Virginia. Then sent East, and was with Kanawha Division in the Second Bull Run, & at Frederick City, South Mountain and Antietam. Was then sent West, and in the Army of the Cumberland and so at Chickamauga, Missionary Ridge, Buzzards Roost & Resaca. The regiment was mustered out in June, 1864.

Never had an opportunity to see the President.
Have been in Washington since, and shook hands with Presidents Harding and Coolidge.

Am now in my 83d year and enjoy comparatively good health.
Am a Past Post Commander of the G.A.R. and a member of the Sons of Veterans.

Very truly yours,
Jn. A. Marietta
11th Ohio Volunteer Infantry

Arthur E. West

George H. Thomas was under the command of William T. Sherman in the campaign in Tennessee and Georgia in 1863. Sherman had known Thomas at the beginning of the war and all through the fighting around Chattanooga, and the advance to Atlanta, he had the utmost confidence in the Virginian, and when Thomas was sent to protest Tennessee while Sherman made his famous march to the sea, Sherman knew the state would be ably defended, and he wasted little energy worrying about what might happen in his rear.

On June 1, 1862, writing to his brother John, the General said, "There are two A. No. 1 men there, George H. Thomas and Captain Gykes. Mention my name to both and say to them that I wish them all the success they aspire to, and if in the varying chances of war I should ever be so placed, I would name them for high places. Thomas was never brilliant but always cool, reliable and steady, maybe a little slow."

Grant did not seem to believe in Thomas as much as did Sherman, and would have relieved him at Nashville in December, 1864. If he had delayed battle with Gen. Hood's army a few more days. A group with great power in the government had no faith in Thomas's leadership, more because he went ahead and did things without a grand hurrah; and at the moment when they expected failure, Thomas, with his thorough preparations gained a signal victory. The General was never promoted or rewarded as he deserved, but he said nothing, as much as he resented the injustice, and gave his best whoever was placed over him. His men called him "Old Slowfoot," or "Pap," and they trusted his ability so much, they never hesitated to go even farther than they were sent, even to climbing the steep sides of Missionary Ridge, and gaining a signal victory against an equal number of the enemy strongly entrenched. When he died, March 28, 1870, he was tenderly carried from San Francisco, Cal., to Troy, N.Y., and buried in the family plot of his father-in-law, he having carried Francis L. Kellogg on November 7, 1852. The Old Dominion could not claim him any longer as a son. He wanted to sleep in the loyal states and among the people who willing sacrificed so much to preserve the Union.

Out in San Diego, Cal., lived a man in 1928, who at 16 enlisted in the 57th Indiana Volunteers. He fought at Shiloh, Stone River, and Missionary Ridge, was one of the Old Pap Thomas' soldiers and justly proud of the part he took in the Civil War under that great leader. His name was Arthur E. Vest, and he said "I am more than proud to be one of the boys that responded to the call of our immortal Lincoln for the first three hundred thousand men, enlisting in December, 1861 and staying in the service until January 3, 1866. I passed through 18 hard battles, including Shiloh, Stone River, Missionary Ridge, Franklin and the Atlanta Campaign, serving 4 years and 10 days."

San Diego, Calif.
Feb. 27 1928

Mr. John E. Boos
          Albany, N.Y.

Dear Sir:— Your letter of Feb. 7" just reached me and was read with much interest, also your address at the banquet of Ten Eyck Camp.

I am more than proud to be one of the boys that responded to the call of our immortal Lincoln for the first three hundred thousand men. I had just passed my sixteenth birthday (Nov. 25 1845) and on Dec. 21 1861 joined myself to Co. I, 57th Indiana Vol. Inf.

After serving two years we were asked to reenlist for three years longer, which I did with the other men. After going through eighteen hard battles, Shiloh, Stone River, Mission

Ridge & Franklin for example, we went on the Atlantic campaign and after serving four years & ten days we ceased to be an organization. On Jan. 3rd 1866 we were paid off and returned to our homes.

I never had the pleasure of meeting our beloved President Lincoln. I am now in my 83rd year. My four years experience would furnish matter for good sized book, but this will answer the purpose I hope.

Arthur E. West

Enoch F. Byng

Gen. Forrest with his cavalry was striking federal outposts and garrisons at many points in the district under Thomas' command, while Hood concentrated on the Tennessee, waiting for the two armies under Thomas and Sherman to move. The moment the Confederates discovered the March to the Sea had begun, their army of about 55,000 commenced the move against Thomas at Nashville. The federals immediately began to draw in their forces, fighting one battle at Columbia, Ga., another at Spring Hill, and a terrific fight at Franklin. The federals had thrown up a light breast-works, but when the Confederates charged, they brushed aside everything before them, taking many prisoners and almost sending the Union troops in a complete rout back to Nashville.

Opdyke's command had been in the advance. They were immediately turned around, ordered to charge, and they drove the Confederates back, re-capturing all that had been lost and re-forming the lines of troops that had been so badly defeated a short time before. The charge had been a complete surprise to the Confederates, the flying federals giving them confidence the day had been won, and though Gen. Hood threw heavy masses of troops against the works he had lately captured, the heroic Opdycke and his men, aided by the stragglers that were fast re-enforcing the lines beat them back with severe loss. The battle raged until 10 p.m., and though assault after assault shook the line, it held firm, the wagon trains were saved, and at midnight the troops left the trenches and moved back to Nashville. On the first of December, 1864, Hood prepared to invest the city and try to capture it.

Gen. H. Thomas, in his report said "At the battle of Franklin, Opdycke displayed the very highest qualities as a commander. It is not saying too much to declare that, but for the skillful dispositions made by him, the promptness and readiness with which he brought his command into action at the critical moment, and the signal personal gallantry he displayed in a counter assault on the enemy, when he had broken our line, disaster instead of victory would have fallen us at Franklin."

Enoch F. Byng was in the Western Army, having enlisted in the 26th Iowa Infantry, August 15, 1862 at Clinton, "I was in the battle of Arkansas Post, where we suffered heavy loss. Later was through the siege of Vicksburg and Jackson, Miss. Later in the year at Missionary Ridge. Was in the Atlanta campaign from Reseca and in many minor engagements, thense to Atlanta. I was wounded July 28, 1864 near Atlanta, in left shoulder and was sent home at once. I did not recover in time to go on the "March to the Sea." I was assigned, early in my career to clerk to Adjutant, was promoted early in 1864 from private to 1st lieutenant of Co. B. and took command of a the company, but several times acting as A.A.A.G. of the First Brigade, being in that capacity when wounded.

April 21st 1928.

Mr. John E, Boos.
                Albany , N.Y.

                Dear Sir;
                        In compliance with your request for my autograph , and part I took in the Civil War.
            I submit the following,
                I never saw Abraham Lincoln as I was with the western armies all the time.
                I enlisted August 15th 1862, at Clinton Iowa in Company "C" of the 26th Iowa Infantry, later assigned to the First Brigade , First Division . Fifteenth Army Corps. was with that Command during my servise , was in battle of ~~Rxxxxxx~~ Arkansas Post . Ark . where we suffered heavy loss. later was through [Siege] of Vicksburg and Jackson Miss, later in year at Missionary Ridge, in late 1863 —, Was in the Atlanta Campaign from Resacca and in many minor engagements, thence to Atlanta
            I was wounded July 28th 1864 near Atlanta, in left shoulder was sent home at once. did not recover in time to go on the March to the Sea, much to my regret, I resigned December 1864.
            I was assigned early in my career to clerk to Adjutant, was promoted early in 1864 from Private to First Lieut, of Co. B. and took command of the Company, but was several times acting as A.A.A.G of First brigade and was in that capacity when wounded.

                        Respectfully Submitted.
                                            Enoch. F. Byng

am now past 89 yelars. Still vigorous...

Joseph A. Barrall

In 1895, J.R. Gilmore wrote a vivid account of Garfield's ride from Rosscran's headquarters in the field to Thomas with a message to hold on until dark, if possible, and then fall back to Rossville. Corps after corps were in retreat, Chickamauga was lost unless Thomas could withstand the shock and Garfield rode almost in the face of the Confederates, a distance of 6 miles to reach the one man he felt sure would hold, if holding the line was humanly possible.

"Garfield's horses had been struck," wrote Gilmore, "but the danger had given him the spirit of a lion, and he plunged forward at a breakneck pace, through ploughed fields and tangled forests, and even broken and rocky hills, for another four miles, until they climbed a wounded crest, and were within view of Thomas. In a slight depression of the ground, with a small group of officers about him, he stood in the open field, while over him was sweeping a storm of shotted fire that fell in the thick drops on the high foothill that Garfield was crossing. Shot and shell and canister ploughed up the ground all about Garfield, but as he caught sight of Thomas he halted in the midst of the storm, and with uplifted arm, shouted, 'There he is! God bless the old hero! He has saved the army!' For a moment only he halted; then he plunged down the hill through the fiery storm, and in a few moments more was by the side of Thomas.

"As the two men embraced each other, the noble horse that has so bravely borne Garfield through that hurricane, struck by another bullet, staggered a step or two, and fell dead at the feet of Thomas.

"In hurried, broken sentences Garfield tells Thomas that his outflanked, and that the whole Confederate army of seventy thousand is closing down upon his right wing to crush into fragments his weary force of 25,000. He must withdraw his right wing, and form lines again upon the crested horse shoe which is before them at the base of the mountain. Quick the order is given, and quick the movement is made, yet not a moment too soon; for yonder, from behind a clump of woods, emerges the head of Long-street's bristling columns."

One of the soldiers who passed through those terrific days was Joseph A. Barrall, and in 1928, he wrote from his home in Brooks, K.Y., "I joined the 28th Kentucky Vols., Nov. 15, 1861. Never met Abraham Lincoln, as I was in the Army of the Cumberland. I was in the battles of Franklin and Nashville. Saw hard service and suffered various privations. Was in the Atlanta campaign. ON Christmas day 1864, I had three ears of corn parched for my dinner."

GEORGE H. THOMAS

Brooks Ky
March 29, 1928

Dear Sir

Yours was received a few days ago have been in bed all winter, been almost blind for two years had cattaract removed from one 4 weeks ago, am 83 years old ___ the 28th Ky. Reg. Co. C. Infantry ___ 15, 1861. Never met Abraham ___, as I was in the Army of ___ Cumberland. I was in the battles ___ Franklin and Nashville Tenn, ___ hard service and suffered various ___ ations, was in the Atlanta Campaghn Christmas day 1864 I had three years of ___ parched ___ grounds mixed with ___ molasses for my dinner

Respectfully
Joseph A. Barrall
Brooks Ky

The monument of John E. Wool can be seen from many parts of Troy, Watervliet, Gohoss and Waterford, N.Y. It is like a beacon shinning in many directions, marking the site of Oakwood Cemetery on a high ridge within the city limits. Gen. Wool was a resident of Troy, an officer in three wars, and he made a notable record in the Mexican War.

Not far from Gen. Wool's grave is another, whose occupant made a creditable record in the war against Santa Anna and his Mexican legions, and who became an outstanding figure in the Civil War. He saved the Union army at the battle of Chickamauga, and cut a rebel army to pieces at the battle of Nashville. "Old Pap," his soldiers called him because they loved him; "Old Slowfoot," spoke many leaders, because he moved steadily and sure, and "The Rock of Chickamauga," cheered the whole Western Army, they knowing a real leader from their training under the invincible Sherman.

"George H. Thomas' is carved on a beautiful stone in the midst of a fine large space of green, surrounded by trees and shrubs. The lot is owned by an old Troy family, the General having married Frances L. Kellogg, November 7, 1852.

Thomas was born in the Southland, July 31, 1816; the state that claimed the birthplace of Washington, Jefferson, Madison, Johnston, Jackson and Lee, but unlike the latter three he cast his lot with the Union and defended the nation at the State of his birth and her allies. He died at San Francisco, March 28, 1870, and it seems the homeland, defiled by rebellion and succession, could not take him to her bosom. He would rather sleep among the people and in the land that stood loyal to the government of Washington, and who gave the full measure of devotion to prevent a new Capitol and a States Rights, slave owning government at Richmond. He was brought back to the land that preferred Lincoln to Davis; one nation undivided; one people, all free. Bishop William E. Boane of Albany preached the funeral service, and on the evening after he was laid to rest, Gen. Steward L. Woodford, Ex-Lieutenant-Governor spoke on his life and services to a great mass of people.

Gen. Thomas talked very little, and though he knew Lee, Johnston, Bragg and other officers very well, better in fact than most of the northerners in the army, they knew well where he stood, and when Fort Sumter was fired on, another loyal Virginian, Gen. Winfield Scott, spent no time wondering where "Old Slowfoot" stood. I have a letter in my possession, written from Nashville in 1866, in which he said: "I remember very well in answer that I wanted them buried in such a manner as to create the impression of National care, not sectional or state, as we have had enough of States Rights. Those being my sentiments, I have no objection to your quoting them in your article on the National Cemetery at Chattanooga."

Gen. Thomas graduated from West Point, ranking twelve in the class of 1840. In the next year he took part in the Seminole War and was brevetted 1st Lieutenant "for gallant and good conduct in the war against the Florida Indians." August, 1845 fond him in Texas, and from then on he was in close touch with the Mexicans, fighting in the battles at Monterey in 1846 and received a compliment for his bravery from Gen. J.P. Henderson. In 1847 he was in the battle of Buena Vista and received brevet of Major for bravery, Capt. T.W. Sherman saying in his report, "Lieutenant Thomas more than sustained the reputation he has long enjoyed in his regiment as an accurate and scientific artillerist." On July 19, 1847, the citizens of Southampton Co., Va., purchased a sword and sent it to him in honor of the fine record he made in the war.

He was made Major Thomas when the Civil War started, but he was immediately appointed Colonel of the 2nd U.S. Cavalry in place of the famous Confederate General Albert Sidney Johnson. On August 24, 1861 he was promoted to Brigadier-General of the Volunteers, and on January 19, 1862 won his first battle against odds at Mill Springs, Va., where the enemy was routed, and the first decisive victory was won for the Union. The commission of Major-General of Volunteers came on April 25, 1862. Then came the battles of Perryville and Stone River, and in 1863 the famous stand at Chickamauga to save the army from capture and the loss of Chattanooga.

Charles A. Pana, writing to the famous cavalry leader, James H. Wilson on October 3, 1863 said, "I would also tell you that Gen. Rosecrans came to Chattanooga after the rout of the left, and consequently bore no part in the glory of the afternoon's battle. He seems in consequence to have lost some of his great popularity with the soldiers, whose idol is now very naturally the man whose saved them, and indeed saved us all, Thomas. For my own part, I confess I share their feeling. I know no other man whose composition and character are so much like those of Washington; he is at once an elegant gentleman and a heroic soldier."

On October 16th, Thomas succeeded Rosecrans as commander of the Army of the Cumberland. Then came Lookout Mountain and Missionary Ridge, the troops advancing under Sherman to Atlanta, Ga. On October 26, 1864, Thomas was in command in Tennessee, and on December 15th, he opened the battle of Nashville, the fighting continuing until the night of the 16th, completely crushing the Confederates under Gen. Hood. That ended the Rebellion in the State, and Stanton said "No commander has more justly earned promotion by devoted, disinterested and valuable service to his country." He immediately prepared Wilson's Cavalry for a raid through Alabama and a part of Georgia, which ended in April, many miles of railroad having been destroyed, the unlickable Forrest being defeated and Jeff Davis captured.

S. McAulliff

S. McAulliff was a member of the 1st Connecticut, 13th and 39th Massachusetts Volunteers during the war and he had the honor to see Gen. Thomas a number of times in 1861, although he never served under him. He saw Pres. Lincoln on a dispatch boat of Alexandria, Va., in May 1861, and saw the flag floating from the Marshall House in that town a day or two before Col. Ellsworth took it down and was for doing so by the owner.

W.H. BISBEE

William H. Bisbee enlisted in the United States army in his 21st year as a private in the 2nd Battalion 18th Infantry on September 2, 1861, and he was retired from that army on October 1, 1902 with the rank of Major-General.

The General was born in Rhode Island, January 28, 1840 received a common school education and was working when war was declared between the states. He had been advanced through the ranks to Captain when the war ended, but making the army his life-work, he remained in the service, holding the Captain's rank until May 18, 1893, when he became a Major in the 17 Infantry.

All of his service in the Civil War was spent in the Western Army, taking part in the Atlanta Campaign in 1864 and also serving under Gen. Thomas in some of the prominent battles. He was wounded at the fight in Hoover's Gap, Tenn., June 25, 1863, but soon recovered and went back to his regiment.

In 1866, Captain Bisbee built Fort Phil Kearney in Dakota, and he participated in a number of engagements with the Sioux Indians. In 1895 he was in command of a battalion at the fight in Jackson Hole during the Bannock Indian campaign.

Gen. Bisbee commanded a regiment in the Santiago campaign in the Spanish-American War, and from 1899 until his retirement in 1902 commanded troops in the Philippines. Writing in 1917, he sad,–"I regret to say that I did not have a personal acquaintance with Mr. Lincoln. My service was with the Western Army of Cumberland and my first visit to Washington not until 1869."

Gen'l WILLIAM H BISBEE. U.S.A.
1928 BEACON STREET.
BROOKLINE, MASS.

Mr J. E. Boos
My dear friend,
I regret to say that I did not have a personal acquaintance with Mr Lincoln. My service was with the Western army of the Cumberland and my first visit to Washington not until 1869

Yours sincerely
William H Bisbee
Brig Genl
USA
retired

Part Five: The Lincoln Guards

Lincoln's Soldiers

I want to dedicate this volume to Thomas Goldie, Senior, and to Thomas Goldie, Junior; two men who were sincere friends until the City was ruled by a Democratic Mayor, when they became bitter enemies, they claiming I had become a Flopper, because I was fortunate enough to hold my place in the Public Baths when the Democrats came into power.

I have never changed my Republican enrollment while Tom, Jr., changed from Republican to Democrat, and Tom Sr., from Republican to Democrat.

"Consistency, thou art a jewel."

Lincoln's Body Guard.

Men who had the honor to be near the great War President, nearer than the average man could get; men who guarded his person, who loved him in life and revered him after death. I have bound together a few letters from these soldiers of the Union whose sworn duty was to guard the person of the Chief Executive during the bitter days of a great Rebellion. How I wish I could have had more of these letters and could have met more of the men who took a turn guarding the White House and the President's Summer Home near Washington.

John E. Boos.
1939.

George C. Ashmun

"I am George Ashmun, but I am not the man who was President of the Convention that maintained the Railsplitter in 1860, not the man who was a member of the Committee officially notifying him of that great honor. He lived in Springfield, but the city was in Massachusetts, not the Illinois Capital, and if I am not mistaken, he did not live more than five years after the war.

"But I did see Lincoln many, many times.

"I can still see him riding down the dusty streets of Washington and out into the country for his night's rest and a little time of quiet at the Soldier's Home. I say a time of quiet, but he had very little time to himself and not many hours of rest, even darkness and the lateness of the hour did not top the dispatch bearers, or prevent men and women coming out to the grounds to be an audience with him.

"I was a sergeant of his guards for a time, and a Lieutenant when he was assassinated. We were proud of our great Leader, and we closely guarded him. Had our men watched him that night the foul assassin could never have entered his box.

"We soldiers loved Lincoln, and we wanted to stop every person coming to guard the lines, but the great man insisted all should be allowed to see him if they had references as their character.

"The guards at the Home could often see him through the window, could watch him reading the dispatches while the bearer, usually a lad of 8 or 10 years old stood at a respectful distance. At some, his face twitched with pain, at others, it would light up, and often a smile would come. If there was an answer to be made, he did it with few words, handed the notes to the boy, and how often have I seen him put his arm around the lad's shoulders, talk a few minutes, and then announce he was ready for visitors. There were from one to a dozen every night. All had a hearing, and though some had justice, some received more than they deserved.

"Yes, I can still see our little escort riding beside him down the dusty street, and if you rode with us you would wonder how he could tip his hat so many times without getting a cramped arm. Every person who nodded, or stood at the curb to see him pass, received a sign of recognition. Often groups or companies or regiments of soldiers came marching down the street, and he would stop, lift his hat and watch them. Usually all thought of discipline was forgotten, and they would cheer, wave their hats and yell, 'Hello Uncle Abe,' or sing one of those great marching songs that only an army of young men could sing. You wonder why I thrill at 'John Brown's Body.' You should have heard these soldiers sing it, tired, dirty, hungry as they were, while they swung past our little group, their clear voices and enthusiasm making you feel their weary appearance was a sham.

"Oh, he used the carriage more than the horses, and when Mrs. Lincoln was along she talked every minute, and he seldom said more than a short answer, as she usually seemed to be giving him advice he did not accept happily.

"When Tad was along, he talked and laughed every minute; that is, the minutes the little fellow was not talking he was laughing, but he seemed to talk all the time. How Lincoln loved that boy! and I sincerely think his love for Tad is what kept him alive.

"Our tents were in a grove, and often when the weather was very hot, Lincoln came over, sometimes alone, and often with some official or prominent citizen. He would walk among our tents, or sit with the officers and listen to their talk. The men understood him, and if he stopped at a group, their discussion did not stop, and he often took part in it. Though we respected him as our President, we thought of him as a sincere friend, and never felt embarrassed when he was near. We looked for his company, and every member of the guard delighted to hear his comments, especially when he referred to the Army as 'His Boys.' And we were his boys! Every man of that million or more, and we knew no leader gave us more thought, more sincerely looked out for our welfare, and none worked and prayed more fervently for peace to come.

"We would damn the Rebs, but the President always spoke kindly of them, and no man dared curse them in his presence. Remember we were all young men and we always referred to him,–but not in his presence of course,–as Uncle Abe, Old Abe, or Father Abe, but when he was within hearing, it was Mr. President. Do not think we meant to be disrespectful, but those names seemed to fit better, just as you would call a tent-mate by a nickname that at times seemed absurd.

"I have always believed Mr. Lincoln never had a particle of fear. He never seemed to worry about assassins. He would mingle in any crowd, and whenever he visited the army, he went where he pleased and once he nearly got into trouble, I well remember that day. It was a terrific hot day in July, 1854. Gen. Farly's troops were entrenching at the very outskirts of Washington. Every civilian able to bear arms was in the forts, or helping to build new breastworks. Troops from the front were being rushed to the city, and for a time it seemed as though the Johnnies would break through and capture the city. The President rode out to Fort Stevens. It was in that section the fighting was going on. The newly arrived troops from the famous Sixth Corps were deploying in line of battle to attack the Rebs, and the President, anxious to get a better view of the flight stood on the parapet, refusing to get down until a soldier was wounded by a Confederate sharpshooter a few feet from him.

"Well, your man, your question of how I became a member of the guard is simple. Early in 1863, Governor Ted of Ohio raises a company of one hundred picked men to be used as a mounted guard for the President. Permission being granted, they were picked from all parts of the State, and I happened to be fortunate enough to be chosen. Few of that old guard remain, and we are all proud of our contacts with the great President who liked to call those who were the Union Blue, 'His Boys.'"

Mr. Ashmun was born in Talleadge, Ohio, January 31, 1841, and when the war started he was in Medical College, which he immediately left and entered the army.

At the end of the war he finished his medical education, and in 1873 was given the M.D. at Western Reserve University. From that year in 1886, he was the United States Examiner for Pensions at Cleveland and he also held the position of Health Officer of that city from 1881 to 1891. From 1893, almost to the time of his death, he was a Professor at Western Reserve University and a lecturer on Hygiene Case School of Applied science since 1903. He had also been a member of the Cleveland City Council.

> George C. Ashmun —
> 1. 2° Reg't Ohio. Vol. Cavalry, Aug 1861 – Sept 1862
> 2. "Union Light Guard," 7th Indpt Co Ohio Vol Cav —
> This company was recruited, one man from each county in Ohio, Nov & Dec 1863, and served as body guard and escort of President Lincoln until his death — It was mustered out in Washington, Sept 9th 1865. During the summer of '64, Mr Lincoln for a short time rode a horse with the company, in the trips between the White House and the "Old Soldiers Home," where the family were staying — As one man may see another, we saw Mr Lincoln, nearly every day, without intimate contact other than an occasional word or grasp of hand — He was President, and we were soldiers on duty —
> I was a Sergeant and 2° Lieutenant in this company —

Henry G. Baird

Mr. Baird was another of the men Governor Tod picked to make up the group that would act as guard to the President. He lived in Lanesville, Ohio, and writing in May, 1916, he said,–

"I saw Mr. Lincoln many times, and I think that he who said 'With malice toward none, with charity for all,' stands before us in history, as the greatest character in the list our country's greatest men."

William P. Bogardus

I did not interrupt, because I was afraid he might stop and I would loose some of the never heard before stories about the great War President. One of the stories was about a burning barn in Washington, though I know Lincoln was strong and athletic, I hardly think he vaulted a six foot fence without loosing that beaver hat, as Mr. Bogardus expected me to believe, unless the President was a juggler.

Mr. Bogardus also told me how he went to the President's New Year's reception and was surprised to see the white kid gloves he wore, look black as far from the hands of the many that had grasped them. "they were filthy," the old gentleman exclaimed; "You would think people could keep their hands cleaner."

The story of the group of men who stopped the unguarded carriage with only Tad in it is a story I had never heard before, but the older soldier said it was the truth, and from then on, every move on the President was closely watched, at least one guard being near him every minute.

I laughed when Mr. Bogardus told me how the horse would go trotting along, a guard at each side, with at least two following, and the President seemed as comfortable as any of the riders, though the soldier were always expecting the stovepipe hat to go sailing through the air at every jump of the horse. The hat seemed to be a part of the President, and it never once left his head on the many rides through the streets and into the country.

The old soldier, though he had been transferred to a Second Lieutenancy in the 34th U.S. Colored Troops was in Washington on March 4th, 1865, and had the pleasure of hearing the Second Inaugural. He later had the sad honor of being one of the funeral escorts when Lincoln's body was brought to Independence Hall to like in state in Philadelphia.

Mr. J.E. Boos
    20 Dudley Heights
           Albany N.Y.

Sir;-

In answer to your letter of the 26th of May that came just as I was leaving for the East and from where I just came Saturday last would say that I enlisted ,as a private in the 7th. Independent Company of Cavalry of Ohio. to serve as an escort to Mr. Lincoln.

We arrived in Washington Dec. late in the month. My first sight of Mr. Lincoln was on New Years day when I went up to the reception that has always been given by the president until the present incumbent changed the custom.

The thing that attracted my attention most as I passed along by the president was and shook his hand was the soiled condition of his gloves. He had on white kid gloves, and by the time I had reached him they were in a filthy condition. Almost as black as tar.

When the barn burned in --- one of the boys and I went up to see the fire. As we stood th watching the burning building some one put a hand on the tight board fence that surrounded the barn and vaulted over. The fence was over six feet high As he came up to where we were and stood by us he remarked "Well boys this is a pretty how-dodo" and then we recognized that it was Mr. Lincoln There were twenty five of the onehundred men of the company selected to act as his mounted escort on his rides to and fre from the Soldiers Home, where he spent the hot months of the summer. At first he rode in a closed carriage, something like a hack. but one afternoon he was not ready at the usual time and let "Tad", his son use the carriage to go on an errand down street. As he passed out of the gate the carriage was stopped by a c cre ud of men, but as soon as they learned that it was but a child in the carriage they permitted the carriage to proceed. After that Mr. Lincoln always rode horseback on his trips to and from the Soldiers Home. He always wore a stove pipe hat.

it was always a surprising thing that he did did not lose it. He was one of the very few that could ride a trotting horse and keep a stove pipe hat on.

After a service in the company of a little over a year I passed examination and was promoted to a first Lieut in a colored Regiment, but as there was a long list of FirstLieut's I took a Second Lieutenancy in Co. E. 24th. U.S.C.T. and was mustered into that regiment March 6 1865. I remained in Washington, however long enough to hear the second inaugeral address of Mr. Lincoln.

Our regiment was encamped at Camp William Pen at the time Mr. Lincoln was assasinated, and fo formed a part of his escort as his body was brought to Independence Hall, there to lie in state for a few days.

Company 7th Independent Cavalry of Ohio (President'Lincoln's body guard) afterwards
2nd. Lieut Co. E. 24th U.S.C.T.

William P. Bogardus

Mt Vernon Ohio.

WILLIAM M. CLARKE

"Will be passing through Albany Monday and would like to meet you at the train;" read the telegram which had been sent from Boston.

I was sitting for that train long before it pulled in the Union Station, and was hurrying down the corridor of coach 373 before it had really come to a full stop. Near the front sat my soldier looking out of the window for me. I knew he was my soldier, because he wore the uniform of Blue, and he was the only old soldier in sight.

"Hello, you man. I have been looking for you. Sit down and let's have a chat about before the train moves again."

I had never seen him before, and he had never seen me, but some sort of sacred sense seemed to bring us together, and in the midst of the noise, the dust and the hurry, I spent a delightful twenty minutes with the man who had stood guard with his company when Lincoln made his first inaugural address. He was a member of the Washington Light Infantry, and it was his company that was ordered to stand between the President and the crowd, because of the many threats uttered by the Southern sympathizers.

Folks called him an old soldier; he had passed eight-one, but he seemed young to me, his clear voice, fresh complexion, quick movements, and carefree ways made me feel skeptical he had seen so much of life and taken part in historic events.

The window was open, as it was a fine September day, and I had brought cigars, because I thought the old soldier could dream better if he learned back in he seat, and puffing slowly on a good cigar, old scenes would come to mind much easier, and old memories would be more vividly portrayed. The smoke could float out of the window, the ashes could be knocked off on the sill, and the trainman could overlook the rule, "No Smoking."

As he puffed, and talked, I thought of that beautiful poem of James Whitcomb Riley, in which he says,

> "The lamplight seems to glimmer with a flicker of surprise,
> As I turn it low to rest ? of the dazzle in my eyes,
> And light my pipe in silence, save a sigh that seems to yoke
> It's fate with my tobacco and to vanish with the smoke."

Reminiscences, old memories, stories of the days when the fate of the Union hung in the balance, intertwined with smoke, and I went back again to the days when the regiments swung down the dusty Washington streets signing "John Brown's Body," or "When Johnny comes marching home."

He talked until the warning whistle blew and I had to say a reluctant farewell, going home to value the ?, the following letter he had written a few weeks before, and in which he said,

"I was a member of Co., C., of the Washington Light Infantry and was one of that company's personal guard at the inauguration of President Lincoln on March 4th, 1851."

William H. Clarke was born in Washington, June 19, 1842. At ten, he was working in the Ordnance Department at the Washington Navy Yard, was a page in the House of Representatives in 1856, and from 1858 to 1860, acted as Secretary to Colonel A.H. Redfield, the first agent of the Yancton Sioux Indians. At the beginning of the War, he was a member of the Washington Light Infantry, and from 1863 until mustered out at the end of the War he was regimental quartermaster-sergeant of the Second Illinois Light Artillery. After the War he became a traveling salesman.

WILLIAM B. CARY

Ira Harris was a Senator from New York, and a close friend of the President; so close, the Harris and Lincoln families were intimate; so much so, Senator Harris' daughter and his step-son were in the box at Ford's Theatre as members of the party when the assassination sent the bullet into the great leader's brain.

In July, 1861, a cavalry regiment commenced to organize in New York State, and its leaders took the name of the Ira Harris Cavalry. When it was mustered into the Federal Service it was given the designation, 5th New York Cavalry, and in its long service, terminating at the end of the War, it had taken part in almost every battle and skirmish of the Army of the Potomac. It lost 951 men, killed, wounded and missing, more than a hundred of them dying in Confederate prisons.

William B Cary joined the regiment at Plain, N.J., on September 5, 1861, as First Sergeant of Company L. He was promoted a Second Lieutenant in April, 1862, a First Lieutenant in June of the same year and became Captain in March, 1864, being mustered out of the service October 23, 1864. While in command of a scouting party in August, 1862, near Orange Court House, Va., he captured J.E.B. Stuart's headquarters, finding many valuable papers, among them a plan of attack on Gen. Pope. The papers were sent to the General, who immediately formed the line of battle to resist an intended attack by General Lee.

On August 27, 1862, Lieut. Cary was detached with a squadron to act as escort to Gen. Heintzleman, and was in Washington a sort time. He rode in the escort of President Lincoln on several occasions from the White House to the Soldier's home. He rode on the President's left, while Captain James G. Bennett was on the right. One evening Mr. Lincoln invited him into his rest, where the great President talked with him late into the night. "We talked over war experiences and politics, and he seemed so tired, fagged out with anxiety and care, I realized I was not alone entertaining, but relieving and resting the mind so overwrought."

it was always a surprising thing that he did did not lose it. He was one of the very few that could ride a trotting horse and keep a stove pipe hat on.

After a service in the company of a little over a year I passed examination and was promoted to a first Lieut in a colored Regiment, but as there was a long list of FirstLieut's I took a Second Lieutenancy in Co. E. 24th. U.S.C.T. and was mustered into that regiment March 6 1865. I remained in Washington, however long enough to hear the second inaugeral addres of Mr. Lincoln.

Our regiment was encamped at Camp William Pen at the time Mr. Lincoln was assasinated, and fo formed a part of his escortas his body was brought to Independence Hall, there to lie in state for a few days.

        Company 7th Independent Cavalry
        of Ohio (President Lincoln's body
        guard)   afterwards
           2nd. Lieut Co. E. 24th U.S.C.T.

        William P. Bogardus
           Mt Vernon Ohio.

placed in command of Dept Washington, with Hd of Qrs at Arlington, then at Washington. While on this duty I rode in the Escort of President Lincoln on several occasions from the White House to Soldier's Rest. I rode on his left side. Capt Jas G. Bennett on his right. Lincoln invited me into the House with him at the "Rest", and I sat with him late into the night talking of experiences in camp &c &c "at his request". He was tired, fagged out with anxiety and Care, and I was for a time as a means of diversion. Advanced to 1st Lieut — Rejoined regiment when Heintzelman went West. In the Fall Campaign of 1863. In Kilpatrick's raid on Richmond Mch/64. "Wilderness" opened by me Mch 5" 64. 6 A.M. was on "Wilson's Raid" June. Thence to the Valley under Sheridan, fought Winchester Sept 19" 64. Fisher's Hill Oct 9th and Cedar Creek Oct 19"/64. Advanced to Capt June/64.

Horace E. Clough

I did not see Mr. Clough write his autograph, but if he did sign his name to the sheet, he has a marvelous hand for a man of ninety-one years. He was a private in the 3rd Vermont Volunteers, and though he was not a member of the President's body guard, he said "the last time I saw Lincoln he was on his way to Fort Stevens. His body guards (100 men) made a very showey turn out. They were from Ohio, and every man was six feet or more tall, while the horses were all jet black and stood sixteen hands high."

Soldiers Home   Dec 5, 1933
Bennington Vt.
    Hon. John E Boos,
     21 Dudley Heights
Dear Sir and Comrade.
Your letter with other papers were duly recieved and were something of a surprise. my age prevents me from doing what I would like to. I saw Mr Lincoln several times voted for him for president in 1864 the last time I saw him he was on his way to fort Stevens his body guard (100 men) made a very showey turn out the men were from Ohio I was told every man was 6 ft or more high while the horses were all jet black and stood 16 hands high. It has cost me quite an effort to write this hope you can make some use of it
     Very sincerly
       Horace E. Clough

*Soldiers Home
Bennington VT*

*Horace E. Clough,
Co. I 3d VT
Age 91   Dec 5, 1933*

COL. W.H. CROOK

There died in Washington on March 13, 1915, a man who for nearly four years stood guard at President Lincoln's door through the night hours. If he left the building, this man followed, and stayed at his elbow every minute, allowing no one to get between him and the President. His name was Col. W.H. Crook. He was familiarly known as "Lincoln's Night Watchman," and though advanced in years, he attended to his duties until a few days before his death. At the theatre, at the War Office, and at receptions, Col. Crook was ever near, and woe to the one who should attempt any harm to the President.

On the fatal night when the President entered the box at Ford's Theatre, the guard was ordered to sit near the box and allow no person to enter. From his station, he could see neither actors nor the stage, and being very much interested in what the performers were saying, he walked down the aisle and took an unoccupied seat. He soon became so interested in the play, he forgot about his duty until he heard the report of the pistol.

Col. Crook always regretted that he was not allowed to accompany the President's party that night. He realized from experience the danger of leaving the President unprotected for a single minute, and would never have left the box entrance; while the guard, who was a new one in the White House, could not know the great importance of exercising unceasing vigilance. The realization of his neglect so prayed on the poor fellow's mind that he slowly pined away and soon after died.

According to Col. Crook, there is a big difference between the Presidential receptions of today and those which were held during Lincoln's time. It was not uncommon sight to see men come to greet the President, wearing cowhide boots and big slouch hats, some of them personal friends. They received a hearty welcome, "For to Lincoln, clothes meant nothing, manhood, truth, honor and hard work meant everything."

> *W. H. Crook, Private,*
> *Dist of Columbia Vols.*
> *last living body guard*
> *of Abraham Lincoln.*
> *My story of Lincoln have*
> *already been published,*
> *Nov. 20. 1911,*

WILLIAM E. PATTERSON

It was almost Christmas, but the warm sun and fresh foliage made a person feel the date should be nearer Independence Day, than the mid-winter anniversary of the birth of the child Jesus. The old soldier had come South to escape the hard weather and snow of the North. Came to one of those States the great Army he was a member of fought back into the Union fifty years before, and he was loud in praise of the fine Florida climate.

He was basking in the shade of his porch at White Springs and he insisted it was perfect day, but moisture as trickling down my back and the perspiration was softening my collar. It was the Christmas season, and though Florida days are warm, I would much rather see the snow and listen to the ice-tipped wind-blast in old New York State than swelter in the land of Johnny Reb and Damned Yank

The heat did not prevent me enjoying Mr. Patterson's stories of the War and of the regiment that pursued Booth to his hiding place on the Garret farm in the Old Dominion. Boston Corbett, the man who took aim through a knot-hole in the old barn, and shot Booth, was an intimate friend, Corbett afterward telling Mr. Patterson he had to do it, because the assassin would not put down his gun. Mr. Patterson did not take part in the capture, he being in the hospital with typhoid fever at the time.

The 16th New York Cavalry was one of the fighting regiments in the Civil War, and the old soldier also did service in the 3rd Provisional Cavalry, the 13th New York, and the 8th Illinois Cavalry.

Speaking of President Lincoln, he said,–"I have the distinction of being one of the 20 cavalrymen who formed Mr. Lincoln's military body guard, and guarded him from the White House and back again. He lifted his hat to us at the west gate and we presented sabers to him."

in refering to my Regt and the capturing of Booth our Regt went after him I was in the Hospital just recovering from a severe case of Typhoid an Pneumonia I was convalesing, and was made corporal of the guard in camp. I was intimately acquainted with Sergt Boston Corbett who shot Booth he told me he had to shoot him as he would not put down his gun or agree to surrender.

I saw Mr Lincoln in Frederick city M d after the Battle of sauth mountain or perhaps after the battle of Gettles burg he was on horseback I admired him as a leader and statesman soldier and Christian Gentleman.

White Springs Fla. Dec. 20th/1913

William E. Patterson
Co G. 16th N.Y. vol. cav
also Co A. 3rd Regt of Provisional
cav.. vol.
by consolidition
of 16 Ny cav
" 13 " " "
" 8 Ill " " "
we were mustered out at
Camp Barry Washington D &
discharged at Hearts Island
N.Y.
I have the distinction of being one of the 20 cavalrymen who formed Mr Linolns military body guard and guarded him from the whitehouse to the Capitol and back again he lifted his hat to us at the west gate and we presented Sabres to him it was real inspurring to us. I am a true Lincolnite Wm E. Patterson

Smith Stimmel

"I was one of those hundred Ohio men that were sent to Washington by Governor Tod to become Lincoln's bodyguard. I had served three months in the army, had been discharged and was at my home on a farm near Columbus when I heard of the call of the Governor for his body of selected men to go in the army for special duty. A friend of the family who was a member of the County military committee gave me a letter of recommendation, and I went to the capitol, where the Governor talked to me a few minutes, gladdening my heart with information I would be accepted, and then telling me what the service would be. Then I went to the barracks, I found a splendid lot of men, nearly all of whom had seen service, one having been discharged with the rank of Major. We were quickly equipped, supplied with black horses, and given title of the Union Light Guard.

"On our arrival in Washington, we were placed in a camp close to the city and stationed as guards at the front entrance of the White House grounds, acting also as an escort to the President whenever he used a carriage or rode horseback. We especially enjoyed acting as his escort in the summer when he rode to and from the Soldiers Home, his family occupying a modest two story brick house on the grounds. It was a very pleasant place on an elevated plot of ground, surrounded by a fine grove of trees, and our camp was placed a short distance from the building. Members of our company acted as an escort morning and evening, and in this way we saw much of him and became acquainted with his daily habits.

"I often saw him walking down one of the paths in the early evening, usually alone, and moving slowly as though he was studying the trees and the landscape in an effort to forget the trying hours of the day. We always avoided him, but if we did come upon him unexpectedly, he showed no lack of surprise, and he always spoke pleasantly, often stopping to talk a few minutes. He talked commonplace; the scene about him, how nice the trees looked, how fresh the grass was, or how pleasant the evening seemed. It was not unusual to see him walking in our company street with some visitor, or talking to one of our officers, or have him look in the tents and ask us how we were getting along. We never met him at the White House grounds, or when he was leaving each soldier of the escort. We always addressed him as Mr. President, but behind his back he was Uncle Abe; not as a nickname, but it made us think he was closer to us, the word President making us feel too far removed from such a high personage. We loved him, and were very proud to be near him."

Smith Stimmel was speaking in his Fargo, North Dakota home. He had seen Lincoln nearly every day for two years, and being a very intelligent young man, studied him closely, and was able in later years, to give vivid impressions of the great leader, in lectures which he delivered before many societies. On July 4, 1914, he represented North Dakota at the unveiling of the bust of Lincoln at Christiania, Norway, where he made the principle address. He was brought up on a farm, his first enlistment being in the 88th Ohio Volunteers in 1862, and in the summer of 1863 became a member of the 7th Independent Troop, Ohio Volunteer Cavalry, also known as the Union Light Guard. He graduated from Ohio Wesleyan University, and later moved to North Dakota where he practices law.

> I was a private in Co. H. 88. O.V.I, in 1862. Enlisted in a Cavalry troop in 1863. which was assigned to duty at the White House as President Lincoln's mounted body guard, and served until after the close of the war. Was present at the President's public reception given on the evening of the 8th of March 1864, and saw President Lincoln and

Gen.l Grant met for the first time that they ever met

My Motto is "Our Country and our flag".

My sentiment is, "Eternal vigilance is the price of liberty."

Sincerely yours

Smith Stimmel

Fargo N.D. Feb. 1 1916

A.M. WHITE

Mr. White Moved from Ohio to Nebraska after the War. Speaking of the history of his company, he said,–"in 1863 the governor of Ohio told Secretary Stanton he could organize a body guard for the President, and he accepted the offer. The governor therefore made a request for a picked man from each County in Ohio, but did not say what the service would be. Each man thought he was going to the front and he enlisted with that idea.

"When they arrived in Washington they were informed they were to be President Lincoln's body guards, and served as such until his death. They were stationed on the ellipse south of the Treasury, some being on guard every hour of the time, two hours being the limit for each day and night. There were 105 men in the company, being mustered in at Columbus, Ohio, December 17, 1863, the enlistment being for three years.

"The mustering officer was Capt. Elmer Otis, 4th U.S Colored Troops. They left for Washington, December 22, 1863, and reported to the Secretary of War. They were not all kept about the White House, but were scattered about Washington and the forts surrounding the city, but always a goodly number of them were kept near the President."

"I was commissioned First Lieutenant of the company, and while on duty at the White House I met the President almost every day, finding him one of the most wonderful men I ever met."

Bostwick Neb
May 29th 1914

Mr J. E. Boos
Albany, N.Y.

Dear Sir

Replying with your favor of 22d inst.

I first met Mr Lincoln in 1861 as he was on his way to Washington to take up his great work, at Columbus Ohio

In 1863 I was made 1st Lieut of the Union Light Guard 7 Squadron Ohio Cavalry; Raised for Body Guard to Mr Lincoln

While on duty at the White House I met the President almost every day finding him one of the most wonderful men I ever met. Others have said so much that I can add nothing to make him greater than he was. Respectfully &c

A. M. White Late First Lieut U.S.?

Henry M. Kieffer

Crowds love to mass on the famous board walk at Atlantic City to watch the bathers, criticize the dresses of the fine ladies, or look over the near-great who visited the famous resort each summer. I became interested in an elderly gentleman who seemed to be enjoying the comfort of a beach chair and getting real pleasures from the antics of a group who swim better in the sand than in the water. When I drew near I was surprised to see the Little Bronze Button on the lapel of his coat, and without begging pardon or excusing myself, I rather bluntly asked if he had seen Lincoln.

The older gentleman,–he was 83,–was a little surprised too, at my ignorance, I imagine, but he smiled broadly when he saw it was intense interest instead of rudeness that made me ask the question without really waiting to get acquainted.

"Yes," he smiled, "I saw that great American many, many times. Two of the companies, D and X, were detailed as guard at the Soldiers Home from September, 1862 to November, 1862, when we were sent to our regiment and Co. K, stayed in Washington until the end of the war. I joined the Pennsylvania, officially known as the 160th Pennsylvania Volunteers as a Drummer Boy in August, 1862, and I was with my comrades until the end of the war, becoming the Hospital Steward and later Brigade Steward. I was one of the fortunate ones, never having received a wound, or reporting sick, and I was on all the marches and in all of the battles of my brigade. So many memories of those days come to mind, especially when I talk to young people; the pleasant sights, the terrible scenes and the terrors and excitement of battle, never seem to fade.

"The colors! The Grand Old Flag! How we loved it! One of my comrades wrote the following short paragraph that shows how we cared for it, guarded it, and thrilled with it unfurled at the head of the line.

"On the march the colors of the regiment were kept encased in their leather coverings, and carefully guarded by 'the Color Guard'. When the column came at length upon the field of battle, and forced in line, often on the double-quick (as on that ever memorable first day at Gettysburg) and the command was given, 'Color Guard, Unfurl the Colors!' and the leather coverings were quickly stripped out to the breeze-no one who witnessed the scene can ever forget the sublime thrill that ran along the line at the sight of 'Old Glory.'

"But I forgot to tell you about the President. He spent most of his nights until late Fall at the Soldiers Home, and we were camped on the lawn near the building during those two profitable months we acted as guards about the grounds. I saw him almost every day and I am sure I woke him out of his sleep more than one morning when I sounded reveille. I saw him step out of his carriage on many evenings, his haggard face and weary step showing plainly how the great responsibilities of the office were wearing him down. Little Tad often played in our camp and Mrs. Lincoln did not fail to do many acts for us. We loved them all and it was an honor to be called 'Old Abe's Soldiers,' or as many Copperheads called us, 'Lincoln's Hirelings.'"

I forgot about Atlantic City and all it meant and I sat in the sand beside the regimental campfire,—so it seemed,—listening to the stories of the great war until lunch time when the survivor of the famous Backtails had to go, and as he faltered on the sand, I thought of a verse of one of his own poems, which reads,

> *"Oh comrades, we are marching*
> *With the sunset in our face,*
> *And behind us fall the shadows*
> *That are lengthening space.*
> *The column's moving slowly*
> *Toward the setting of the sun,*
> *And our ranks are growing thinner,*
> *For our march is nearly done."*

Dr. Kieffer wrote eight books, one of the best being Recollections of a Drummer Boy, and a number of poems. He was born in Mifflingburg, Pa., on October 5, 1845, joined the army at seventeen, and when he was discharged in 1865, returned to school, receiving an A.B. from Franklin and Marshall College in 1870, and graduated from the Theological Seminary of the Reformed Church at Lancaster, Pa., in 1873. He almost immediately became the Pastor of the Reformed Church at Morristown, Pa., where he stayed until 1884 when he took up the work in the Reformed Church at Easton, retiring in 1903, when he joined the Episcopal Church. My visit with him was a great experience, an hour filled with vivid incidents of the War for the Union and of delightful stories about Abraham Lincoln from the lips of the kindly person, who as a drummer boy say much of him, and who as an old man spoke his name in reverence.

NEVER was there a more pleasant camp than ours on the green hillside, across the ravine from the President's summer residence. We had light guard duty to do, and that of a kind we esteemed a most high honor; for it was no less than that of being special guards for President Lincoln. But the good President, we were told, although he loved his soldiers as his own children, did not like being guarded. Often did I see him enter his carriage before the hour appointed for his morning departure for the White House, and drive away in haste, as if to escape from the irksome escort of a dozen cavalrymen, whose duty it was to guard his carriage between our camp and the city. Then when the escort rode up to the door, some ten or fifteen minutes later, and found that the carriage had already gone, wasn't there a clattering of hoofs and a rattling of scabbards as they dashed out past the gate, and down the road to overtake the great and good President, in whose heart was "charity for all, and malice toward none."

   Boy as I was, I could not but notice how pale and haggard the President looked as he entered his carriage in the morning, or stepped down from it in the evening, after a weary day's work in the city; and no wonder either, for those September days of 1862 were the dark, perhaps the darkest days of the war. Many a mark of favor and kindness did we receive from the President's family. Delicacies, such as we were strangers to then, and would be for many a long time to come, found their way from Mrs. Lincoln's hand to our camp on the green hillside; while little Tad was a great favorite with the boys, fond of the camp, and delighted with the drill.

Henry M. Kieffer, in his 83rd year —
Drummer Boy, Co. D, 150th P.V. "Bucktails."

*Autograph of
Henry M. Kieffer
at the age of 83 —
Late Drummer Boy,
Co. D, 150 Penna Vols
"BuckTails"
Later Hospital Steward
of his Regiment — and
later Steward of his
Brigade — First Brig.
First Div — Fifth Army
Corps —
Written — Atlantic City, N.J.
July 23 – 1928.*

Dr. A.H. See

Dr. See lived in Ralira, Kansas, on the prairies John Brown fought over and which was stained by the blood of the Free State men, also be the gore of the Border Ruffians, when the Old Abolitionist decided to use that old testament phrase "a tooth for a tooth, and an eye for an eye." After he had killed a few of the Missouri guerillas, the anti-slavery people were left alone and Kansas got a fair deal, coming into the Union as a Free State.

I met the old soldier sitting on a bench in a park during one of the Grand Army Encampments, and I found him a strong believer in John Brown's methods. He enlisted in the 150th Pennsylvania Volunteers, became one of the company that guarded President Lincoln for nearly two years, and after the war studied for the ministry. He was Pastor in a number of churches and had traveled all over the prairies, preaching in many out of the way places where there was no settled minister.

The old soldier knew Boston Corbett, and in his talk he said, "I first met him at a prayer meeting in McKendree Chapel, Washington, the week after President Lincoln was assassinated. I shall never forget the eccentric prayer he offered on the occasion, that the assassin might be speedily brought to justice. It was but a few days till his prayer was answered by his own revolver.

"I didn't see Corbett again until our Methodist Episcopal Church conference at Concordia, Kansas, in 1881. He was present, though not a member. Many remember how some of the timid ones jumped when he shouted. I was stationed at Concordia that year, and met Corbett often. He said Booth had his gun leveled and was about to fire when he drew his revolver and fired. He knew he was violating orders, but it was either disobedience of orders or the death of a comrade, and he did not hesitate. He eccentricity amounted to insanity at times.

"In 1886-7, I was running the Methodist Book Store at Topeka, and it was at that session of the legislature that he was elected doorkeeper. He visited my store often. One noon he came in very nervous and excited. That morning three strangers had been questioning him at considerable length about the killing of Booth, and he suspected that they were after him. He had his revolver with him and I could not persuade him to leave it with me. The same three men commenced on him again, and he took out his revolver and chased them through the cloak rooms. They finally escaped, but he went crazy, and for some time held the house in terror, till finally the police bound him and sent him to an asylum. When an opportunity offered he jumped from the second story window and, mounting a pony that was hitched nearby, rode off to the southern part of the State to a Friend's house."

Beulah Colo. June 28. 1915

John E Boos.
Dear Sir:—
Your letter of June 15. requesting my autograph & sentiment about the immortal Lincoln, as from one who had seen him and taken his honest hand, was forwarded me from Topeka Methodist Episcopal Home for the aged. We are summering here.

I was privileged to be one of the White House (& Soldiers Home) Guards. (Co. K. 150 P.V.) for the last 16 months of the war & saw President Lincoln almost daily till his death. We saw more of him because his son Tad was at our Camp nearly every day and frequently took dinner with us at Camp & we loved him as a brother.

Words would fail to express the regard esteem, and almost worship, we had for the president. We regarded him as Gods agent, raised up, preserved & guided by Him to preserve the nation. As He prepared Moses to lead Israel so He prepared Lincoln to lead us. I believe He designed Israel to bless the world too. I believe He designs our Nation to bless the world & will preserve & bless us if true to Him.

Yours truly
A. McKee

75 years old today

A.P. SIMMONS

Mr. Simmons was a member of the 49th New York Volunteers. The regiment was organized at Buffalo and mustered into the Federal service on September 18, 1861. It lost 322 men and was in the more than two score battles, including the Seven Days fights, Antietam, Gettysburg, Cold Harbor, Cedar Creek and the Appomattox campaign.

Mr. Simmons saw much hard service, and where I met him he was as sturdy and as vigorous as any man could be for his age. Of Mr. Lincoln, he said, "Saw our leader at the White House, and many other times while going up 7th St., to his summer retreat at the Soldier's Home."

The old gentleman told of the wild cheers and rejoicing that went down the line when the news spread that Lee had surrendered, and I thought the same kind of excitement cheered the people when the Mexican War was going on, because I had just read an ad in the Albany Freeholder of May 10th, 1847, which said,–

"Victory! Victory!
General Taylor

Whips the Mexicans, and
Joseph Ehrich & Co.,
No. 336 Broadway, will sell
Dry Goods!
As cheap if not a little cheaper than they can be bought anywhere this side of the Rio Grande.
Their present stock consists of Broad Cloths, Cassimeres, Vestings, Sattinetts, Tweeds, Kentucky, Jeans, Gambroone and Summer stuffs of all kinds."

"If an ad appeared in one of our local papers at the present time we would be going to the store to see what Gattinetts and Cambroons were like."

S. O. Smith Co. B 27th Iowa Inft
Saw Grant at Vicksburg

A. P. Simmons
  Co. K 49th N. Y. Vol.
Saw Lincoln at White House
and at many other times while
going at this xxxxx Home up 7th St.
        Soldiers

At Rochester, Pennsylvania

When it was announced Mr. Lincoln was going to leave his home in Springfield early in the morning of his birthday, and would proceed slowly to Washington, his train to stop wherever a crowd had gathered so that the people could get acquainted with him, as he aptly expressed himself, and that he would talk in the principle cities along the route, the whole country became excited, and many traveled long distances to see and hear him. To many, the Union had been proven a failure, and before the new President could be inaugurated, new confederation would have been formed and an independent nation of at least eight states would separate the Slave from the Free States. This loyal people were very much discouraged, a great majority being sure the tall, untrained man from the West would be unable to hold what the fathers of the nation founded.

In their anxiety to see him and if possible read what was in his mind, or to hear him say an encouraging word, they waited for hours at crossroads, at village stations, and in the larger cities, praying he would be the man of the hour, his appearance and his words giving them new hope and confidence that the nation would be saved. He spoke, but said nothing about his plans and what he would do about the states in rebellion, but his manners gave them new hope, while the disloyal element was encouraged, and they were sure he could do nothing but let them for their slave government in peace. The disunionists looked into the homely, sad face, and saw nothing but failure, they being unable to see the resolution and determination in it to bring the rebellious states back regardless of cost and sacrifice.

How bitterly they cried after Gettysburg and Vicksburg, shouting dictator and tyrant at the tall, weary man, and how loudly they shouted for the Union when the gentle soul lay cold in death. Peace Democrat, Knight of the Golden Circle and Copperhead hurriedly changed their accursed skins and wrapped themselves in the Stars and Stripes.

ROBERT A. SMITH

One of the big crowds that had patiently waited for hours to see the presidential train, stood in the cold at Rochester, Pennsylvania, and a sixteen year old boy stayed close to the rails when the train stopped, working his way to the rear car, where he stood almost within arm's length of Mr. Lincoln when he stepped on the rear platform to be welcomed by the Mayor, and answer the cheers, because the citizens of Rochester were 100 percent loyal. The boy was Robert A. Smith, and shortly before he died in 1926, he said,–

"When Mr. Lincoln had spoken a few words we commenced to move up to the platform and I had the pleasure to shake his hand. Behind me was Henry Pillion of Beaver Borough, who laughingly said, 'Let's measure, Mr. Lincoln.' The crowd gave a big laugh, because everybody knew Henry, and he was considered the tallest man in Beaver County. Mr. Lincoln immediately turned his back, and when it was announced he was slightly taller, the crowd cheered, and shouted, 'Come down, Henry, you're out-measured.' That crowd went home sure Mr. Lincoln was going to do something about the secessionists, and shortly after the war started, I enlisted in the 100th Pennsylvania Volunteers, known as the Roundheads, and I served in that regiment almost to the end of the war.

"I saw Mr. Lincoln but once again, and that was when we passed through Washington in September, 1862, having come from the battlefields of Second Bull Run and Chantilly. We were on a forced march, hurrying to the train that was to take us to the front and check Robert E. Lee's forces moving toward Pennsylvania. We sang 'We are coming Father Abraham, three hundred thousand more,' and he stood at the curb with his tall silk hat in his hand, waving the other at us. How it cheered us, because the army was badly demoralized, the incident taking place after the Second Battle of Bull Run."

Mr. Smith lived in Rochester, where in his old age many local societies heard well told stories of his experience in the war.

> During the brief period of un Mr. Lincoln stopped at Rochester Pa. when on his way to Washington to be inaugurated we all shook hands with him & then was 16 years old. one man a head taller than all the rest named Henry Dillen a resident of Beaver Borough jumped up on the platform of the car and said, "let us measure and the backs of the two men met. but old Abes height was a little greater. this man considered about the tallest man in Beaver County. It raised quite a laugh I tell you on our march through Washington in early Sept 1862 from the Battlefields of second Bull Run and Chantilly Va. we were commanded by Gen. Geo B. McClellan a great favorite with us and set on a force march had no time to stop, to check Robt E. Lee from reaching Penna We sang "We are coming Fath. Abraham three hundred thousand more. Mr. Lincoln held his old silk hat in his hand and wore his hand at us. Remember our army was then badly demoralized caused by our terrible defeat at Bull Run with the awful slaughter. Yours truly Robt. A. Smith

George E. Smith

Did you ever feel the desire to sit in an old rocker on the front porch of a little house on a side street so near the ocean you could hear the swells gritting and grinding on the shore, Hear the pleasant,–at least to me,–creaking, straining and cracking of another old rocker beside you in which sits a clear-eyed, keen-minded old soldier crowding close upon his 89th birthday?

It is moving day in New York State,–May 1st,– and it seems the elements delight to make that day disagreeable for those who must take their worldly goods from one house and deposit them in another. The tearing up and replacing; the weariness, fatigue and uncertainty of it all is not enough, but the rain must beat, or the winds blow raw to make life even more uncomfortable on the day they must go the new home.

The winds of Newport, R.I. were kind; they were soft and warm, the sun perfect, and the trees swelled with new leaves, while the songsters sang glad tidings of the beautiful days soon to come.

The old soldiers were fast leaving, the many thousands of my boyhood had dwindled to scores, and I had long wanted to meet one with whom I could chat an hour, or two hours if he would be patient and willing to answer a battery of questions about the war and the great leader who brought victory to the Union arms. I had read many stories of the almost unbelievable sufferings of the men in the prison pens, and heard some of the survivors of Belle Isle, Salisbury and Danville tell of horrible treatment at the hands of prison guards, who I believed , should have been "hanged by the neck until dead," with the Rebel commander of Andersonville, and when I read that George B. Smith was Commander, Adjutant, Chaplain, Auditor and Trustee of Lawton Warren Post, G.A.R. I returned to loop but the man who could hold so many offices at the same time in one organization and do the work well, the next time I went to the noted summer resort. The time had come when the charter stayed alive until the last man had passed away, and I believe that was the case with Warren Post, Mr. Smith having been the last of the many that once gathered for meeting.

The old rocker creaked and strained so much I feared it would fall apart, but the dear old soldier was content, and I could readily see he enjoyed its comfort.

"So you came way down here to see me, did you?" he commenced, looking real serious and speaking in a tone of displeasure, though I knew he was inwardly tickled pink, and overanxious to visit with one interested in the story of the Rebellion.

"Rebellion," he called the South, and "Johnny Rebs," was the name he gave to the men who wore Gray. He talked very kindly of the Confederate Army, but he did hate Jeff Davis and the other leaders, calling them "Fire-eaters," and "Bloody Shirt Wavers," men too cowardly to go to the front, and yellow enough to skedaddle to Mexico and England when the army was licked, instead of standing with their soldiers as brave men should."

He talked excitedly at times and pounded his cane on the porch rail to emphasize his remarks, but he soon cooled, and then I treated to a fine long talk about his regiment.

"Our Governor knew war was coming as soon as Lincoln was elected, and in December, 1861, the Audit-General of Rhode Island sent a request to our Captain asking how many men the Newport Artillery could furnish at short notice if they were needed. We had only 39 members, but when Fort Sumter was fired on that memorable morning of April 13th, a meeting was immediately ordered to be held at the armory, which was filled, and when the call for recruits was read, we had 112 enrolled before our patriotic meeting was over. Our drilling commenced the next day, and at noon April 17th, we were on the way to Providence, where we were quartered with other companies in Railroad Hall. Here we became one of the companies of the First Rhode Island Detached Militia, with A.E. Burnside as Colonel. Before our time expired our Colonel left us and became a Brigadier-General. On Saturday, the 20th, we marched aboard a boat bound for New York and from there to an ocean steamer, arriving at Annapolis, Maryland on Wednesday, 24th.

"Within a week we formed a regiment, were nearing the front. That was quick work, I want to tell you young fellow." I thought so myself, but I imagined most of the men had been in military companies and knew something about the art of war.

"Early on the morning of the 25th, we commenced the march to the Junction to board the train for Washington, and when we reached the place Friday morning, we were told the track had been torn up for some distance and parts of the engine had been stolen. There were a number of railroad men in the outfits arriving and they were detailed to make repairs, which they did, and to the surprise of everybody, the train was ready to move in the afternoon, and we arrived in Washington in the early morning.

"Very few members of the regiment had ever been in the city, and when we were called to attention after leaving the cars, our orders were to march over a route that would take us past the White House, and we were surprised to see the President and Gen. Scott standing at the curb. Great cheers greeted them and the two leaders answered by waving their hands. We were quartered in the Patent Office, and every day was taken up with drill and instruction in army life.

"On May 2nd, we were drawn up in front of the White House to take part in a flag raising. Mr. Lincoln and his Cabinet were on the roof, and when our band played the Star Spangled Banner, the President raised the flag amid the cheers of a crowd that had gathered. It was a very inspiring sight, and I shall never forget it."

The old soldier kept rocking, and the rocker kept creaking. He had become silent while a robin sang the inspiring notes of welcome to sun and warmth.

"I love a robin," he said. "On the march to the battle of First Bull Run, we were pretty jittery listening to the cannonading in the distance, we never having been in a battle before. Suddenly a robin in a tree near the road sang as though inspired, and I never heard gunfire afterward that the robin's song did not come to mind and give me new courage.

"It was on the afternoon of the flag-raising that we were called to attention on the Capitol grounds, and the federal oath was administered to us by Col. Loomis of the regular army. A few nights after that Col. Ellsworth's Fire Zouves from New York arrived and I think everybody in the city turned out to welcome them. Their uniforms were so strange, so different, so flashy, and their fame had gone ahead of them. They wore loose, baggy, red pants, white leggings, French blue cutaway jackets with yellow clover leaf on back and arms, a red sash, red skull cap with long flowing yellow tassel, and they carried Enfield rifles.

"There were a lot of skulking Rebs in the city, some as spies, others to make as much trouble as they could without getting caught. Near midnight, a fire broke out in a building next to Willard's Hotel, the city firemen refusing to respond. The Zouaves, who had been New York firemen, rushed with their Colonel to the fire houses, smashed in the doors and it was not long before the apparatus was working and the fire was out. As a reward, the guests in the hotel made up a purse and the Zouaves were given a fine breakfast the next morning.

"I watched that fine regiment march by more than once. Saw Col. Ellsworth, who was later killed by Jackson the hotelkeeper of Alexandria for tearing down a rebel flag that was on the hotel, and passed Ellsworth's coffin when he lay-in-state in the White House. I also knew Brownell, the man who shot the hotelkeeper, and it makes me get the blues when I realize not one man of that regiment is alive today."

At this point I had a chance to talk, and I told the old soldier Ellsworth's uniform, sword, and the rebel flag hang in the capitol in Albany, and that I had often seen them. That brought out more Fire Zouave stories, and I was delighted to hear so much about the young Colonel and patriot who was born near Albany.

"I went through the war, took part in a number of battles and was one of the few lucky ones to come home without a scratch. I saw Mr. Lincoln a number of times. He was always dressed in a black broadcloth suit, a very tall silk hat,–swallow-tail coat,–black boots, I think a black vest and necktie, and on damp or cold days at our cap, a grey shawl over his shoulders.

"We had our afternoon review at five o'clock, and as often as possible Mr. Lincoln with his wife and Cabinet, some members of Congress and a large number of citizens were present standing near Col. Burnside and Governor William Sprague. Sprague was the youngest Governor in the country and a manufacturer or calico at the great factory of A & W Sprague at Cranston, R.I., known as the Cranston Print Works. Miss Chase, with her father was also seen at the camp.

"After the review, the President came to the quarters of each mess of 18 men while we were at our evening mess which was directly after the parade and naturally we arose from the long bench upon each side of the table.

"He had no time to say much as he wanted to go to all the messes to see the thousand or twelve hundred men and in our mess, which was that of our second

Sergeant Burdick of Co. F., and the only words he said as he entered the doorway was 'Don't get up, Boys,' then shoot the hand of each one. We then resumed our places as he passed on.

"I feel very proud to have seen him a number of times, because there were not many who saw him more than once. When we began to thin out, those of us who did see him looked upon the fact as a special distinction, and we often bragged about it at Post meetings and at our reunions."

The sun was getting far west, and the robin raised his voice again, as though in warning to advance, which I did with regrets, leaving the old soldier and the comfortable chair with the hope I might come again. I was earnestly invited to make another visit, but alas, time stepped in before I could return, the old soldier having laid down his arms, and been mustered out of active life to the immortal. "God bless him," is my prayer, and may it be his great privilege to meet again his beloved "Father Abraham."

> Dear Comrade Boos –
>
> In answer to two of your questions I would say that whenever we were in close touch with the President (Lincoln) it was always after our evening dress parade at 6 O'c when we were seated about the table at supper. We were divided into messes of 18 men each and when he came in and took the hand of each he had only time to say "Don't get up Boys" (for when he came in we all stood up.)
>
> The other is in regard to Gov. Sprague. At that time he was considered rich, and of the firm of calico printers under the name of A. & W. Sprague Mfg. Co. –
>
> His great fault was drink –
>
> He was the youngest Governor in the country and was very popular in society

If you don't get tired of this long story and need more let me know.

I hope I have covered all you wish this last may take the place of the first which might be destroyed

Yours &c   Geo. B Smith
Commander of Lawton Warren Post
135 Gibbs Avenue

I shall be 89 the 2nd of July —

John E. Boos

Trades in the Regiment.

173 Jewellers — 85 Clerks — 70 Carpenters
70 Machinists — 52 Laborers — 51 Painters
58 Moulders — 37 Farmers — 37 Spinners
33 Sailors — 23 Shoemakers — 19 Weavers
21 Blacksmiths — 16 Masons — 17 Students
15 Accountants — 15 Tin workers — 12 Merchants
13 Brass finishers — 13 Silver smiths — 11 Butchers
11 Musicians aside from the Am. Band.
11 Teamsters — 10 Gas fitters — 10 Lawyers
10 Printers — 8 Tailors — 7 Dentists
7 Carriage makers — 7 Druggists — 7 Drivers
7 Engineers — 7 Engravers — 7 Gentlemen
7 Manufacturers — 7 Hostlers — 7 Grocers
7 Physicians — 6 Die sinkers — 6 Carders
6 Rule cutters — 6 Stone cutters — 4 Porters
5 Boot makers — 4 Plumbers — 4 Bath makers
5 Cabinet makers — 5 Harness makers — 3 Artists
4 Rubber manufrs — 4 Tobacconists — 3 Barbers
3 Chemists — 3 Coloriests — 3 Coopers
3 Curriers — 3 Dairians — 3 Traders
3 Photographers — 3 Scythe makers — 2 Bakers
2 Bar leaders — 2 Map makers — 2 Clergymen
2 Calico printers — 2 Casars — 2 Draughtsmen
2 Equestrians — 2 Express Messengers — 2 Firemen
2 Fishermen — 2 Gilders — 2 Hatters
2 Lapedaries — 2 Mechanics — 2 Peddlers
2 Roofers — 2 Sash makers — 2 Tanners
2 Shoe dealers — 2 Tradesmen — 1 Actor
1 Aeronaut — 1 Bag maker — 1 Banker
1 Bank Cashier — 1 Bonnet maker — 1 Bottler
1 Book binder — 1 Book seller — 1 Brakeman
1 Brass finisher — 1 Brass founder — 1 Brewer
1 Broom maker — 1 Brush maker — 1 Civil Eng
1 Carriage trimmer — 1 Cigar maker — 1 Clock maker

1 Cloth Inspector — 1 Coachman — 1 Coal dealer
1 Confectioner — 1 Copper smith — 1 Cotton Broker
1 Designer — 1 Door maker — 1 Cutler
1 Draughtsman — 1 Engine builder — 1 Dyer
1 Engine turner — 1 Farrier — 1 Finisher
1 File Cutter — 1 Horse Jockey — 1 Ice man
1 Instrument maker — 1 Ins. Agent — 1 Miller
1 Lithographer — 1 Lumberman — 1 Mule spinner
1 Lumber dealer — 1 Master builder — 1 Music teacher
1 Correspondent — 1 Opperative — 1 Opperator
1 Pattern maker — 1 Provision dealer 1 Pedler
1 R.R Treasurer — 1 Salesman — 1 Piecer
1 Soap boiler — 1 Soap Mfg — 1 Plater
1 Stone mason — 1 Teacher — 1 Servant
1 Stove Mfg — 1 Tool maker — 1 Soldier
1 Turner — 1 Upholsterer — 1 Varnisher
1 Vet. Surgeon — 1 Watch Case Mfg. 1 Watchmaker
1 Wheelright — 1 Wood Engraver — 1 Wool sorter
Not returned   134

Out of the 110 in Co F
93 Re-enlisted for the war —

I don't think that I have spoken of the following before this but if I have you may burn it up –

We were quartered in the Patent Office for a few weeks, there we had much to interest us – The Declaration of Independence, The Staff of Franklin, The sword, Uniform and camp chest of Washington and large cases filled with models –

From our quarters and after going into camp the rebel camp fires were plainly seen upon the opposite border of the Potomac. On May 2nd we were drawn up in line in front of the east wing of the Patent Office with Mr. Lincoln and his Cabinet on the roof and at the proper time he raised the flag to the peak as our band played the Star Spangled Banner.

Our camp was built by our own mechanics each building had a one pitch roof like our old wood sheds, there were 6 bunks on three of the sides – a porch where we had our meats. This may give you some idea of our buildings – no chairs but a bench on each side of the eating table – and the best cooks in the country and a large brick furnace – and when the 1st and Second regiments were in camp it required 960 Gal. of Coffee 10 Barrels of flour, 1300 lbs of meat and for a treat occasionally 150 large pans of gingerbread – and always hot bread –

I will just give a receipt by the cooks it may be of interest to the young folks –

Pork and beans — 1½ barrels of Pork
3 barrels of beans,
A boiled dinner — 1 barrel of Pork
325 Cabbages — 3 " " Beef
A berry pudding — 180 quarts of berries
8 barrels of meal — ½ barrel of flour
20 Doz Eggs — 40 Gal of milk
and spice to the taste —

To use this receipt for a family —
weigh all you can — and divide by
1200 men and you have the receipt for
one person then multiply by the number
in the family —

If you wish more please let me
know

              Geo B Smith

        Born July 2nd 1839.

Mr. John E. Boos.

My dear Sir. Your letter of enquiry has been received and I will give you my own account—

I shall be 89 years old on July 2nd 1928—

On the receipt of President Lincoln's call for 75,000 men which was issued on the 15th of April 1861 The Newport Artillery Co. which has been engaged in every war since its organization in 1741 had on its roll 39 members and the above call came to us on the 16th at 3 O'c— The guns called the pride of the Armory and the old place was filled — The order of our state calling for 100 men was read — Volunteers were called to fill the number lacking and in Ten minutes we had 110 men—

the next day at 12 O'c we were on our way to Providence to become a part of the 1st Reg. Rhode Island Detached Militia. Every company in the state was uniformed differently so the authorities must go to work and uniform us alike so as to start as soon as possible and be as a little bother to the government as possible, and the flies were thick enough — we got to Annapolis — we left there in the evening and set off on the 20th by way of Annapolis Junction — when arrived 24th leaving there next morning for Annapolis Junction — the track was torn up and engine disabled, but men from some of the regiments re-placed them and we arrived in Washington on Friday the 26th and marched in review before the President — we took up temporary quarters at the Patent Office and later went into camp —

Mr Lincoln was a visitor quite often at our evening review — we had our popular Governor (Sprague) with us in uniform and a fine Colonel (Burnside) and a fine staff —

Frequently while we were seated at our supper Mr Lo. came in and shook hands with us and left a few word —
for June we went into Maryland to drive the rebels out of Harpers Ferry — then on a forced march back to W —
On the 17th of July 1861 we crossed over into Virginia and then to Centreville and on the 21st we were in the Battle of Bull Run

Several of our men were killed and wounded — but — I am still well and am now the Commander Adjutant, Chaplain, Auditor and Trustee of the Lawton Warren Post G. A. R.

Yours in F C & L.

Geo B Smith

"I will write more later"

Newport R.I. May 1st 1928

Dear Mr Boos-

Your kind letter was received this day and in answer I would say that Mr Lincoln was always dressed in a black broad cloth suit, a very tall silk hat - swallow tail coat - black boots - I think a black vest and neck tie and in damp or cool days at our camp a grey shawl over his shoulders -

We had our afternoon review at 5 O'c and as often as possible Mr Lincoln with his wife and Cabinet, some members of Congress and a larg' number of citizens were present standing near Col Burnside and Gov. Wm Spragal - He was the youngest Governor in the Country and a manufacturer of calico at the great factory of A & Wm Sprague at Cranston R.I. known as the Cranston Print Works - Their string teams of several black horses with black fur robes over their shoulders and a good leader - he was very rich at that time - and single -

Miss Chase with her father was also at the camp -

After this review the President came to the quarters of each mess of 18 men while we were at our evening mess which was directly after the parade and naturally we arose from the long bench upon each side of the table.

He had no time to say much as he wanted to go to all the messes to see the thousand or twelve hundred men and in our mess which was that of our Second Sergeant Burdick of Co. F. 1st Reg. R. I. D. M. and the only words he said as he entered the door way was "Dont get up boys" then shook the hand of each one —

We then resumed our places as he passed out.

Yours truly
Geo. B Smith
Commander of Lawton Warren Post.

I Never Saw Lincoln

SAMUEL R. FISHER

In 1925, Samuel R. Fisher lived in retirement at his home in Parsons, Kansas, not because he was worn out, but time had changed since he first rode the box cars and worked up to an experienced railroad executive. Then a man held his job until strength weakened or the mind began to tire, but in this modern age, 70 years is the limit of service and he was compelled to lay down his work and retreat to an easy chair.

Mr. Fisher graduated from Washington Jefferson College in 1868, and in a short time accepted a position with the Rogers Locomotive Works at Patterson, N.J., where he stayed until he went to the Pennsylvania Railroad in 1873 as a member of the Engineering Department. In 1885, he again changed his position by being appointed Chief Engineer of the Milwaukee and Northern Railroad, going from there to Minneapolis, St. Paul and Sault Saint Marie in 1890. In 1893 be became Chief Engineer of the Everett and Monte Gristo Railroad, and in 1895 he again made a change by becoming Chairman of the Valuation Committee of the Missouri, Kansas and Texas, and in 1916 decided to ease up a little by becoming a Consulting Engineer of the Road.

Mr. Fisher was born in Cherry Fork, Ohio on October 24, 1846, and I having a mania to write to every man who was born before the year 1859, I wrote and asked if he had seen the great Civil War President. His answer was, "It was not my good fortune to meet or see him."

Parsons Kan.
May 18 1925

Mr. John E. Boos.
Dear Sir;
Your note of April 30 has been recieved —
In reply I would only state that it has never been my fortune to meet Abraham Lincoln — or even to see him —

Yours truly
Samuel B Fish

Did You See Lincoln?

GEORGE D. SEYMOUR

Though George D. Seymour was not born until October 6, 1859, I thought he might have seen President Lincoln, and it being a great event in his life, he might have retained the experience in his memory. He did not have the good fortune to see the great Emancipator, but he once had the pleasure of speaking to the Vice-President of the Confederacy, who, though one of the real Rebel leaders, always admired the President of the Union.

Mr. Seymour graduated from Hartford High School in 1878, later graduated from Yale and became a lawyer. During his life he was a trustee of the Thomas Lee House of East Lyme, of the Wadsworth Atheneum of Hartford, Chairman of the State Commission on Sculpture, Director of Donald G. Mitchell Memorial Library of Westville, Vice-President of the American Federation of the Arts, and the Society for the Preservation of New England Antiquities, Chairman of New Haven Municipal Art Commission, and of the Sub-committee on medals of the Tercentenary Commission of Connecticut, and Associate Fellow of the Berkley College of Yale. He also wrote a number of historical books.

In 1914, Mr. Seymour purchased the birthplace of Nathan Hale to preserve it as a permanent memorial, an act for which he deserved the thanks of every American.

GEORGE DUDLEY SEYMOUR
223 BRADLEY STREET
NEW HAVEN, CONNECTICUT

March 15, 1940

Mr. John E. Boos
21 Dudley Heights
Albany, N. Y.

Dear Mr. Boos:

I was born, October 6, 1859, and never saw Lincoln and do not get into your gallery, but I once talked with Alexander H. Stevens, in Washington.

That is as near as I get to Lincoln. I wish you luck, as one collector to another.

Faithfully yours,

S/p

George Dudley Seymour

NATHANIAL FOOTE

Justice Foote was born at Morrisville, N.Y., on November 15th, 1849, and, thinking he may have seen Abraham Lincoln, I wrote to him, but the answer came, "No, I never had the privilege of seeing that great American."

In 1905, Mr. Footes became a Judge of the Supreme Court of New York State, and on January 1st, 1912 became an Associate Justice of the Appellate Division, sitting on the bench until the Constitutional retirement age of seventy in 1930. From 1892 to 1894 he was President of the Rochester Bar Association, and in 1894 he was a delegate to the State Constitutional Convention.

August 6th, 1925.

Mr. John E. Boos,
   10 Lexington Avenue,
      Albany, New York.

Dear Sir:—

In reply to your letter of July 30th I regret to say that I never had the privilege of seeing Abraham Lincoln, and therefore am not able to write you such a letter as you request me to write.

Very truly yours,

Nathaniel Foote

F:MHS

I Should have Liked to have Seen Lincoln

Dr. Daniel Fiske

Dr. Daniel M. Fiske was born April 10, 1846 at Hampton, N.H. In 1869 he was given a Ph.B at Brown University, an A.M., and a D.D. by Hillsdale College in 1897. From 1872 to 1886 he was Professor of Biology at Hillsdale Michigan College and in the later year was ordained a Congregational Minister. He held pastorages in Jackson, Mich.; Toledo, Ohio; St. Louis, Mo.; and Topeka, Kansas. From 1899 almost to his death, he was Professor of Sociology at Washburn College, Topeka, Kansas.

Writing in 1925, he said of President Lincoln, "As I was only an Academy undergraduate in New Hampshire when the President was assassinated, it was never my privilege to see him, so my autograph can be of no possible interest to you."

Daniel M. Fiske
Professor-Emeritus of Sociology
in Washburn College
Topeka, Kansas

A Homer B. Sprague Letter

I saw much of Gen. Grant when he was President. He visited Oak Bluffs when I was a summer resident and I accompanied him to Hyannis, Nantucket, etc. I was correspondent of the Brooklyn Eagle, and was much surprised at his extensive acquaintance with Brooklyn affairs. He said he had carefully weighed the merits of the Beecher-Tilton controversy, and was satisfied that Mr. Beecher was in the right. I heard a good story that I have not seen in print illustration of Lincoln's humor.

It is said that he and Gideon Welles, then Secretary of the Navy, were down the Potomac one day, and that Welles had much to say of the importance of mines planted thickly here and there on the bottom of the river. Lincoln asked, "Why important?" "Because," said Welles, "although there is little probability that the enemy's armed vessels shall ever be able to come here, yet, if they should come, it would be a handy thing to have the mines in readiness for such an emergency."

"That reminds me," replied Lincoln, "of the doctor out West, who, when asked of what possible use can the rudimentary breast of a man be, answered that if, at any time, it should be so happen that a man should give birth to a child, it would be a handy thing to have the breasts ready for nursing the infant in such an emergency."

THE BOOK OF JOB

THE POETIC PORTION

VERSIFIED, WITH DUE REGARD TO THE LANGUAGE OF
THE AUTHORIZED VERSION, A CLOSER ADHERENCE TO
THE SENSE OF THE REVISED VERSIONS, AND A MORE
LITERAL TRANSLATION OF THE HEBREW ORIGINAL

WITH AN

INTRODUCTORY ESSAY

ADVANCING NEW VIEWS

AND

EXPLANATORY NOTES

QUOTING MANY EMINENT AUTHORITIES

BY

HOMER B. SPRAGUE, Ph.D.

FORMERLY PROFESSOR IN CORNELL UNIVERSITY, AFTERWARDS PRESIDENT
OF THE UNIVERSITY OF NORTH DAKOTA AND LECTURER IN DREW
THEOLOGICAL SEMINARY, EDITOR OF MANY ANNOTATED MASTERPIECES
OF CHAUCER, SHAKESPEARE, MILTON, GOLDSMITH, SCOTT, IRVING,
CARLYLE, ETC.

BOSTON
SHERMAN, FRENCH & COMPANY
6 BEACON STREET

614 Shirley Street
Winthrop (Beach)
Mass.

June 5, 1911

Mr. J. E. Boos,
Albany, N.Y.

My dear sir:

Yours of the 27th, asking me to write something of Lincoln & Grant, has come to hand here, where I expect to spend most of the hot weather.

When I shall have disposed of matters, which are just now very urgent, I shall take pleasure in complying with your wishes, so courteously expressed.

Cordially yours,
Homer B. Sprague

I heard a good story that I have not seen in print — illustrative of Lincoln's humor.

It was said that he and Gideon Welles, then Secretary of the Navy, were down the Potomac one day, and that Welles had much to say of the importance of mines planted thickly here and there in the bottom of the river. Lincoln asked him, "Why important?" "Because," said Welles, "although there is little probability that the enemy's armed vessels shall ever be able to come here, yet, if they should come, it would be a handy thing to have the mines in readiness for such an emergency."

"That reminds me," replied Lincoln, "of the doctor out west, who, when asked of what possible use can the rudimentary breasts of a man be, answered that if, at any time, it should so happen that a man should give birth to a child, it would be a handy thing to have the breasts ready for nursing the infant in such an emergency."

Ira B. Webster

Ira B. Webster lived in Northeast, some State, when he wrote the enclosed letter on November 11, 1860. It is a letter about the folks home, interesting only to the family, but the last paragraph will make interesting reading for any Lincoln lover. It says,–"You probably have heard before this that Abe Lincoln the Railsplitter will be our next President. We did not receive our N. York paper yesterday, so just when we want it most we have to do without it. Northeast gave 70 majority for Lincoln."

Northeast must have been an anti-slavery town, Hooray for Northeast.

but did not receive the first premium on account of her hose running away with her but she stuck like to him, but there being a premium at the Brockport Fair she thought to try her luck again, and here she took the first prize of $20. besides great churning for Parma.

Uncle Samuel has sold out his brick yard at Chicago and expects to return to Parma within five or six weeks.

You probably have heard before this that Abe. Lincon the rail splitter will be our next President. We did not receive our N. York paper yesterday so just when we want it the most we have to do without it. Northeast gave 70 majority for Lincon.

Yours Ira B Webster.

Senator Simeon D. Fess

The Record of Senator Simeon D. Fees of Ohio is as follows:

Born: On a farm in Allen Co., Ohio, Dec. 11, 1861

Start-in-life: Country school teacher

Career: Son of impoverished log cabin dwellers, he was four when his father died. At twelve he was sent to live with an elder sister, did farm work summers, got a little schooling winters. Aged 19, he passed an examination, received a license to teach. With his earnings he sent himself to Ohio Northern University at Ada. On the day in 1889 that Ohio Northern graduated him aged 27, that Methodist stronghold also appointed him professor of history. Equipped with a law degree, he became president of Antioch College, vocational school at Yellow Springs, Ohio, in 1907. Five years later he entered politics as delegate to the State constitutional convention, where he was the author of an amendment creating a State department of education. Same year he successfully stood for election to Congress from the 6th District of Ohio. He was successfully re-elected until 1922, having resigned Antioch's presidency in 1917. In 1922 with strong female and Dry support he won his seat in the Senate, defeating Democratic Senator Atlee Pomerene.

In Congress: Except for one innocent flutter toward Progressivism in his early days in the House, his Congressional career has been marked by the strictest party regularity. He thinks regular, talks regular, votes regular. As chairman of the Republican National Congressional campaign Committee in 1919-20-22, he did yeoman service by helping rally heavy G.O.P. majorities in the House. Having frequently compared Warren G. Harding's "moral leadership" to Abraham Lincoln's his maiden speech in the Senate was a spirited defense of the discredited President's administration. Never a member of the Ohio gang, he nevertheless branded each investigation of it misdeeds as "an orgy of slander, a spree of muck-racking, a riot of vituperation and incrimination."

With Calvin Coolidge, whom he admired tremendously and whose frequent White House guest he was, he indulged in long intimate hours of what Sen. Pat Harrison called "Political rumbletypog." Bob Fess was bitterly disappointed when Pres. Coolidge refused to run for a third term, was more responsible than anyone else for keeping alive the "Draft Coolidge" movement.

A self proclaimed reactionary, he suspects the New Deal Legislation, believes the Democratic recovery program is composed of "mere relief measures."

"As a party whip he has found little time to pursue any personal legislative bent except public education. For years he was chairman of the Library Committee, which governs the Library of Congress.

In appearance he is red-faced, small (5 ft. 6 in.), a neat dresser. His addresses, delivered in falsetto, are usually admonitory, pedagogical. When his party was in power, he used to wear a wide political smile. Now an annoyed frown is usually to be seen behind his pince-nez. His lack of humor makes him a perennial target for opposition rags. No one questions his sincerity and within his own ranks he is respected for his devotion to the party. Time, June, 1934

Compliments of S. D. Fess

ABRAHAM LINCOLN.

SPEECH
OF
HON. S. D. FESS,
OF OHIO,

In the House of Representatives,
Thursday, February 12, 1914.

HOUSE OF REPRESENTATIVES.
Thursday, *February 12, 1914.*

The House met at 12 o'clock noon.

The Chaplain, Rev. Henry N. Couden, D. D., offered the following prayer:

God our Father, make us worthy of the memory of Abraham Lincoln, a great soul whom thou didst send into the world with a destiny to fulfill, not only for his people but for all the world; a superb intellect; a heart of love; a divination which enabled him to see far beyond the vision of his contemporaries; a courage which swept him on without fear where others faltered; a faith which in the darkest hours failed him not. Surely he belongs to the ages, will live in the ages, and while he lives this Republic will live to bless mankind. "O Lord, God of hosts, be with us yet, lest we forget" his sublime example and the stupendous work he accomplished, ".That government of the people, by the people, for the people shall not perish from the earth." For Thine is the kingdom and the power and the glory forever. Amen.

The Journal of the proceedings of yesterday was read and approved.

The SPEAKER. By special order, the gentleman from Ohio [Mr. FESS] is permitted to address the House for 30 minutes on the life and character of Abraham Lincoln. [Applause.]

Mr. FESS. Mr. Speaker and Members of the House, I esteem it no small privilege or little honor to be permitted to speak to this group of legislators upon what I regard as one of the most remarkable characters in human history. Just 53 years ago yesterday, standing upon the platform of a train that was to bear him to Washington, Abraham Lincoln addressed a large concourse of people in his city of Springfield, in which address he said:

Will you not pray for me that the same Arm that supported the great Washington may be my support? For with that support I can accomplish my duty; without it I can not do anything.

The train stopped at the little town of Tolono, where, as in every town through which the train passed, a large concourse of people gathered. The train stopped for the engine to take

30580—12826

2

water. Mr. Lincoln was not expected to speak, but finally he did respond to the great cry of the people who had gathered, and came out on the platform and said:

> I am upon a journey fraught with a great deal of concern to you and to me. May the words of the poet still be true, "Behind the clouds the sun is still shining." Good-by. God bless you!

He then resumed his seat in the train.

Some men make their place in history by notable utterances, others by notable deeds. Few in the world's history have the credit of both, and to that class belongs Abraham Lincoln. At an early time in his political career, speaking upon the most sensitive question before the country then or since, he showed his courage by saying:

> Broken by it I, too, may be; bow to it, I never will. The probability that we may fail in a worthy cause is not a sufficient justification for our refusing to support it.

In 1855, in a letter to Judge Robertson, of Kentucky, he said:

> The one question that wears upon me is, Can our country permanently endure half slave and half free? It is too much for me. May God in his mercy superintend the solution.

Three years later, in 1858, in a convention in Springfield, Ill., where he was nominated for the position of Senator—for the seat then occupied by Douglas—he announced the same principle, "I do not believe that this Government can permanently endure half slave and half free." This announcement sounded like a fire bell would sound at the hour of midnight in a country village. It was taken up by the entire country. It was quoted in the London Times and other publications of Europe. It was pronounced by many of our statesmen as revolutionary. Stephen A. Douglas, one of the brainiest men of the country, and one of the most courageous as well as patriotic, believed that it was a dangerous doctrine, and announced that he would reply to it in his home city of Chicago on the 9th of July.

Mr. Lincoln went to Chicago to be present on that occasion. He heard one of the most powerful arguments against his position that probably could be made. At the close of that meeting he arose and, in substance, said:

> I shall be here to-morrow night, at which time I will pay my respects to my friend, the judge, who has charged me with an attempt to array one section of the country against the other. I hope some of you will come out to hear my side of the story.

The next night Mr. Lincoln greeted a great audience, upon which he made a profound impression. When Mr. Douglas went to Bloomington, Ill., to speak, Mr. Lincoln followed him. Mr. Douglas noticed while he was speaking that Mr. Lincoln was in his audience again. He referred to the fact with some feeling. On the afternoon of the 17th of July Mr. Douglas spoke in Springfield, and on that night Mr. Lincoln also spoke. Then Mr. Lincoln wrote a challenge to Mr. Douglas; asked him to go on the same platform with him, divide the time, and discuss the question. The result of this was that a series of debates, seven in number, the most notable in American political history, was arranged. In the debate, when Mr. Douglas propounded a series of questions to Mr. Lincoln, Mr. Lincoln replied to them categorically, and then propounded a series, and dwelt upon one as the key to the entire situation. That question was:

> Can the people of a Territory in any lawful manner, against the wishes of the citizens of any of the States, exclude slavery from within its limit prior to the adoption of a State constitution?

30580—12826

He pressed it. Mr. Douglas was the author of the popular sovereignty scheme, as you all know, the authority of control of such questions must be left to the people of the States. The friends of Mr. Lincoln went to him and said, " Do not press that question; if you insist on an answer you can never be elected to the senatorship in this country." Mr. Lincoln replied, " If Mr. Douglas answers my question, yes or no, he can never be elected President of this Nation, and I am looking for larger game." That did not mean that Mr. Lincoln was at that time looking for himself to the Presidency, because that debate was in 1858, and as late as 1859 Mr. Lincoln replied to a letter written to him by a friend about being Vice President, " I am not fit to be Vice President of the United States." Mr. Lincoln in 1858 was simply stating that if Mr. Douglas answered that question he, Mr. Douglas, could never be elected to the highest position in the gift of the people of the country. In 1859 Mr. Lincoln made that notable speech in Columbus, Ohio, one of the greatest contributions to the political literature of his day. Then in February of 1860, speaking in the heart of New York City at Cooper Union he gave, I think, the finest type of the periodic sentence in a long speech to be found anywhere. From the standpoint of the rhetorician as a critic this long speech is a gem in American political literature. This is the meeting over which the eminent poet Bryant presided and introduced Lincoln as a " distinguished citizen of the United States." I believe, gentlemen, that the Cooper Union speech is the finest exposition of the sensitive issue, and that it was put in the most rhetorical form of any long speech in our literature, and he did it with such magnanimity. He said:

If slavery is right, then all that the South asks we can readily grant. If slavery is wrong, then all that the North asks the South can readily grant. Their thinking it right and our thinking it wrong is the precise point upon which turns this whole controversy; but thinking it wrong, as we do, we can afford to leave it where it now exists by virtue of the law, but can we afford to allow it to go into new territory?

There, for the first time the real issue was presented by Mr. Lincoln; not the issue of the abolitionist, but the issue of Mr. Lincoln of the constitutional power of the Congress to control property in a Territory, which was to give rise to an organization of public opinion that was not to abate until slavery was no more. That was in 1860. In 1861, in his famous inaugural, he said:

Friends can make laws easier than enemies can make treaties. We must not be enemies; we must be friends. Though passion may have strained, it must not break the bonds of our affection. The mystic chords of memory stretching from every battle field and patriot's grave to every heart and hearthstone all over this broad land will swell the chorus of the Union when again touched, as it surely will be, by the better angels of our nature.

With his keen perception of the mighty issue he was also wonderfully magnanimous.

This magnanimity that was uttered at that time had been uttered in the town of Steubenville, Ohio, a little while before, when on his way to Washington, looking across to the State of Virginia, his father's native State, he said to that concourse of people on the Ohio side:

Only the river divides us, and you on the other side are just as sincere in your contention as we on this side.

On this trip he addressed the Legislatures of Indiana, Ohio, New York, and Pennsylvania, all notable speeches, teeming with

30580—12826

evidence of his grasp of the situation facing him. When he reached Philadelphia, out in front of old Independence Hall, he said on the occasion of raising the American flag over the hall:

What principle has kept our States so long together? It is not the mere fact of separation from the mother country, but it is the principle found in the Declaration of Independence, penned by the immortal Jefferson and adopted in this hall, that gave promise not alone to the people of our own country but to all the people of all the world that ere long the weight shall be lifted from the shoulders of all men and all shall have an equal chance. Now, my fellow citizens, can the Nation be saved upon that basis? If it can and I can help to save it I am the happiest man in it, but if it can not I was about to say I would rather be assassinated on this spot than to surrender it.

That was on the 22d day of February, 1861, in the famous Independence City, out in front of Independence Hall. I mention these historical utterances, so notable and significant in their meaning, because I would like to have this body recall this wonderful ability in expression, the like of which probably is not known in any political orator or figure in our country. Why, it was none other than Prof. Bailey, a professor of rhetoric in a famous American college, who had been so charmed with the pure English of this plain statesman of the West that he sought an interview to ascertain the secret of his power. Mr. Lincoln at first expressed surprise that he had any power in utterance, but when pressed he substantially said: "Well, all I can remember is that when neighbors would come to my father's house and talk to father in language I did not understand, I would become offended, sometimes, and I would find myself going to bed that night unable to sleep. I bounded it on the north, south, east, and west until I had caught the idea, and then I said it myself, and when I said it I used the language I would use when talking to the boys on the street." Prof. Bailey said: "That is one of the most splendid educational principles I have ever received from any man." To which Mr. Lincoln expressed great surprise.

Mr. Lincoln's ability to express the English language consisted in the use of the small word. Eighty-five per cent of his words are monosyllabic. He never employed a big word when a little one would do. He never clouded his thought by a multiplicity of words. His sentences were always short and their meaning never involved. In a word, he never spoke to be heard, but always to be understood; and therefore he was not always elegant from the standpoint of the rhetorician, but wonderfully expressive. For example, he would say, "I dumped it into a hole"; but Douglas, the rhetorician, would say, "I deposited it into a cavity," which is a good deal better from the standard rule of expression. Lincoln would say, "I dug a ditch"; Douglas would say, "I excavated a channel." Lincoln said, 'My defeat by Douglas in 1858 was due to bad luck; I ran at the wrong time"; Douglas said, "It was due to a strange fortuitous combination of importune contingencies that nobody could have foreseen." Here stands Stephen A. Douglas, a master of rhetoric; Abraham Lincoln, a master of logic; Stephen A. Douglas, eloquent in words; Abraham Lincoln, eloquent in thought; Stephen A. Douglas appealing to expediency; Abraham Lincoln, appealing to right. Douglas said, "I do not care whether you vote slavery up or vote it down." Lincoln said, "I care very much about what most people care most about." He turned his back upon his

30580—12826

audience and spoke to Douglas, "Is it not a false philosophy to build a system upon the basis that you do not care anything about what most people care most about?" It was for that sentence that Mr. Douglas paid him such a tribute in three weeks after the close of those debates. Mr. Lincoln was powerful in this series of debates, and it was here that his wonderful ability as a thinker and debater was first disclosed to the public. I say to you men of Congress that Abraham Lincoln had not an equal on the American platform in the use of pure Anglo-Saxon.

If you think that I am overstating, I have two items of evidence that any lawyer will accept as fairly conclusive. In Oxford University, England, you will hear the finest English taught and spoken of any place in the world. An American visiting this great seat of learning will be led to a corridor where can be read one of the famous letters written by this man, known to the world as unlettered, or illiterate, because he was not a collegiate, the letter to Mrs. Bixby, the mother of five sons, all of whom gave their lives for their country:

> DEAR MADAM: I have been shown in the files of the War Department a statement of the adjutant general of Massachusetts that you are the mother of five sons who have died gloriously on the field of battle. I feel how weak and fruitless must be any words of mine which should attempt to beguile you from the grief of a loss so overwhelming. But I can not refrain from tendering to you the consolation which may be found in the thanks of the Republic they died to save. I pray that our Heavenly Father may assuage the anguish of your bereavement and leave you only the cherished memory of the loved and lost, and the solemn pride that must be yours to have laid so costly a sacrifice on the altar of freedom.
> Yours, very sincerely and respectfully,
> ABRAHAM LINCOLN.

This letter, thus permanently preserved, is pronounced by the savants of Oxford as one of the finest letters of condolence ever written in our language. Note its beauty, its purity, its sublimity.

If that is not sufficient evidence, then go to the British Museum, where can be found books enough, if put on a single shelf, to reach 40 miles. Ask the authorities there what their judgment is as to the finest short speech in the English language. You will be handed at once this splendid piece of rhetoric and high mark of literary appreciation, as well as statesmanlike delivery, at Gettysburg, November 19, 1863:

> Fourscore and seven years ago our fathers brought forth on this continent a new Nation, conceived in liberty and dedicated to the proposition that all men are created equal.
> Now we are engaged in a great civil war, testing whether that Nation, or any nation so conceived and so dedicated, can long endure. We are met on a great battle field of that war. We have come to dedicate a portion of that field as a final resting place for those who here gave their lives that that Nation might live. It is altogether fitting and proper that we should do this.
> But, in a larger sense, we can not dedicate, we can not consecrate, we can not hallow this ground. The brave men, living and dead, who struggled here have consecrated it far above our poor power to add or detract. The world will little note nor long remember what we say here, but it can never forget what they did here. It is for us, the living, rather to be dedicated here to the unfinished work which they who fought here have thus far so nobly advanced. It is rather for us to be here dedicated to the great task remaining before us—that from these honored dead we take increased devotion to that cause for which they gave the last full measure of devotion; that we here highly resolve that these dead shall not have died in vain; that this Nation under God shall have a new birth of freedom; and that government of the people, by the people, for the people shall not perish from the earth.

30580—12826

6

When he finished, the orator of the day, Edward Everett, walked over to the President, took his hand, and in substance said: "Mr. President, if I could congratulate myself upon the belief that in two and a quarter hours I had been enabled to put the issue as clearly as you have done it in two and a quarter minutes, I would regard myself as a happy man."

This speech the British Museum authorities regard as one of the finest short speeches uttered in the English language. Who is this man that he could thus speak and write? Born in a hut, of the most humble surroundings, at the age of 7 he accompanied his parents and sister into Indiana, where they lived one winter in an open camp with but three sides to it. And yet, without ever having, as a pupil, a lead pencil or a piece of paper, a slate pencil or a slate, without having gone to school but six months all told, according to his own statement, here is a man thus starting with no convenience who has reached a plane, an ability to speak the English language, not yet reached by scholars of the day. Where is the secret? I think that it might be found in the sort of books he read. What are they?

The one book with which he was quite familiar was King James's version of the Bible. I once heard Parks Cadman, pastor of the greatest Congregational Church in the world, say that Abraham Lincoln's verbal knowledge of the Bible was not equaled by the theologians. I would not state that upon my own authority, but I cite it upon his authority. He knew Shakespeare, and in the darkest hours of the Nation's life, in the midst of great depression, often when the Cabinet was in session, Mr. Lincoln would throw himself back in an armchair and quote page after page of Shakespeare, until the scholarly Seward would turn to him and say: "Why, Mr. President, our understanding has been from the beginning that you have never gone to school, and yet you quote Shakespeare as I do not, and I am regarded as somewhat of a Shakespearean scholar."

Bunyan's Pilgrim's Progress was another book that he read. Feed a growing mind upon the English of these texts and you will have a choice of English. I concede the speeches before mentioned to be a high rank of expression, but I think the high-water mark was reached on another occasion, when looking back over four years of awful war, a period of the bitterest hatred and almost vicious calumny, on the part of his foes at least, and during which period no man's heart was bleeding more than his, he said:

> Both read the same Bible and pray to the same God, and each invokes His aid against the other. The prayers of both could not be answered. That of neither has been answered fully. The Almighty has His own purposes. If we shall suppose that American slavery is one of those offenses which in the providence of God must needs come, but which, having continued through His appointed time, He now wills to remove, and that He gives to both North and South this terrible war as the woe due to those by whom the offense came, shall we discern therein any departure from those divine attributes which the believers in a living God always ascribe to Him?
>
> Fondly do we hope, fervently do we pray, that this mighty scourge of war may speedily pass away. Yet, if God wills that it continue until all the wealth piled up by the bondman's 250 years of unrequited toil shall be sunk and until every drop of blood drawn with the lash shall be paid by another drawn by the sword, as was said 3,000 years ago, so still it must be said: "The judgments of the Lord are true and righteous altogether." With malice toward none, with charity for all, firmness in the right as God gives us to see the right, let us strive on to finish the work we are now in, to bind up the Nation's wounds, to care for him who shall have borne the battle and for his widow and his orphan, to do all which may achieve and cherish a just and lasting peace among ourselves and with all nations.

30580—12826

Here is one of the finest prose poems in the literature of our language, and, in my judgment, is the highest reach in refinement of utterance we have from this remarkable leader of men not only in thought but as well in deed.

And I think of how he suffered in the White House as the head of the Nation, so distracted by civil war and he helpless to end the strife. One night he said to Frank Carpenter at the dead hour of midnight, standing with his hands in this shape [indicating]: "Oh, Carp, Carp, what would I give to-night in exchange for this wearisome hospital of pain and woe that they call the White House for the place that is occupied by some poor boy that sleeps under the sod in a southern battle field? I can not stand this thing much longer. I have got to have some relief." When I read from Carpenter, the painter of the famous emancipation picture, I instinctively say: "Oh, Jerusalem, Jerusalem, how oft would I have gathered thee as a hen gathereth her chicks under her wings, but ye would not."

Oh, my dissatisfied countrymen, you who can not understand the suffering and the heartbeats, the great distress of the head of the Nation, how changed would be your attitude if you could but see him in his agony for the Nation. If we could have understood his sufferings, we would not have had the feelings of bitterness that were so often expressed. My friends, this hatred was not confined to any one section of the country, as you well know. I was rocked in a cradle over which was sung the lullaby:

> Old Abe Lincoln is dead and gone.
> Hurrah! Hurrah!

And I am not the only one in the State of Ohio who was taught that he was not a patriot. But when I come to look into his words and to study his acts and with regard for his magnanimity, together with his intellectuality, I can easily understand why, in the lapse of half a century, there is such universal approval now of the characteristics of that great man in all parts, not only of our Nation but of the world.

I once asked one of the best editors in this country or in any other, Charles A. Dana, who knew Mr. Lincoln as perhaps no other man knew him during the period that covered the war, what he thought was Lincoln's secret of greatness. Quickly he said: "His control of men." And then he added: "If a man can not control other men, then his power is limited to what he can do alone. On the other hand, if he can control men his power is multiplied just to the number of men he controls."

In view of this theory I am not so sure but that we might possibly for a moment pause to fix our eyes upon the White House now, with reference to that quality of leadership. But this is not the place nor the hour for making comparisons. They might be misunderstood. Mr. Lincoln had that ability to differ from men and yet to win them. Note how he struggled with the great commoner, Thaddeus Stevens. When Lincoln insisted upon his method of Reconstruction, which Stevens denounced as his shorthand method, destined to swamp the American Congress by Confederate leaders, Lincoln put it in this homely way, or substantially in these terms: "Stevens, you want what I want, but we do not go after it in the same way. Concede that my policy, which you criticize, is now in its beginning to what the policy is when it is finished, as an egg is to the chicken when it

30580—12826

is hatched. do you not think you will get that egg quicker by hatching it than by smashing it?" A homely illustration that carries in it a sound philosophy.

That is an example of the way he had of reaching Mr. Stevens. He had his own way of dealing with the leaders of the day, such men as Mr. Seward, and especially Mr. Stanton, both of whom he regarded as the greatest Secretaries of their respective departments. In the early part of the administration the country looked upon Mr. Lincoln as a much inferior man to Mr. Seward. None knew this better than the great Secretary. This explains the strange suggestion of Seward.

He reminded Lincoln that after so long the Government was still without a policy, and said that while he did not seek it, if the President desired, he would assume the responsibility. The reply by Lincoln is historic, and discloses his rare talent to control men. The policy was forthcoming, but it was not that of any Cabinet officer. A similar instance is when he rejected Seward's proposed adjustment of the Trent affair and directed it himself by taking Seward's proposed plan and blue-penciling two-thirds of it as useless and dangerous. In spite of this wide difference between them, the time came when Mr. Seward said, "I know the men of my time, and I believe Mr. Lincoln was truly the best man I ever met in public life."

On the night of the second election quite a scene took place between Lincoln and Stanton. Dana said. "Whitelaw Reid came in, and I, as a matter of courtesy, withdrew and went into another room, where Stanton was. It was not long before I noticed that Stanton was quite indignant. He was walking the floor greatly disturbed. I said to him, 'What troubles you, Mr. Secretary?' and he pointed his hand through the door toward Lincoln." Dana said that Lincoln at that moment was a very comical figure. He was sitting leaning back against the wall, his legs crossed, and laughing convulsively. He had just read to Reid something from the writings of Petroleum V. Nasby, the editor and humorist of the Toledo Blade, at that time almost as popular a writer as was Mark Twain later. "Stanton noticing that he was reading Petroleum V. Nasby seemed so angry," says Mr. Dana, "that he turned to me and said, 'Look there. There sits the man around whom the heartstrings of this Nation are wrapped to-night, being amused over a damned mountebank.'" Evidently Mr. Lincoln must have heard him, for he immediately called to Mr. Stanton, "Mr. Secretary, have you ever read anything written by Petroleum V. Neesby?" And Whitelaw Reid, who was sitting by, said, "Nasby; Mr. President, Nasby," when Mr. Lincoln repeated Nasby. Mr. Stanton replied, "No; I haven't time for such buncombe." Mr. Lincoln said, "Here is some buncombe that you would enjoy." He added, "Nasby says there are three kinds of fools. There is the natural fool and the educated fool, and when you take a natural fool and try to educate him, you have a damphool." [Laughter.] Dana said Stanton did not enjoy the joke at all. [Renewed laughter.]

Mr. Stanton seemed so different from Mr. Lincoln, and people are speculating now as to whether they were friendly to one another. The difference was one of temperament. They were equally sincere and patriotic. The brusk demeanor of the Secretary was ever in sharp contrast with the childlike kindness and affectionate regard of the great President. The two men

30580—12826

quite frequently clashed for the moment over policies. These differences usually grew out of Lincoln's pardoning habit. You will recall that Lincoln ordered some persons that had been imprisoned at Baltimore upon the charge of treason for the sale of goods to the Confederacy to be liberated, against the wishes of Stanton, and Judge Holt——

[Here the hammer fell.]

The SPEAKER. The time of the gentleman from Ohio has expired.

Mr. YOUNG of North Dakota. The gentleman from Ohio [Mr. FESS] should have an extension of an hour.

Mr. WILLIS. Mr. Speaker, I ask unanimous consent that my colleague be allowed to proceed to the conclusion of his remarks.

The SPEAKER. The gentleman from Ohio [Mr. WILLIS] asks unanimous consent that his colleague [Mr. FESS] be permitted to proceed without limit. Is there objection? [After a pause.] The Chair hears none.

Mr. FESS. Mr. Speaker, I thank you and the Members of the House for this courtesy, and I shall certainly respect it enough not to keep you very long. [Cries of "Go on!"] That gavel knocked out of my mind what I was saying. [Laughter.]

A MEMBER. You were talking about certain kinds of fools. [Laughter.]

Mr. FESS. It was the incident over in Baltimore. It was said that Judge Holt, of Kentucky, went over in confidence on the order of the President and made some arrangement to let the people out without regard to Mr. Stanton's wishes. Mr. Stanton was very much enraged, and he called Mr. Holt, a subordinate, "on the carpet"; but Judge Holt defended himself on the ground that the President had ordered him to do it. It is reported that Mr. Stanton said, "Did Lincoln order you to do that?" Holt said he did. Stanton hesitated a moment and then said, "Holt, the only thing left us is to get rid of that baboon in the White House."

That is a very serious statement to make on the floor of this House when regarded from the standpoint of the relation between chief and subordinate, but it is in the reminiscences. When the matter came to the notice of Mr. Lincoln he said in good humor, "Did Stanton say that?" He was assured that he had, and another person speaking with him said, "I would not endure the insult." Lincoln said, "Insult? That is no insult. All he said was that I was a baboon, and that is only a matter of opinion, sir," and then added, "and the thing that concerns me most is that Stanton said it, and I find he is usually right." [Laughter and applause.]

Oh, such magnanimity, when a difference clothes itself in language of insult as well as ridicule, in such a great soul; to differ from men and still hold their respect to the last was a quality possessed in abundance by the great Lincoln.

On one occasion when Stanton chided the President for allowing a mother-in-law to impose upon him on behalf of her daughter whose husband was to be shot for desertion, in which the Secretary expressed a doubt whether the old lady really cared about the fate of the man, Mr. Lincoln replied, "It may be she did not. I did not see the lady while she was speaking. I only saw the poor young woman who was so soon to become a widow unless I interposed."

30580—12826

10

Here is but one of scores of incidents to show his magnanimous spirit to his inferior, and at the same time that beautiful temper of mercy of which many were beneficiaries.

In evidence of this power over men note this incident: A retired Presbyterian minister said to me recently, "My inspiration and success as a preacher came from Lincoln, when after I had made my report to Congress of the work of the Sanitary and Christian Commission, Mr. Lincoln said to me, 'The good God has blessed you, young man, with power to influence men. Go on in the way you have started. Pay more attention to the hearts of men rather than to their heads.'" That became my guiding principle.

What is the secret of Mr. Lincoln's ability to control men like Seward and Stanton and Stevens, and other men who were so wonderfully different in temperament and eminently superior to him in all that went to make up modern standards? I think I can give a solution to the mystery. It is in a combination of two qualities that are usually found in leadership. The one is that wonderful fund of humor and the other is that deep sense of pathos. At one moment Mr. Lincoln would make you laugh. At another moment you would want to cry. Strange as it may seem, these seeming contradictories are generally present in the same person. If Lincoln was the most comical man in public life, he was certainly the saddest. The world tires of the person who plays on but one string.

I distinctly recall an incident that is told by Carpenter. Mr. Lincoln frequently went out here to the hospital near Washington, not simply to be in the presence of sorrow but to comfort the wounded soldiers, many of whom were dying by the inch. On one occasion he had spent a good deal of time out there—most of the day. Just as he was ready to get into the carriage to return, somebody rushed out and said to one of the men with him, "I wish you would tell the President that in a part of the hospital that he did not visit there is a Confederate soldier, and he is dying; he wants to see the President." The matter was referred to the President, and he said, "I shall go back." He excused himself for a moment, and was led back to where the Confederate soldier was lying upon the cot, and when he came to the sufferer all that he could hear the soldier say was, "I knew they were mistaken; I knew they were mistaken."

Evidently he had been told that Mr. Lincoln was the sort of a man that I had been taught he was, and he had found that he was not. When Mr. Lincoln took his hand and asked him what he could do, he said, "The surgeon says I can not get well; I do not know anybody here, and I wanted to see you before I died." When Mr. Lincoln asked him what he could do, there was something said by the poor boy in regard to what he wanted sent home, and then Mr. Lincoln stooped and took his hand in his two. The President, standing in that fashion, said, "Now, my boy, is there anything else I can do? I have been here most of the day; I am busy, and I must go." The boy said, in broken tones, "Oh, I thought, if you did not mind, you might stay and see me through." And there stood the President bending over the dying soldier and copious tears dropping upon his coat sleeve.

Men of this House, that is the most beautiful picture in American history. If I were a painter and wanted to paint Lincoln, I would have to seize upon some particular moment

30580—12826

of time, because you can not paint duration in a picture, and I would seize the moment when the President of this Nation, the mightiest Republic on earth, stooped and wept over a dying Confederate soldier, dying away from home. That is a most beautiful representation of the real Lincoln. [Applause.]

He has been misunderstood in regard to the slavery agitation. Mr. Lincoln's greatest work, gentlemen, was in the preservation of the Union. Do you not remember in 1863 what a bitter letter he received from Horace Greeley, published in the New York Tribune as an open letter to the President, in which Greeley called him "an opportunist"? Mr. Lincoln replied to it—and I want to give you exactly his reply; and, therefore, you will allow me to read that reply. It is one of the suggestive utterances of his life. He replied:

> As to the policy I seem to be pursuing, I have not meant to leave anyone in doubt. I would save the Union. I would save it in the shortest way under the Constitution. The sooner the national authority can be restored the nearer the Union will be the Union as it was. If there be those who would not save the Union unless they could at the same time save slavery, I do not agree with them. If there be those who would not save the Union unless at the same time they could destroy slavery, I do not agree with them. My paramount object is to save the Union and not either to save or to destroy slavery. If I could save the Union without freeing any slave, I would do it. If I could save it by freeing all the slaves, I would do it.

Then he added:

> I am ready to accept new views as soon as they are proved to be true views.

I do not mean here to minimize the title of the "great emancipator." I simply mean that the one supreme purpose of his career was to preserve the Union. This does not and should not detract from his achievement as the leader who, by the stroke of his pen, lifted a race out of human chattelhood into the atmosphere of American citizenship. But that achievement was destined to take place; if not by his hand, then by another's. The institution of slavery was indicted by the civilization of the centuries and had to succumb. However, this could not be said of the preservation of the Union. The greatest single achievement in the history of civil government in the world is the preservation of republican form of government. Since the close of the Civil War this idea has spread over the world like the waters cover the sea. There is not a single country that is not feeling the mighty impulses for self-government, the finest example of which is our own Republic. In fixing Lincoln's place in history it will not be so much the emancipator of a race as the savior of a nation and republican government on the earth. Both of these accomplishments demanded the best talent of head and heart.

He had other elements of statesmanship. His heart throbs for liberty never carried him to the shoals of license. On the other hand, reverence for law was fundamental with him. On one occasion he said:

> Let reverence for the law be breathed by every American mother to the babe that prattles on her lap; let it be taught in schools and colleges; let it be preached from the pulpit, proclaimed in legislative halls, and enforced in courts of justice. And, in short, let it become the political religion of the Nation, and let the old and the young, the rich and the poor, the grave and the gay, of all sexes and tongues and colors and conditions, sacrifice unceasingly upon its altars.

When he was criticized for the appointment of Stanton, who had not supported him, a friend said to him, "Why, Stanton has not been in your favor." Mr. Lincoln said, "That is no matter. I met him down in Cincinnati in a lawsuit where I tested his mettle, and I know his power." And then the interested party said, "But you are the first President of a new party, and you would have a splendid opportunity to build up a political organization." Members of Congress listen to Lincoln in reply: "We will save the Union first and build a party out of what is left." That is another element of statesmanship, it seems to me.

On the other hand, notice the humor. May I give you an incident that Dana gave me? Lincoln was pestered with office seekers, strange to say, in that day as we are not so much (?) in this. These office seekers came from every place. One day Mr. Lincoln saw three men coming up the walk toward the White House. At the time he seemed in exceptional spirits with humor bubbling over. Lincoln was looking out of the window. He said, "Dana, look. Those three men have been here before. This is the third or fourth time they have come. They want an office. I do not know even where it is. I do not know whether it is in Missouri or Illinois. It would not make any difference whether Tom, Dick, or Harry had it. It will not pay over $180 a year." Dana urged him not to receive them, when Lincoln replied, "Oh, yes; I will receive them." About that time the man whose duty it was to announce callers to the President came in and told him there were three men from the West who wanted to see him, and asked what he should say to them. Lincoln said, "Bring them in and let them sit down here." I wish I could tell this story as Dana told it, but I can not. Dana said the three men came in and took their seats, and Mr. Lincoln, after greeting them, said to them, "Excuse me, gentlemen, until I finish a story I was telling Dana." He had not been telling any story at all, but he began: "I think I was about 13 years old. Our fashion was to meet in Sunday school, where we would read sometimes in the Old Testament and sometimes in the New. On this particular day we were reading in the Old about the three Hebrew children. In that class we always would stand in line; the first boy would read and then the next, and if anybody made a mistake the fellow next to him would correct him, turn him down, and go up. There was one fellow in the class, about as tall as I was, who never had learned to read, and he always stood at the foot. (Just excuse me, gentlemen, in a few minutes I will be through with this.) When it came this fellow's turn to read, he read something like this, holding his finger on the page to keep the place, and reading in a loud monotonous tone, hesitating on every word: 'And — a — part — of — the — kingdom — was — to — be — ruled — over — by — by — by —' 'Well,' said the teacher, 'read on, read on.' 'By — Meshach, — Shadrach, — and — Abed-nego.' (Just excuse me, gentlemen, in a few minutes I will be through.) Then the next boy read, and then the next one, and it came around to this boy at the foot again, and the teacher said to him, 'Read that fourteenth verse.' It was the same verse. So he read the same verse again, and in the same hesitating way: 'And — a — part — of — the — kingdom — was — to — be — ruled — over — by — by — by — well, if there don't come them same three gol durned fools again.'" [Laughter.]

The leader said, "Mr. President, we will come some time when you are not so busy." As soon as they were out Lincoln said to Dana, "Didn't we fetch 'em this time?"

30580—12826

If you link the quality of humor, which is always present, to the other quality of pathos, which was instinctive with him, you have the elements in combination that made him the leader of men. It would be easy to illustrate the two qualities by the great number of incidents similar to these I have mentioned in his life.

Then there are two other abiding qualities in the man that I find in my study of him that I think this House ought now to think about. They are the fundamental qualities that make his name an increasingly important one in our history. The first one is faith in the people. I do not believe America shows in her history any man who had equal faith in the common goodness of mankind. It welled up in both word and deed upon every hand, in season and out of season. I have the greatest admiration for Samuel Adams, of Massachusetts—the man of the town meeting and one of the country's most distinguished democrats, past or present. I have also the greatest admiration for Thomas Jefferson, of Virginia, the author of the Declaration of Independence and the founder of the Democratic Party.

As a man who has lived all his life in the study of history, I have a wonderful admiration for the hold those men had upon the people, in their faith in the people. But, Members of this House, with due regard for the faith of the fathers, I think Abraham Lincoln was in the truest sense a man of the people, one among the people, and in sympathy with the people beyond any man in our history. I do not think any man can come to his shoulders in this attribute if measured by what he said, by what he did, by what he really was in that respect. When a man said to him, "The people will go wrong on this matter," he replied, "Intellectually, probably they may; morally, never." The collective wisdom expressed in morals is always better than individual wisdom. "In the multitude of counsel there is safety," said he, quoting it from the Good Book. I could give you numerous suggestions falling from his lips, expressions like these: "God must have loved the common people, for He made so many of them." "You can fool all of the people some of the time, some of the people all of the time, but you can not fool all of the people all of the time." You know people have said it was Barnum who said that. It was not. It was Lincoln. It is Lincolnian. He believed in the people. In other words, he did not think the Government was going to the bowwows if attempts were made at some innovation, or changes were inaugurated in the interest of the public. He never failed to see the distinction between an attempt to suppress public opinion and to direct public opinion. The first is unwise; the second is rational. He fearlessly indicted the cowardice of such procedure. After the fugitive-slave law was made a part of the Compromise of 1850, both of the leading platforms, Whig and Democratic, declared that the Compromise was the settlement of the slavery issue and forbade its further discussion. Lincoln knew such cowardice was like resolving the tide should cease to flow. Our business is to direct public opinion in the right channels, and not to attempt to suppress it. That was Lincolnian.

Another quality of his nature was his deep religious convictions. I do not believe we ever had any man in the presidential chair who was so profoundly religious in nature as Abraham Lincoln. Prof. Brooks, who was at the head of the

30580—12826

educational movement in Illinois, came to him with the query, "Mr. Lincoln, we have been discussing your religious convictions." Mr. Lincoln said, "Well, what about it?" "We wondered how much time, if any, you devote to your relationship with your God." Mr. Lincoln turned to him and said, "Professor, I spend more time upon the thought of my relationship with my God than upon all other questions combined." That was Lincoln at a time when he had no reason to assert anything untrue about his belief. You will remember that when the brilliant, peerless leader, Stonewall Jackson, was almost within reach of this Capital City and the Cabinet was very much alarmed, Mr. Lincoln said, "The thing I fear about Stonewall Jackson is that he is a praying general; he prays before he goes into battle." A high tribute by the head of the Nation to that peerless soldier.

Mr. Lincoln had an abiding faith in God. Notice his statement at Springfield when he bade farewell to his neighbors on February 11, 1861, and called upon them to give him their prayers. Notice his statement in his first inaugural:

Is not a firm reliance upon Him who has never yet forsaken our favored land sufficient to adjust our differences?

Notice him in his second inaugural. His judgments are righteous altogether. Hear him saying to Brooks, "I would be the veriest blockhead if I thought I could get through with a single day's business without relying upon Him who doeth all things well."

I want to say to this body of legislators, from the standpoint of a close study of the life of Mr. Lincoln, that his was the most profoundly religious nature of any of our great Presidents. Why, then, you ask, did he not belong to a church? I answer you, I hope as a consistent member of the Methodist Episcopal Church, Abraham Lincoln was too great a soul to be circumscribed by the narrow denominational lines of the day in which he lived. [Applause.] I say it not in antagonism to churches, for I believe in them and I am a member of one of them. But the bitterness that was then felt between branches of the Christian church was such that it was pretty hard for a man of that great heart of his to subscribe to a good deal of this bitterness. But let no man, because of this, quote him as against religion. He was profoundly religious, and always gave his voice and influence to the things for which the church stands.

He once said:

Show me the church which writes over its portals "Thou shalt love thy God with all thy strength of heart and mind, and thy neighbor as thyself," and I will join that church.

I close with this suggestion: As Mr. Lincoln was closing his career he was more concerned about the Reconstruction of the Seceded States than any other one subject. He made his last speech from the Executive Mansion on the 11th of April. He spoke about Reconstruction, and said that that was one of the things that had most deeply impressed his heart during all these years, and then he said, in substance:

Let us not now enter into a controversy as to whether the States are in the Union or out of the Union. That question can only have the mischievous effect of dividing our friends. We all admit that the States are out of their practical relations with the Union. Let us strive to reinstate the relation as it existed before the war, and when that is done, then let us each one alone take pleasure, if there is any pleasure in it, in seeing whether they were ever away from home. Finding themselves safely at home, it would be utterly immaterial whether they had ever been abroad. Let us not bring that up now, for it can only end in mischief.

30580—12826

To the South he said:

It may be my duty to make some new announcement to the people of the South.

That announcement was never made. Four days later the bullet of the assassin closed his lips forever, and he was not to make an announcement on that or any other great subject. But the one situation he yearned so much to see adjusted was the preservation of the Union as it had been before 1861. His death removed the one insurmountable obstacle to the success of radical measures in Reconstruction. As I once said before, his rare magnanimity, illumined by an intellect equally rare, peculiarly fitted him to pilot the ship through the rough breakers that hugged the shore of nationality as he had safely brought it through the stormy Civil War. He was broad enough to know that too much national prerogative was despotism, and too much State rights might lead to anarchy among the States. I want to say that when the bullet of the assassin laid him low the best friend the South had in authority had fallen. [Applause.] Jefferson Davis said that next to the fall of the Confederacy the death of Lincoln was the greatest stroke the South ever received.

What a beautiful thing it is to contemplate the change of attitude toward him. Fifty years ago many a child of that day in the North was rocked in the cradle over which was sung the lullaby:

> Old Abe Lincoln is dead and gone.
> Hurrah! Hurrah!

Then, the people were divided. To-day, 50 years after, our differences, born in the heat of a great national issue that precipitated war, are no more. His name is spoken in reverence by a reunited Nation, whose finest product is embodied in the great war President.

His yearning for the cessation of strife was in his every impulse. When the scene of Appomattox had passed, no one was so happy over the prospects of a return to peace as he.

But in a moment of rejoicing all was changed. Another tragedy was to be added to the series of tragedies. It was not his to live to see the fruits of the war, and to so guide its reconstruction as to rebuild safely with the highest honor to all our people. No. It was his to die. He was surrounded by friends, including his official family, as his spirit went home to its God, with whom it had kept so closely throughout the dark hours of civil war.

Stanton, at the head of the bed, now virtually the head of the Nation, Seward having been attacked in his sick room, broke the silence of death when he said, " Now he belongs to the ages."

The next day the great Secretary, who had so often differed from his great chief, looked upon his face now asleep in death, and pointing his hand toward him said, " There sleeps the mightiest man that ever ruled a nation."

It was thus left to one of his critics, who differed with and yet loved him, to pass the highest encomium upon him.

In my judgment Abraham Lincoln is the truest type of the American statesman, the broadest in comprehension, the sweetest in disposition, the deepest in humanity of secular history. And now as we are facing to-day as great problems as ever faced him in his day, let us renew our obligations to our common country by pledging ourselves in his words our last full measure of devotion in the hope that the Government of the

30580—12826

people, by the people, and for the people shall not perish from the earth. [Applause.]

Mr. GOULDEN. Mr. Speaker, I ask unanimous consent to address the House for two minutes.

The SPEAKER. The gentleman from New York asks unanimous consent to address the House for two minutes. Is there objection?

There was no objection.

Mr. GOULDEN. Mr. Speaker, I feel that I should apologize to the House, as well as to the distinguished gentleman from Ohio, who has just completed his splendid patriotic address. Perhaps I am the only man on the floor of the House who heard Lincoln's famous speech at Gettysburg. [Applause.] That is my excuse for injecting myself at this time. By the grace of God and the will of the Speaker, nine veterans of the Civil War, six who wore the gray and three who wore the blue, all that are left of that memorable struggle, were honored by an appointment to accompany the Vice President and himself to the fiftieth anniversary of the great Battle of Gettysburg last July. While standing there on the memorable spot on which Mr. Lincoln stood 50 years before, I heard that famous speech of his. I first heard—and I can assure my colleagues that I was tired and weary—the splendid oration of Edward Everett, a brilliant speaker of that day, which lasted two hours. I know, in my youthful impatience, I hoped that he would finish quickly so that the great war President might be heard, but he did not. He truly made a magnificent speech. I want to ask, Mr. Speaker and gentlemen of the House, how many of you can recall or could repeat even portions of the beautiful oration of Edward Everett on that occasion, while on the other hand the brief, touching speech of President Lincoln is known to every schoolboy and every schoolgirl, not only in this country but in many others. I stood within 30 feet of the platform and heard the President. As Mr. Lincoln stepped to the front, with that pathetic, sad look upon his face, the great audience of 25,000 people started an applause loud and long. A smile went over his countenance, and when he smiled you forgot the homeliness of his rugged countenance. He then made that famous address of his, which lasted less than three minutes, making a most profound impression on his listeners, at least one-half of whom could hear him distinctly. I saw Edward Everett step over and shake his hand, but I could not hear what he said; but we are told what he did say was that he would give his two hours of effort for the three minutes of Mr. Lincoln; and he was right. That was a great occasion, upon a battle field that more than 200,000 as brave men as ever lived fought three days for what they thought was right. It was one of the greatest in the history of this or any other nation, marked to-day by more than 500 splendid monuments.

We do well, Mr. Speaker, to call to mind the deeds of our great men, those who have so greatly aided in making the Nation a world power, respected everywhere, and I think none carries with it a greater lesson of patriotic sentiment so worthy of emulation than that of the lamented martyred President of the United States—Abraham Lincoln. [Loud applause.]

30580—12826

○

WASHINGTON : GOVERNMENT PRINTING OFFICE : 1914

Part Six: JOHNSON BRIGHAM
THAT MAN SAW LINCON

Bringham, Memory Pictures of Lincoln

"I was riding my horse when I caught my first glimpse of President Lincoln. Accompanied by Mrs. Lincoln, he was driving in his carriage to his temporary residence, the Soldiers' Home. It was in the summer of 1864. I had been promoted from hall-ball in the central office of the Sanitary Commission to be the chief clerk's first assistant, and one of the perquisites of the position happened to be the privilege of riding the chief clerk's horse-a coal black stallion with a running record on the Long Island course. Many regarded the horse as the most beautiful horse in the district, and I, at least knew him to be one of the fastest.

"One evening, as I was passing the President's carriage, I was quick to notice that the man who sat leaning forward with his elbows upon his knees was the President himself. He was quite as quick to notice the points of the horse I rode, and, out of respect for the noble animal, he waved his hand and bowed to the young rider. After that informal introduction, he watched the stallion as he pranced or flew past the carriage, and he never omitted the salute-which I rightly interpreted as a mark of respect for the handsomest horse in the District.

"The thing I remember most vividly about the President's face at that time was its extreme sadness. I had read much of Lincoln's quaint humor and of his fondness for telling droll stories; I was therefore shocked to find that the real Lincoln's countenance was the saddest I had ever beheld. I afterward learned that the position in which I first saw him-his elbows on his knees and his hands supporting his head-had become habitual. The break in his physical strength had already begun.

"Years afterward Schuyler Colfax told me that in the summer of 1864 the President was conscious that his load was greater than he could physically bear. Fully a year or more before his assassination his nearest friends realized that he was breaking in health and that he could not long survive the end of his second term.

"Now let us pass over into the eventful year, 1865, and consider Lincoln the orator.

"The fourth day of March, the day of his second inauguration, was raw and disagreeable. About eleven o'clock that Saturday morning the sun came out and somewhat enlivened the scene at the east entrance of the Capitol-a somber scene at best. Thousands of people stood in the mud and patiently waited for the President to appear. I had never heard the man whose debates with Douglass had inspired my boyish admiration, and I was expecting great things from his oratory.

"President Lincoln, fresh from the solemn inauguration ceremonies in the Senate Chamber, took his stand at the top of the steps leading to the east entrance of the Capitol, and after a few preliminaries began to read his now world famous Second Inaugural Address. His face was so solemn that I wondered that anyone could think him light and trifling. At first I was disappointed. I looked for oratorical flourish; but there before me stood only an earnest man with a few sheets of manuscript in his hand, from which he was conscientiously reading. He was bent only on uttering certain words that needed to be spoken. Occasionally he would look up over his old-fashioned, heavy-rimmed spectacles at the listening thousands, and would repeat a clause or sentence from memory. At such times his voice gathered power, and his audience felt the thrill of his suppressed emotion and the force of his intense earnestness.

"As he neared the close of his address, he scarcely looked at his manuscript. With grandly simple, almost pathetic, eloquence he uttered those historic words-words that can never grow commonplace: "Fondly do we hope, fervently do we pray, that this mighty scourge of war may speedily pass away. Yet if God wills that it continue until all the wealth piled by the bondsman's two hundred and fifty years of unrequited toil shall be sunk, and until every drop of blood drawn with the lash shall be paid by another drawn with the sword, as was said three thousand years ago, so still it must be said, 'The judgments of the Lord are true and righteous altogether.'"

"Then, with fatherly counsel and injunction, he added the oft-quoted closing words: " With malice toward none, with charity for all, with firmness in the right, as God gives us to see the right, let us strive on to finish the work we are in,–to bind up the nations wounds, to care for him who shall have borne the battle, and for his widow and his orphan,–to do all which may achieve and cherish a just and lasting peace among ourselves and with all nations."

"Let me present another aspect of this many-sided character. During the momentous week when Grant was hammering at the gates of the Confederate capital, the President, feeling in every fiber of his being that the end was near, took passage for City Point, in order that with his own eager eyes, weary with long watching, he might see the last act in the drama of war-and, I doubt not, that he might check any overt and unseemly act, should occasion require.

"Late one afternoon, while he was resting from his writing on the gunboat River Queen, he observed several little kittens, hardly able to stand, blindly crawling about the floor. He lifted them tenderly to his desk, and for some time watched their movements, as if pondering the greatest of all problems-the mystery of life. Seeing a loosening film over the eye of one of the kittens, he carefully wiped it away with his handkerchief and, as he placed the little fellow on the floor again, said gently, "There little one, I've done for you what even your mother couldn't do." As I have time and again recalled to my mind that incidental use the word "mother," I have thought that at that moment there must have come to the President some recollection of the delicate, hard-worked woman who had toiled and struggled for her son, and who yet in her poverty felt that she could do so little for him. What the word "mother" meant to this man can be inferred from his oft-quoted saying to a friend: "All that I am, or hope to be, I owe to my angel mother-blessings on her memory!"

"A few days later, I saw still another side of Lincoln's nature. The incident occurred in the rush of events following the close of the war and has escaped the attention of biographers and historians. It was the afternoon of April 10, 1865. The end that the President had unceasingly prayed for and struggled toward had come. Richmond had fallen. Lee had surrendered, and-although we could hardly realize it-the war was over. Some two hundred youths, mostly employed in the departments, headed by the band of music engaged for the occasion, marched to the White House to welcome President Lincoln back from the front. Strikingly different was the Lincoln of 1865 from the Lincoln a few years before. The lean, muscular man who in 1861 had come out of the West had sadly aged. His black frock coat fitted him loosely. The deep lines of care on his sallow face had deepened into furrows. His cheeks were sunken , his cheek bones unduly prominent. But a marvelous change had come over him since I had last seen him. The wearied look was gone, and his deep-set gray eyes flashed with a jubilant expression that told the story of a lifted burden. After listening to the music, the President good naturedly complied with our demand for speech. He said that, as he was then in the midst of preparing a speech on reconstruction, which he had promised to deliver on the following evening, he would now say no more than that he appreciated the tribute of regard from the youths and young men of the departments, and profoundly rejoiced with them in the thought that the nation was saved. Then the old humorous expression of other days came to his now habitually sad face and, turning to a reporter at his elbow, he remarked that he did not dare to say anything more lest the reporter should fail to quote him right to the country, "Such things have been done you," he added with a smile. Then turning to the leader of the band, he said:

"The Confederacy has one tune I very much like, and, since we've captured the Confederacy, I think the tune goes with it. Just to please me, will the band strike up, 'Dixie?'"

The leader gave the word, and the band played the familiar air of the Confederacy. The President kept time with his foot, and a genial smile made his strong, homely face almost beautiful.

"On the evening of April 11th, about two thousand people-perhaps more-gathered in the driveway and upon the lawn in front of the White House to listen to the President's speech on the all-important subject of the hour-reconstruction. It was a dark night and rain was falling; hundreds of umbrellas massed together made an imperfect covering for the shivering crowd. The dim lights from the outdoor gas jets and from the executive mansion gave a weird appearance to the throng, and the hollow sound of raindrops falling upon the canopy of umbrellas accentuated the strangeness of the scene.

"Soon after eight o'clock some one raised the historic east window over the front entrance of the White House, and presently the tall, angular form of the President was silhouetted against the background of light. Without formality he began to read his speech-one for which the country had impatiently waited, and one which, except for the untimely death of its author, would undoubtedly have led to a wide settlement of viewing question of the hour.

"The somewhat metallic voice, in which was a suggestion of the quaintness of the man behind the voice, was clear and distinct to those within the limits of the semicircular driveway; but it did not carry much further. Conscious of the importance of the subject, the President rarely lifted his eyes from the manuscript, and then only to round some familiar period. That historic address related to an experiment in reconstruction then going on in Louisiana. The President pointed out the difficulties that surrounded the whole question of reconstruction, then going on in Louisiana. The President pointed out the difficulties that surrounded the whole question of reconstruction, chief of which was the adverse criticism of certain journals in the north. He frankly declared that, should his Louisiana experiment fail to work satisfactorily, he would promptly abandon it. He showed that it was foolish to discuss conflicting theories about the status of the seceded states, for the problem was a practical one-merely that of pacing them in normal relations with the general government.

"Let us all join," he said, "in doing the acts necessary to restore the proper practical relations between the states and the Union, and "-with a smile on his face-"each forever after innocently indulge his own opinion" whether the states had been brought back from within the Union, or had never been out of it.

"The next time I saw the President, on April 17th, he lay in his coffin in the East Room of the White House. His pale, calm face not at all suggested the terrors of that fateful night of April 14, when, in the midst of his rejoicing and at the height of his great fame, he was laid low in death. That night of horror! I recall it with a shudder even now.

About eleven o'clock, while on my way to my room on F Street, I looked down the street and say a crowd gathered in front of the theatre. Thinking that it was an ovation to the President, for the newspapers had said he was to see Laura Keene's presentation of the then popular play, "Our American Cousin" I ran down the street and was soon part of the crowd. A tall, black-visaged young fellow was fiercely gesticulating under a lamp-post to a crowd of excited men. I knew that something terrible had happened, for consternation was written upon every face. I asked a man at my side what had happened. He looked at me in astonishment and in a broken voice exclaimed "Happened! My God, boy, they've killed the President!"

"I joined the eager crowd of youths and young men that, under the leadership of the tall workingman who had witnessed the tragedy from the gallery, vainly searched for the assassin in the alleys, and stables, and all out of the way places. Failing to find him, we mingled with the throng in front of the Peterson home opposite the theatre, to which the President had been carried. There was waited, hoping against hope, until well on into the morning. We took no sleep that night. Soon after seven o'clock on that black Saturday the solemn tolling of bells

President Lincoln, fresh from the solemn inauguration

That Man Did Not See Lincoln

of Apiex, following his return from City Point in '65; also his last formal address, on "Reconstruction," from the east window of the White House on the evening of the 11th of April, '65. I had tickets for Ford's Theatre on the night of his assassination but was prevented from attending. On the following Tuesday, I saw his remains lying in the coffin in the East Room of the White House, and on the following Wednesday I looked for the last time upon his face as his body lay in state in the Capitol.

This is in response to the request of Mr. Boos. Johnson Brigham.

State Library, Des Moines, Iowa.
August 15, 1916.

The child is father to the man. Mr Lincoln would not have been "honest Abe" at forty if he had not been "honest Abe" at fourteen. He would not have been a minister of justice to a race as President if he had not been a minister of justice as a local lawyer. To pin the best service one can pin, whatever his task, whether it is digging a ditch or guiding a nation, is the essence of honesty. Greatness of character is not the same as greatness of achievement. The real character does his work well, whatever the work & whatever the reward — whether it is fame or blame, whether it is money or martyrdom. So to live that you can say, My world is a little better because I have lived in it, is the lesson which Abraham Lincoln has taught us.

Lyman Abbott.

President without starting anew the flow of tears.

I took my place at the end of the line at an early hour, and it was not long before hundreds were lined up behind me. For hours we stood waiting for a last look at the face of our beloved President. Nearer and nearer we drew, one slow, short step at a time, until at last I found myself in the historic East Room, looking down into the face of the man whom I had grown to know and love. The look of rest and peace upon his marred countenance held no suggestion of the tragic experience through which he had passed. I stood for a moment looking through my tears into the coffin of my friend; then some one told me in an undertone to move on.

On Wednesday the President's body was borne to the Capitol, and thence, as the reader knows, to its last resting place in Springfield.

I followed the funeral procession far down Pennsylvania Avenue--where only a few weeks before I had witnessed another procession escorting President Lincoln from the White House to the Capitol. As before, the avenue was lined with thousands. But instead of cheering and shouting, all of the spectators were now silent, and many were in tears. I vividly remember the riderless horse of the dead President, immediately following the casket--eloquent symbol of the general loss.

Johnson Brigham

Des Moines, Iowa, Jan 24, 1916.

Mr. Kearney

Mr. Kearney was in the Navy, and he was more anxious to write down the vessels he was on then to give me any other information. I met him at the annual encampment of the Grand Army in Albany in 1932. He was a fine robust man and appeared to be one of the leaders of the little group of 55 delegates. The last time the old soldiers met in Albany there was hundreds of delegates present.

Iowa State Library
Des Moines, Iowa   May 11, 1916

Mr. J. E. Boos,
20 Dudley Heights,
Albany, N. Y.

Dear Sir:-

I am at present at work on a book on Lincoln and Washington during the last year of the war, to be submitted, on invitation, to Messrs. Little, Brown and Company. Will keep your request in mind, and when relieved from present pressure of this work and of revision of another work, will fill your pages.

Yours very truly,

H. J. Kearney
U.S.S. Portsmouth
" " Jean Nat—
" Pensacola
" Tuscarora

THAT MAN DID NOT SEE LINCOLN.

     Mr. Kearney was in the Navy, and he was more anxious to write down the vessels he was on then to give me any other information. I met him at the annual encampment of the Grand Army in Albany in 1932. He was a fine robust man and appeared to be one of the leaders of the little group of 55 delegates. The last time the old soldiers met in Albany there was hundreds of delegates present.

ABRAHAM LINCOLN'S RUM SWEAT

A VIGOROUS REMEDY THAT HELPED HIM DURING HIS PRESIDENTIAL CAMPAIGN

BY

GEORGE P. FLOYD

"I have not suffered by the South; I have suffered with the South. Their pain has been my pain; their loss has been my loss. What they have gained I have gained."

FIRST met Mr. Lincoln at Springfield, Illinois, in February, 1856. He was then practising law with W. H. Herndon; "Lincoln & Herndon" was the firm-name. Their office was in a small room in the second story of an old frame building on Sangamon Street. The floor was bare; the furniture consisted of two small desks, a little table, a few old chairs, and a long wooden bench. I remember that large pictures of Washington and Andrew Jackson hung on the wall. Books and papers were scattered about. Mr. Lincoln wore a long, old-fashioned frock-coat and a tall "plug" hat; his breeches hardly reached to his ankles. He had on blue socks, an old-fashioned high dicky, and what was called in those days a "stock." Mr. Lincoln was made up of head, hands, feet, and length, yet it required but a very few words with him to dispel any unfavorable impression of him that might have been formed. His kind, gentle voice and manner would draw any one to him.

I had leased the Quincy House, at Quincy, Illinois. The property was owned by a widow, Mrs. Enos, who lived at Springfield. I employed Mr. Lincoln to execute the lease for me. He sent the lease to me at Quincy, but said nothing about the pay for his services. Thinking twenty-five dollars would be about right, I sent him that amount. In a few days I received a letter from Mr. Lincoln, of which the following is a copy:

SPRINGFIELD, ILLINOIS,
February 21, 1856.

MR. GEORGE P. FLOYD,
Quincy, Illinois.

Dear Sir:—I have just received yours of 16th, with check on Flagg & Savage for twenty-five dollars. You must think I am a high-priced man. You are too liberal with your money.

Fifteen dollars is enough for the job. I send you a receipt for fifteen dollars, and return to you a ten-dollar bill.

Yours truly,
A. LINCOLN.

Lincoln's Dangerous Breakdown during the Debates with Douglas

During the summer of 1858 Abraham Lincoln and Stephen A. Douglas stumped the State of Illinois in joint debate. The first meeting was at Clinton, August 20. From there they went to Jonesboro, Charleston, Galesburg, Quincy, and ended at Alton, October 28. While Mr. Lincoln was always temperate in all things, the "little giant" Douglas generally carried a comfortable load of the "juice of corn." On October 15 they reached Quincy, where an immense crowd assembled to listen to the debates. While Judge Douglas was very eloquent, fascinating, and rhetorical, Mr. Lincoln was neither rhetorical, graceful, nor brilliant, and used very little gesticulation. But in a little time the crowd was unconsciously and irresistibly drawn by the clearness and closeness of his argument. His fairness and candor were very noticeable. He ridiculed nothing, burlesqued nothing, misrepresented nothing. Instead of distorting the views held by Judge Douglas, he very modestly and courteously inquired into their soundness. He was too kind for bitterness and too great for vituperation.

The strain on body and mind had begun to tell on Mr. Lincoln. After he had finished his speech, he almost collapsed from sheer fatigue. He was taken by friends to his rooms in the hotel, which I was then keeping. They

303

laid him on a lounge in his room, and Mr. Lincoln remarked: "I tell you, I'm mighty nigh petered out; I reckon I'll have to quit and give up the race."

How Mrs. Floyd's Rum Sweat Saved the Campaign

My wife stood watching him. She was a great believer in old-school remedies, and suggested that Mr. Lincoln be treated to a "rum sweat."

"Rum sweat!" said Mr. Lincoln. "Why, I never drank a drop of liquor in my life."

"You don't have to drink the rum," replied my wife. "It's an external treatment."

"Well," said Mr. Lincoln, "if you think it will do me any good, just crack your whip and go ahead. Any port in a storm, and, I tell you, I am mighty near overboard."

The treatment was administered as directed by my wife. A pan of New England rum was placed under a cane-seated chair. The patient was stripped, seated in the chair, and covered all over with blankets. Then the rum was set afire. The fumes or vapor of the rum caused

"'WHY, I AM FEELING LIKE A TWO-YEAR-OLD'"

profuse perspiration, after which the patient was put to bed, covered with woolen blankets, and given a decoction of hot ginger tea. The sweating continued.

The next morning, to our surprise, Mr Lincoln made his appearance bright and early We asked how he was feeling. "Why," said he, "I am feeling like a two-year-old. I can

"ABRAHAM LINCOLN'S RUM SWEAT"

jump a five-rail fence right now, I swanny! I've heard of folks drinking liquor, and rubbing their bodies with the bottle for ailments, but I never yet heard of driving the stuff through the pores of the hide to get a man full. If Mrs. Floyd would only join us in this campaign and prescribe for me, I think we could beat out Judge Douglas slick and clean."

Civil War Days

Abraham Lincoln never forgot a favor. Seven years rolled by before I met him again. In 1861 I was in business in Montgomery, Alabama. In February of that year the Confederate government met there and remained until it was removed to Richmond, Virginia.

Although I was a slaveholder before and during the war, I was not imbued with the spirit of secession, and fortunately I was exempt from military duties, for I had mail and other contracts with the Confederate government.

During the Civil War the people in the Confederate States, hemmed in as they were through the blockade by land and sea, were obliged to depend on their own resources. They had no factories of any kind, no foundries, no powder-mills, tanneries, or cotton-mills. They had worlds of cotton, but no means of manufacturing it. The extremes to which the Southern population was forced during the war, the sufferings, deprivations, and sacrifices they endured, have never been half told. Yet all the while they were surrounded by millions upon millions of wealth which they were unable to utilize. Bales of cotton innumerable were stored away in every nook and corner of the Confederacy. It was estimated that during 1864 there was cotton enough in the Confederacy, if it were sold at the market price then ruling in the North, to pay one half of the whole war debt of the North. From the commencement of hostilities the Confederate government imposed a war tax on all the cotton raised in the Confederacy. This percentage of the crop, pressed into bales marked " C. S. A.," was stored in warehouses throughout the Confederacy.

To President Lincoln for Protection

When the Federals captured cotton, it was sold at auction, and the proceeds were deposited in the United States Treasury, subject to the decision of the Court of Claims. In December, 1864, about forty thousand bales were captured by General Sherman at Savannah, Georgia, and sent to New York to be sold at auction. The proceeds of this sale, amounting to many millions of dollars, went into the United States Treasury. There is to-day in the treasury a large deposit representing the proceeds of cotton captured during the war, which has never been successfully claimed.

In December, 1864, I concluded to leave the Confederate States. I left Montgomery, Alabama, December 15, going from Charleston, South Carolina, to Nassau on the blockade-runner *Arrow*, thence to New York on a regular steamer.

Since I left a considerable amount of perishable property in the South, I was anxious to

"'I HAVE NOT SUFFERED BY THE SOUTH,' HE SAID; 'I HAVE SUFFERED WITH THE SOUTH'"

GEORGE P. FLOYD

get protection papers from the Federal government, to save it when the Federals should capture Montgomery. Armed with letters of recommendation from Governor John A. Andrew of Massachusetts, Governor Joe Gilmore of New Hampshire, and a very strong personal letter from General Ben Prentiss (whom, together with his staff, I had befriended while they were prisoners of war in Selma, Alabama, in 1863), I proceeded to Washington. At that time, on account of the hundreds seeking interviews, it was very difficult to get an audience with Mr. Lincoln.

Lincoln at his Desk in the White House

After five or six days' waiting I succeeded in reaching him. It so happened that I was the last visitor before the closing hour of business. When I entered his rooms, he was sitting in his office chair with his long legs resting on the desk. His feet were incased in old-fashioned carpet-slippers. His face as it looked at that time I shall never forget. He "looked like death." His pale, haggard features, furrowed with wrinkles, his sunken eyes and care-worn face, made me hesitate to trouble him.

For a few moments he did not move a muscle, and seemed to be gazing at something a thousand miles away. At last, taking up my card and without changing his position, he said in a very kindly voice, "Well, my friend, what can I do for you?"

"Mr. President," I replied, "you look too tired and care-worn to do anything for anybody. I hate to trouble you."

"Oh, I'm all right," he replied. "What can I do for you?"

I laid my papers before him. He commenced reading them. He had read but a few lines of General Prentiss' letter, when he jumped up, grasped my hand, and said: "Why, I have seen you before, sir; I remember you very well. I believe your wife saved my life when I was at Quincy in 1858. Yes, and I have taken that 'rum sweat' that she prescribed for me many times, and I have prescribed it for some of my friends. It has always been a dead shot." And quickly, as if the keeper of the lighthouse had lighted the beacon-light, the cloud lifted from his face, his eyes snapped, and his thoughts seemed to hark back to the bygone days of 1858.

The President's Tea which Became a Cabinet Meeting

"You must come up and take tea with us to-night," said he. "I want to talk with you about matters and things in the South. Ben Prentiss tells me that you are well posted about things down there."

I accepted his invitation, and, before we got through with the confab, it proved to be quite a cabinet meeting. We were joined by Mr. Fessenden, then Secretary of the Treasury, O. H. Browning, Secretary of the Interior, and Edwin M. Stanton, Secretary of War.

My mail and other contracts with the Confederate government during the war had enabled me to keep behind the scenes and observe some of the workings and tricks of the misguided officials who sailed the water-logged Confederate craft into rough and ragged rocks, to shipwreck and destruction.

The Plan to Save Confederate Cotton

I was enabled to give Mr. Lincoln some information of which he had never dreamed in regard to the Confederacy. Before I left Montgomery, in December, I had procured a list of all the cotton in eight warehouses in the city, and a list of many of its claimants. In the eight warehouses were stored one hundred and twenty-eight thousand bales of cotton, subject to the order of the various claimants. Twenty-three thousand bales of that cotton were the property of the Confederate States government and marked "C. S. A." The balance, one hundred and five thousand bales, belonged to different persons, fifteen hundred bales of it being my own. At that time cotton was selling in New York and New Orleans at about eighty cents a pound. If the twenty-three thousand bales of Confederate cotton could be captured or saved, it would be worth — eleven and a half million pounds at eighty cents — $9,200,000, which would go into the United States Treasury as confiscated property. The balance, one hundred and five thousand bales, fifty-two and a half million pounds, would have sold for $42,000,000. I laid a plan before Mr. Lincoln and Secretary Fessenden to save the cotton in Montgomery. They both favored my plan and at once promised to give me every facility to prosecute it successfully. My idea appealed especially to Mr. Lincoln, who had always been in favor of drawing all the cotton out of the Confederacy.

The Confederacy Like Bill Sikes' Dog

The President was forever illustrating his theories by telling some funny story, as he did in this case. Said Mr. Lincoln: "The Confederacy is like Bill Sikes' dog. Old Bill Sikes had a yaller dog, a worthless cur. His strong holt was to run out and bark at passers-by, and scare horses and children. The boys in the neighborhood decided to have some fun with the no-account canine brute. They procured a small stick of giant-powder, inserted a cap and fuse in it, wrapped a piece of meat around it, lit the fuse, laid the little joker on the sidewalk, whistled, and climbed the fence to see the fun. Out comes the dog with his usual 'wow, wow!' He scented the meat and bolted the bundle. In a few seconds there was a terrible explosion. Dog-meat was flying in all directions. Out comes Sikes from the house, bareheaded. 'What in hell's up?' yelled old Bill. 'Why, the dog's up,' cried the boys on the fence. While old Bill was gazing around in wonderment, something dropped at his feet. He picked it up, and found it was his dog's tail. While looking sorrowfully at the appendage of his departed canine friend, he exclaimed, 'Well, I'll be damned if I think old Tige'll amount to much after this as a dog.' And," said Mr. Lincoln, "so it would be with the Confederacy. Take all their cotton away from them, and it wouldn't amount to shucks. It would fry all the fat out of them."

"I have Suffered with the South"

Mr. Lincoln's feelings toward the South during the war were more of sympathy than of hostility.

"I have not suffered by the South," he said; "I have suffered with the South. Their pain has been my pain; their loss has been my loss. What they have gained I have gained."

I was appointed agent at Montgomery to take charge of all the cotton that was captured when the city fell into the possession of the Federals. With proper credentials, I left Washington for Montgomery March 21. Reaching Mobile April 2, I at once started across country on horseback, overtaking General A. J. Smith's troops about seventy-five miles south of Selma, on their way to capture Montgomery. I made arrangements to have the advance-guard of his army surround the warehouses as soon as they entered the city, to protect the cotton from fire and pillage. Pushing on, I reached Montgomery two days ahead of the Federals. The city was then in command of the Confederate General Beaufort.

The Confederates had decided to evacuate the city without a fight. A number of gentlemen, who owned a large portion of the cotton stored in the warehouses, formed a deputation to wait upon General Beaufort. I joined them, and we used every argument to persuade the general to leave the warehouses intact when the city was evacuated, offering to account to him for the net proceeds of two thousand bales of cotton. The general was at first in favor of complying with our request.

The Burning of the Cotton

Everything looked favorable to our plan for saving the cotton. Then, all at once, General Beaufort began to "crawfish." The fact was, the general had been taking what was known in Confederate parlance as "pine-top," which had unbalanced his craft and changed his course of sailing. He became as stubborn as a mule. We couldn't budge him an inch.

At twelve o'clock that night he ordered the torch applied to every cotton warehouse. In spite of all we could do, the eight warehouses, containing one hundred and twenty-eight thousand bales of cotton, worth $51,200,000 in good money, went up in smoke, without a cent of insurance, doing no one a particle of good. In many cases the cotton was all that the owners had saved out of the wreckage of the war. Men who had always lived in affluence, and who had never known what want was, were reduced to abject poverty by that cruel, uncalled-for, wanton act.

Mr. Lincoln's wife was Miss Mary Todd of Kentucky. Her brother, Thomas Todd, lived in Alabama during the war. In April, 1865, while I was at Montgomery, Alabama, I received a personal letter from Mr. Lincoln requesting me to attend to a little matter concerning Mrs. Lincoln and her brother, which I did. That letter was dated at Washington, D. C., April 10, 1865. Four days later Lincoln was assassinated.

Part Seven: The Failed Assassination Attempt

May 26, 1898

Edward K. Black

"I have been asked to give a statement of the run which saved the life Abraham Lincoln February 22, 1861.

"So long a time has elapsed that only the main facts now remain in my memory. But I will try to tell them as briefly as possible.

"In 1861, I was running a passenger train on the Pennsylvania railroad from Philadelphia to Harrisburg, with engine 161. February 22nd I was called upon to take a special train (consisting of one ordinary coach, no. 29, and one special, no. 160) containing Lincoln and his family to Harrisburg on their way to Washington. They were to spend the night in Harrisburg and go by way of Baltimore the following day. I was introduced to Lincoln and after a few words, he shook my hand, handed me a cigar, and passed to the train. Could I only have foreseen what was to occur in the next few years, I think that cigar, instead of being smoked, would have been kept as a precious and hollowed remembrance.

"The run so far was uneventful. We stopped at all of the station, Lincoln making a few remarks at each. After arriving at Harrisburg, Lincoln and family were taken to the Jones Hotel where they were to remain till the following day. In the afternoon, he spoke to a large crowd from the balcony of that house. In the meantime, there came quietly to me orders to take the car 29 (the ordinary coach), and run about one mile east from Harrisburg station, stopping near Hanna Street, and there await further orders. It was then about 7 o'clock in the evening. I had been told that Lincoln would not be allowed to pass through Baltimore alive, and we must secretly get him to Washington in another way. In a short time I had my train in readiness awaiting further developments.

"I had only been there a few moments when a closed cab drove up as far as Front Street in which Lincoln, quite alone. He quietly walked down the track to the car, went to the saloon and laid down. I remember well how he looked. He wore a long circular cloak, and a Scotch cap. Awaiting him on the train was Enoch Lewis, general Superintendent, Thomas A. Scott, and Division Superintendent Charles Franciscus.

"There are one or two men in public life today who claim to have been in that car. I am sorry to spoil, but they were not there. It had been rather difficult matter to persuade Lincoln to leave his family to go on to Washington alone, and accept the plan made for him. He declared he had no fear of violence at Baltimore or elsewhere. But, after considerable persuasion, he consented to be guided by his friends.

"I was told to make no stops, and when obliged to take water, to do so at the most secluded places I could, to keep a sharp lookout, and to arrive at Thirtieth Street, West Philadelphia by 10 o'clock sharp.

"Feeling great responsibility upon me, you may be sure I looked after things mighty sharp. I have often wondered what the people thought of that short train whizzing through the night. A case of life or death, perhaps, so it was.

"Lincoln remained in the saloon all of the time. Even some of the trainmen did not know he was aboard, and thought that the night run was simply to get the officials of the road back to Philadelphia.

"At 10 o'clock we reached Thirtieth Street. A closed cab was waiting. Lincoln walked directly from the car to the cab and was driven to Broad and Prime Streets which was then the station of the P.W. and B.R.R. Everything was so timed and arranged that he arrived just as the night line for Washington was ready to start, and was quietly on board without any one being the wiser.

"The next morning when the whole United States was at breakfast, the news had been flashed over the wires that President Lincoln was safe in Washington, while the station thought he was in Harrisburg. That he would never have reached Washington alive, but for our own night run is now well known, and the dreadful tragedy which occurred later would have been enacted in Baltimore then."

Daniel E. Garman, Lebanon, Pa,
Fireman of Engine 161
that carried Pres.-elect
Lincoln from Hby & Phil
in Eve of Feb. 22, 1861.

M.G. Brumbaugh
5324 Walnut St
Phil.

L 314
Lot E001

To
HENRY HIRSCHFELD.

A Judge who would much rather judge men
for their good traits rather than their
bad.

Henry Hirschfeld
July 20, 1931

Ridgway's
BAILEY BUILDING
PHILADELPHIA

ERNEST E. JOHNSON, EDITOR
ALBERT J. STOOKER, ADVERTISING MGR.
NORMAN R. HOOVER, CIRCULATION MGR.

Nov 27th, 1906.

My dear Doctor:

I respectfully beg to remind you of the story about David Black, the engineer, and David Garman, fireman, of the historic Lincoln train. If you can favor me with the data in your possession I shall take it as a great favor.

Sincerely yours
Ernest E Johnson

the night in Harrisburg, and go by way of Baltimore the following day. I was introduced to Lincoln and after a few words, he shook me by the hand, [handed me a cigar], and passed into the train, [Could I only have foreseen what was to occur in the next few years I think that cigar, instead of being smoked, would have been kept as a precious and hallowed remembrance,]
The run up was uneventful. He stopped at all of the principal

I have been asked to give a statement of the run which saved the life of Abraham Lincoln Feb 22 1861

So long a time has elapsed that only the main facts now remain in my memory, But I will try to tell them as briefly as possible.

In 1861, I was running a passenger train on the Pennsylvania railroad from Philadelphia to Harrisburg, with Engine 161. Feb 22nd I was called upon to take a special train [consisting of one ordinary coach no 29, and one special No 160] — containing Lincoln and his family stations, Lincoln making a few remarks at each.

After arriving in Harrisburg Lincoln and family were taken to the Jones Hotel where they were to remain till the following day,

In the afternoon he spoke to a large crowd from the balcony of that house,

In the meantime there came quietly to me orders to [take the Car 29 (the ordinary coach) and] run about one mile east from the Harrisburg Station, stopping near Hanna street, and there await further orders. It was then about 7 o'clock in the evening. I had been told quietly that Lincoln would not be allowed to pass through Baltimore alive, and we must secretly get him to Washington in another way. In a short time I had my train in readiness awaiting further developments.

I had only been there a few moments when a closed cab drove up as far as Front street in which was Lincoln quite alone. He quietly alighted walked down the track to the car, went to the saloon and laid down, [I remember well how he looked. He wore a long circular cloak, and a Scotch cap.] Awaiting him on the train was Enoch Lewis, general Superintendent, Thomas A. Scott and Division Superintendent Charles Franciscus.]

There are one or two men in public life to day, who claim to have been in that car. I am sorry to spoil a good story, but they were not there.

It had been rather a difficult matter to overshadow Lincoln

to leave his family, to go on to Washington alone, and accept the plan made for him,

He declared he had no fear of violence at Baltimore or elsewhere. But after considerable persuasion consented to be guided by his friends,

I was told to make no stops [and when obliged to take water, to do so at the most secluded places I could, to keep a sharp lookout] and to arrive at Thirteenth Street, West Philadelphia by 10 o'clock sure.

Feeling the great responsibility

upon me, you may be sure I looked after things mighty sharp. [I have often wondered what the people thought of that short train whizzing through the night. A case of life or death perhaps and so it was.]

Lincoln remained in the saloon all of the time. Even some of the trainmen did not know he was aboard, and thought that the night run was simply to get the officials of the road back to Philadelphia.

At 10 o'clock we reached Thirtieth Street. A closed cab was in waiting nation thought he was in Harrisburg.

[That he would never have reached Washington alive, but for our night run is now well known, and the dreadful tragedy which occured later would have been enacted in Baltimore then]
        Edward A. Black,

Phila May 26th, 1898.
1489, N. 32nd Street.

Mr Brumbaugh.

Dear Sir

You asked Mr Black for a statement of the Lincoln incident. He has so little time, but he scribbled it down, and I have copied it.

I hope it is satisfactory and will be of use to you,

Sincerely,
Celia S. Black.

Daniel Yarman

"Engineer Edward Black and I, Daniel E. Yarman, firemen with engine no. 161, took President Abraham Lincoln to Harrisburg from Philadelphia where he was to take the Northern Train to Washington. Late in the afternoon superintendent G.C. Francicus called to me very much excited and asked me where Mr. Black was. I told him and he said I should go look after the engine and have her ready while he went to look for Ed.

"I quickly went and oiled up the engine and lighted the head light and turned up my fire. Soon after Ed came running down the back, mounted the engine and asked whether she was oiled up. I said everything was all ready.

He then backed up and coupled the engine to one car. We ran below town to front street crossing where we stopped for about a minute. Four plumed horses and closed cab dashed up along side of us and President Lincoln boarded with the train along with some of the Pennsylvania R.R. officials.

"The gong rang and we did some lively running. I did not know that we had the President aboard until we stopped to take on water, when I went back and stepped on the hose. In stooping down I looked into the car door and saw the President sitting with his back turned toward me. I knew him because he was so much taller than the rest. I said back to Ed that the Railsplitter was on the train. Then I saw Francicus come to the door and he said to me, 'Dan, you must not mention that the President was on board'.

You bet I kept quiet then.

"When we started, I turned to Ed and asked, 'Ed, what's up?' He said, 'I don't know, but just keep the engine hot', and of course I did. We had a fast ride that night until we got to Philadelphia. As soon as we stopped, the Superintendent came up to us and handed us two ten dollar gold pieces with the President's compliments. One for the engineer and one for me. So we can say that we got the first money for protecting the President.

"When we arrived there four plumed horses and a closed cab stood there. They left a full gallap."

No. date.

Engineer Edward Black, & I, Daniel E. Garman, fireman with Engine No. 161 took President Abraham Lincoln to Harrisburg, from Philadelphia, where he was to take the Northern Central train to Washington but late in the afternoon Supperintendent G. C. Francius came to me very much excited & asked me where Ed. Black was (he was the engineer) and I told him he was at the United States Hotel, then he said I shall go look after the Engine, have her ready while he ~~went to look~~

You bet I kept quiet then]. When we started, I turned to Ed and asked. "Ed what's up," he said "I don't know" but just keep the engine hot" and of course I did [and of course I got a fast ride, I said that night.] He ran so fast, [that when I got a shovel full of coal to put in the furnace I would be laying on the foot board rolling in the coal instead of getting it in the furnace, but with all that I kept up steam until we got in to Phila. As soon as we stopped the

Superintendent came up to us & handed us two ten dollar gold pieces with the Presidents compliments, one for the Engineer & one for me. So we can say that we got the first money in protecting the President.

When we arrived there four plain clothed horses & closed cab stood there, & they got in & went full gallop to Philadelphia, Wilmington & Baltimore Depot.

Part Eight: THE LINCOLN ASSASSINATION AND FUNERAL

Then a Nation Stood Still, the Assassination of Abraham Lincoln

HENRY CLAY FORD

The Fords were very close friends of the Booth family, and both John T. and his brother Henry Clay were immediately arrested when the tragedy occurred in their theatre and thrown in jail, where they were kept in close confinement for more than a month. Henry Clay Ford became sick in his damp cell, lost the use of one arm, and never regained his strength, though he lived to be 72 years old, and died July 22, 1915.

He made his home at Rutherford, N.J., and when his boys grew to young manhood, they and Mrs. Ford, who was a number of years his junior, went on stage, and were successful for years. They took parts in many plays, and became well known and much liked by the theatre going public.

Mr. Ford loved to sit on his porch and talk about the theatre, and of the great actors when he was connected with his brother John, who was one of the best theatrical managers in the country. It was hard to get him to talk of the night Lincoln was shot, and much harder to get him to relate his experience during those terrible days before the trial of the conspirators.

One day he said,–

"I remember the tragedy as if it were but yesterday. The theatre was owned by my brother John, and I was his treasurer, and in the box office at the time. When I heard Booth's shot, which eventually ended Lincoln's life, it occurred to me casually that the pistol used by Sir Edward Trenchard in Our American Cousin, the play that night, had gone off accidentally. Sir Edward, in the play, puts his pistol to his head at the end of the third act.

"In a second, however, an afterthought came to me. I knew it was not the time of the evening for him to put the pistol to his head.

"In the ticket office there was a window, from which I could see the audience. I looked out, and there was Booth on the stage, where he had leaped from the box. I knew him well. The President and his party had been seated in two boxes, which I had helped to make into one, decorating them with flags which we borrowed from the Treasury Department. In the center of the box I had placed a picture of George Washington, with the flags on both sides. It was this picture which caught Booth's foot. I know it, because his spur made a large cut in the picture.

They always say 'Old Glory' delayed him, but it didn't-George Washington's picture did it"

Writing to me many years after the crime, he said, "I knew President Lincoln well, also was acquainted with J. Wilkes Booth."

> H. Clay Ford
> Treasurer of Ford's Theatre
> 1865   Washington D.C.
> Knew President Lincoln well,
> also personally acquainted with
> J. Wilkes Booth.

JENNIE GOURLAY-STRUTHERS

She stood unconcerned, as though waiting for the red traffic signal to turn green; but it was green, and as I stepped off the curb to cross State St., I turned inquiringly and noticed she was sightless. I asked if I might help, she taking my arm from Eagle St., to Pearl, and during that short walk of two blocks was surprised and very much pleased to be told the soft spoken, friendly lady was the daughter of Jennie Gourlay, the girl who was playing her part in Our American Cousin when John Wilkes Booth shot President Lincoln.

Jennie Struthers, though blind, was a teacher of the blind, and, I thought while she talked; I will stop at Montclair when I go to Newark, N.J., Declaration Day, and look up her mother, and tell her I am going to see The Lonely Lincoln sitting in Newark's public square, that realistic bronze of Borglum so well known and so much written about. I will see if I can induce her to tell me just how she felt when she heard the shot, how she behaved when Booth rushed past her in the wings and what her impressions were during the terrific excitement of the next few minutes.

The day set aside to honor the soldier dead found me in the New Jersey city early, and it was not long before I found Mrs. Struther's home. It was not hard when I found the neighborhood, because she was well known in the city, and when she answered the bell, I met a well preserved, fine appearing, very intelligent woman, who smilingly invited me in.

Most folks, when they get older, worry about the other person's comfort, and though I preferred a hard-seated rocker, I was induced to sit in a big, soft armchair, because she said I would surely rest easier.

There was no introduction. I just told her I had come all the way from Albany to meet her, and hear her story of Booth and Lincoln.

"I cannot bring myself to talk about that horrible experience very often," she quietly remarked, "because it depresses me so, and always makes me shudder at the thought of it, the scene staying in my mind as vividly as the night it took place. I have pictures of Booth and Lincoln, and articles by eye witnesses. I preserve them more for the memories of old friends who send them, than to look at them and read them over.

"I knew Booth quite well. Every actor and actress who played in Washington had a speaking acquaintance, though some thought him odd, and others had stronger opinions, thinking him demented at times, and holding a very exaggerated opinion of his own importance. He made a fine appearance, dressing the gentlemen, his fissy black eyses and black hair attracting attention wherever he happened to be. I often saw him in Ford's theatre, playing, rehearsing or lounging, and we girls even envied his acting, he played the parts as though he was the actual person he represented, and though we were anxious for his praise, we rather feared his nasty temper and bitter tongue.

"I have always thought John Wilkes Booth selected a certain part of the play, Our American Cousin, in which I took part, to assassinate Abraham Lincoln. It was near 10 o'clock and his bodyguard left the private box and was sitting in the parquette. The scene I speak of was entirely in the parquette. The scene I speak of was entirely between A.S. Trenchard, who played Mary Meredith. When I came on the stage I saw Booth standing in the lobby looking so strange I hardly knew him. We went on with the scene. I looked again, and he was gone. As Trenchward burned a will leaving his fortune to Mary, the audience are intent listening to this part of the play. I went up the stage and the scene was closed in. One of the scene shifters was Ned Spangler, who was supposed to have been in the private box that day with Booth fixing a bar of wood to place across the door to prevent anyone from getting in after he entered.

"The leader of the orchestra and I were standing behind the scenes talking, when I heard a shot. Not knowing what it was and hearing a loud murmur, I was stopped from looking out by Booth coming from the first entrance with a long knife in his hand. He slashed Mr. Withers with the knife, pushed me out of the way and went out the back door into the alley and rode away.

"Then came the rush of the audience who had jumped to the stage to follow Booth. I went to the first entrance and on to the stage to find that Lincoln had been shot. Everything was in confusion. There was a call for a doctor. Dr. Charles Taft was sent up to the box. There was a call for water. My father, Thomas C. Gourlay, took Laura Keene to the box by a way known to the regular company. They were stripping Lincoln to find the wound. Miss Keene raised his head in her arms when she found blood trickling down her dress. The bar was removed from the door of the box. When another doctor entered, preparations were made to remove the President. My father helped to carry Lincoln from the box to the house across the way, where he died at about seven o'clock the next morning."

Mrs. Struthers talked until visitors came.

I hated to give up my easy chair, but in a few minutes I was on my way to Newak.

I stood in the public square of that city, and there sat Lincoln on a backless bronze bench. Beside him a little girl was arranging the hat of her doll. She had climbed on the seat beside him, her legs dangling, and through the great man idolized children, he took no notice of her. The mind was deep in thought, and the eyes were trying to look into the future,–or was it to the well-being of the nation he loved.

Mrs. Struthers said John Wilkes Book killed Lincoln.

As I looked into that sad, earnest face, I wondered if Booth really did.

I HAVE always thought John Wilkes Booth selected a certain part of the play, Our American Cousin, in which I took part, to assassinate Abraham Lincoln. It was near 10 o'clock and his bodyguard left the private box and was sitting in the parquette. The scene I speak of was entirely between Asa Trenchard and myself, who played Mary Meredith. When I came on the stage I saw Booth standing in the lobby looking so strange I hardly knew him. We went on with the scene. I looked again, and he was gone. Asa Trenchard burned a Will leaving his fortune to Mary, the audience are intent listening to this part of the play. I went up the stage and the scene was closed in. One of the scene shifters was Ned Spangler, who was supposed to have been in the private box that day with Booth fixing a bar of wood to place across the door to prevent anyone from getting in after he had entered.

The leader of the orchestra and I were standing behind the scenes talking, when I heard a shot. Not knowing what it was and hearing a loud murmur,, I was stopped from looking out by Booth coming from the first entrance with a long knife in his hand. He slashed Mr. Withers with the knife, pushed me out of the way and went out the back door into the alley and rode away.

Then came a rush of the audience who had jumped to the stage to follow Booth. I went to the first entrance and onto the stage to find that Lincoln had been shot every thing was in confustion. There was a call for a Doctor Dr Charles. Taft was handed up from the Stage to the Box there was a call for water. my father Thomas C Gourlay. took Laura Keene. to the Box by a way known to the Regular Company. they were stripping Lincoln to find the Wound. Miss Keene raised his head in her arms when she found Blood trickling down her dress. The Bar was removed from the door of the Box. when other Doctor entered. When preperation were made to remove the President. my father helped to carry Lincoln from the Box to the house. across the Way where he died about Seven O'clock. the next morning

Jeannie Gourlay
Struthers

Jacob J. Soles

Jabes Griffiths died at McKeesport, PA., on January 18, 1898; John Corey was drowned in the Alleghany River near Pittsburg in April, 1884; William Sample died in McKeesport, February 25, 1898 from burns received in a steel mill, and Jacob Soles had retired as a coal miner when a Lincoln student discovered in 1931 that he and the three other men had carried Lincoln from Ford's Theatre to the bedroom of the Peterson House on that fatal April 14, 1865.

The four young men were members of Battery C, Independent Pennsylvania Light Artillery at Camp Barry near Washington. They had been given a pass to go into the city, and hearing that Lincoln intended to go to the theatre that evening they decided to see the play, and at the same time get a good look at the President. As Mr. Soles afterward said, many of the soldiers had very little love for a majority of the higher officers, but you seldom found a man in Blue who did not love the President.

Mr. Soles talked as he slowly rocked in his easy chair;–

"Bill Sample, Jabe Griffiths and John Corey and myself, all of Company C, Independent Artillery, went to Ford's Theatre. We four were up in the balcony. We were on the same side with Mr. Lincoln's box. We were back in toward the rear of the theatre, about fifteen feet from his box. We didn't know at first when we heard the shot, that it was in there, but somebody cried help, and we heard a woman crying. We four rushed forward to the box and a man asked us to help carry the President out. We carried him to the stairway of the theatre, then two others helped us carry him out of the building. We carried him with his feet foremost. I was down at his feet foremost. I was down at his feet with one of the fellows and two men at his head. The two others held him in the middle and in this way we six carried him out.

"We held him in the street almost five minutes until a man yelled to bring him across the street. A young man not in uniform directed us to the house, and we placed him on a bed in a small room on the floor. It was a long hall and the room seemed to be in the middle of the building.

"As soon as we laid the President on the bed, we left. The street was jammed and you had to push a way through to get anywhere. We waited near the stoop until the Doctor came out and said the wound was fatal, when we left for camp.

Lincoln students had been trying for years to find who it was that carried the President from the theatre, and the lone survivor was discovered when a young man talked to a neighbor of Mr. Soles at Turtle Creek, Pa., and was told the old soldier was at the performance that evening. He went to the home of Mrs. Laura Leffler, a daughter and was introduced to the old miner. He had lost an eye in a mine accident several years before and he never went below ground again. He was born in Allegheny Co., on July 17, 1845, and in February, 1864, when 19, enlisted with a group of local boys, they being assigned to the Light Artillery to fill vacancies, where they stayed until the end of the war, all returning home and going to work in the steel mills and the mines.

Mr. Soles quietly told his story of the events of the fatal night and though more than 86 years old, remembered every detail from the moment the shot was fired until Lincoln was laid on the bed, and he was asked by a Surgeon to leave the room to make room for other doctors and high officials who would soon be there.

"Sitting close to the President's box, they were at the front of the group standing or pushing to get nearer, and they immediately stepped forward when the call for help came. The audience was wild with excitement and fear, and it was a rather difficult job to make their way down the stairs and out into the street, where another large crowd had already gathered. They worked their way across the street with some difficulty, and shortly after resting the President on the bed they left for their camp.

"Bill Sample, Jabe Griffiths and John Corey and myself, all of Co. C, Independent Artillery, went to Ford's Theatre at about 7:30 o'clock. Lincoln was shot some time later-I can't give the hour accurately; I know the play had gone on for some time.

"We were in the balcony, on the same side Lincoln's box was. We sat in toward the back of the theatre, I should say a little over fifteen feet from the box.

"We did not know at first when we heard the pistol that the shot was fired in the box, but when the cry for help sounded and we heard a woman crying, we rushed to the door of the box. One or two had reached it ahead of us and we were asked to carry the President out of the building. We four picked him up, carried him to the stairway. Then two others fell in and helped carry him. We carried him out of the theatre flat, with his feet foremost. I was at his feet with one of the other fellows, and two men were at his head, while the other men held him in the middle to keep his body from sagging.

"We stood in the street almost five minutes until a place could be found to lay him. A man hollered out to carry him across the street and a young man directed us through the crow to the house. The young man did not wear soldier's clothes and he lead us to a room on the first floor. We went back through a long hallway to about the middle of the building and laid him on the bed in a small room.

"Guards were already there and as soon as we laid him on the bed we were asked to leave. The guards would not let anybody in except the doctors and a few entitled to be there. The street was jammed with people. You had to push your way through wherever you wanted to get to. We waited around until the news was sent out by the doctors that the wound was fatal, then we pulled for camp."

him on the bed we were asked to leave. The guards would not let anybody in except the doctors and a few entitled to be there. The street was jammed with people. You had to push your way through wherever you wanted to get to. We waited around until the news was sent out by the doctors that the wound was fatal, then we pulled for camp.

Company C Independent Artillery — Jacob J. Doles

Oran J. Randlett

Oran J. Randlett spent his declining years in Lawrence, Mass., but when he enlisted in the war, he was a resident of New Hampshire and became a private in the 12th New Hampshire Volunteers. When I asked him if he had seen the President, he said;–

"The first time I saw President Lincoln was at a review of the Army of the Potomac at Falmouth, Va. The next time was in the Hall of Representatives in the Capitol at a meeting of the Christian Commission in January, 1865. I again saw him at the White House about a week previous to his assassination.

"I was in Fords Theatre when he was shot by Booth, and I saw the assassin leap from the box to the stage. I was very close to Lincoln as he was being carried across the street to the house opposite the theatre, and I saw him as he lay in State in the rotunda in the Capitol. He surely was a great man."

Corporal James Tanner

The New York Grand Army held its Encampment in Albany, and among the many delegates was James Tanner. He had lost both legs in the war, and it was rather difficult for him to walk on his false legs, so he seldom stood up. I watched him more than two hours one afternoon sitting in the Ten Eyck Hotel while he shook hands and talked with a steady stream of admirers. He was the real hero among the many who wore the Blue uniform, and he deserved to be, because he was not alone a good soldier, he overcame the terrific handicap of terrible wounds, made himself a leader in the nation almost without education, stood high in politics, while as an orator he was unsurpassed.

He sat in a large armchair, his arms hanging over the sides, his legs having a peculiar shape if a person did not know they were false. He had light complexion, gray hair, eyes almost dead, and he appeared to be very tired, worn-out old man. Standing; and it was difficult for him to do so, he was about six feet tall, rather heavy built, but looked as though he was a very muscular man.

I saw him in Fansull Hall in Boston in 1917 at the great campfire of the Grand Army. Prominent speakers held the crowd, and in turn, Corporal Tanner was helped to his feet. Shuffling to the edge of the platform he stirred the audience to the wildest enthusiasm. The band played, and the crowded house yelled, but never a muscle moved until quiet was restored, and he went on again. He was frequently interrupted, but he neither showed by wave of arm, movement of face, or flash of eye, how he felt; just stood there, and when his hearers were ready he went on again.

"The recruiting officer of the 87th New York Volunteers asked my age, "he said in his speech, and I answered by asking a question.

"Do you think I will make a good soldier? He said I would. Then I am over 18, but please don't ask me over 18 what. I was taken in, but if he had demanded an explanation, I would have to say over 18 months.

"Most of the men in that audience had done the same thing, and what a roar of approval was given, and what a great laugh shoot the rafters.

After the war, Corporal Tanner held a number of public offices, being Register of Wills in the District of Columbia at his death. He was Commander in-Chief of the Grand Army in 1905-6, and he was one of the group that stayed all night near Lincoln's deathbed. It was Tanner who took the orders in shorthand, transcribed them, and handed the transcriptions to messengers to be sent out. Read his remarkable story of his experiences in the house of death that night, and you will realize what a keen mind the legless soldier had.

Letter from Tanner to his mother:

"Among all the characters who loomed large in the public mind from 1861 to 1865, one came to stand alone in supremacy, finally recognized almost unanimously the world over as without a peer. It took the perspective of many years to enable us to get a correct view of the greatness of his character, his transcendent intellectual endowment, the utter unselfishness of his purpose, his absolute devotion to the interests of the nation which had called him to its leadership and the great agony endured by his loving, gentle heart as he staggered under his awful burden, an agony never equaled since the Saviour of mankind passed the night in the Garden of Gethsemane.

"A military guard had been placed in front of the house and those adjoining, but upon telling the commanding officer that I lived there, I passed to my apartment, which comprised the second story front of the house. There was a balcony in front of and I found my rooms and the balcony thronged by the other occupant of the house. Horror was in every heart and dismay on every countenance. We had just about a week of tumultuous joy over the downfall of Richmond and the collapse of the Confederacy and now in an hour people have shown in a thousand ways and particularly in his recent centennial that every atom relating to the life of Abraham Lincoln is of intense and continuous interest to them and because of this and because of the fact that I was a spectator of the final scene of the supreme tragedy of that time on the morning of April 15, 1865, I pen these lines.

"At that time I was an employee of the Ordnance Bureau of the War Department and had some ability as a shorthand writer. The latter fact brought me within touch of events that awful night. I had gone with a friend to witness the performance that evening at Grover's Theatre, where now stands the New National. Soon after ten o'clock a man rushed in from a lobby and cried, 'President Lincoln has been shot in Ford's Theatre.' There was great confusion at once, most of the audience rising to their feet. Some one cried out, 'It's a ruse of the pit-pockets; look out!' Almost everybody resumed his seat, but almost immediately one of the cast stepped out on the stage and said, "The sad news is too true;–the audience will disperse."

"My friend and myself crossed to Willard's Hotel and there were told that Secretary Seward had been killed. Men's faces blanched as they at once asked, "What news of Stanton? Have they got to him too?" The wildest rumors soon filled the air.

"I had rooms at the time in the house adjoining the Peterson House, into which the President had been carried. Hastening down to Tenth St., I found as almost solid mass of humanity blocking the street, and the crowd constantly enlarging. A silence that was appalling prevailed. Interest centered on all who entered or emerged from the Peterson House and all of the latter were closely questioned as to the stricken President's condition. From the first the answers were unvarying,–there was no hope. In an instant all this was changed to the deepest woo by the foul shot of the cowardly assassin.

"It was nearly midnight when Major-General Augur came out on the stood of the Peterson House and asked if there was any one in the crowd that knew shorthand. There was no response from the street but one of my friends on the balcony told the General there was a young man inside who could serve him, whereupon the General told him to ask me to come down as they needed me. So it was that

I came into close touch with the scenes and events surrounding the final hours of Abraham Lincoln's life.

"Entering the house, I accompanied Gen. Augur down the hallway to the rear parlor. As we passed the door of the front parlor, I found Secretary Stanton, Judge David K. Carter, Chief Justice of the Supreme Court of the District of Columbia, Hon. B.A. Hill, and many others.

"I took my seat on one side of a small library table opposite Mr. Stanton, with the Judge Carter at the end. Various witnesses were brought in who had either been in Ford's Theatre or up in the vicinity of Mr. Seward's residence. Among them was Harry Hawk, who had been Asa Trenchard that night in the play "Our American Cousin," Mr. Alfred Cloughly, Col. G.V. Rutherford, and others. As I took down the statements they made we were distracted by the distress of Mrs. Lincoln, for though the folding doors between the two parlors were closed, her frantic sorrow was distressingly audible to us.

"She was accompanied by Miss Harris of New York, who, with her fiancé, Major Rothbone, had gone to the theatre with the President and Mrs. Lincoln. Booth in his rush through the box after firing the fatal shot had lunged at Major Rathbone with his dagger and wounded him in the arm slightly. In the naturally intense excitement over the President's condition, it is probable that Major Rathbone himself did not realize that he was wounded until after he had been in the Peterson House some time, when he fainted from the loss of blood, was attended to, his wound depressed and taken to his apartments. He and Miss Harris subsequently married.

"Through all the testimony given by those who had been in Ford's Theatre that night there was an undertone of horror which held the witnesses back from positively identifying the assassin as Booth. Said Harry Hawk, 'to the best of my belief, it was Mr. John Wilkes Booth, but I will not be positive,' and so it went through the testimony of others, but the sum total left no doubt as to the identity of the assassin.

"Our task was interrupted very many times during the night, sometimes by reports or dispatches for Secretary Stanton but more often by him for the purpose of issuing orders calculated to enmesh Booth in his flight. 'Guard the Potomac from the city down,' was his repeated direction. 'He will try to get South.' Many dispatchers were sent from that table before morning, some to Gen. Dix at New York, others to Chicago, Philadelphia, etc.

"Several times Mr. Stanton left us a few moments and passed back to the room at the end of the hall where the President lay. The doors were open and sometimes there would be a few seconds of absolute silence, when we could hear plainly the stertorous breathing of a dying man. I think it was on his return from the third trip of this kind when, as he again took his seat opposite me, I looked earnestly at him, desiring, yet hesitating to ask if there was a chance at life. He understood and I saw a choke in his throat as he slowly forced the answer to my question,–"There-is-no-hope." He had impressed me through those awful hours as being a man of steel, but I knew then that he was dangerously near a convulsive breakdown.

"During the night there came in, I think, about every man then of prominence in our national life who was in the capitol at the time and who had heard of the tragedy. A few whom I distinctly recall were Secretaries Walles, Usher, and McCullough, Attorney-General Speed and Postmaster-General Dennison, Assistant-Secretaries Field and Otto, Governor Oglesby, Senators Sumner and Stewart, and General Meigs and Augur. I have seen many asserted pictures of the death-bed scene and most of them have Vice-President Andrew Johnson seated in a chair near the foot of the bed on the left side. Mr. Johnson was not in the house at all but in the rooms in the Kirkwood House and knew nothing of the events of that night until he was aroused in the morning by Senator Stewart and others and told that he was the President of the United States.

"With the completion of the taking of testimony, I at once began to transcribe my shorthand notes into longhand. Twice so engaged, Miss Harris supported Mrs. Lincoln down the hallway to her husband's bedside. The door leading into the hallway from the room wherein I sat was open and I had a plain view of them as they slowly passed. Mrs. Lincoln was not at the bedside when her husband breathed his last. Indeed, I think, it was nearly if not quite two hours before the end, when she paid her last visit to the death chamber and when she passed our door on her return, she cried out, "Oh my God! And have I given my husband to die."

"I have witnessed and experienced much physical agony on the battlefield and in hospital, but of it all, nothing sunk deeper in my memory than that moan of breaking heart.

"I finished transcribing my notes at six forty-five in the morning, and passed back into the room where the President lay. There was gathered all those whose names I have mentioned, and many others, about twenty or twenty-five in all, I should judge. The bed had been pulled out from the corner, and owing to the stature of Mr. Lincoln, he lay diagonally on his back. He had been utterly unconscious from the instant the bullet ploughed into his brain. His sterorous subsided a couple of minutes after seven o'clock. From then to the end only the gentle rise and fall of his bosom gave indication that life remained.

"The Surgeon-General was near the head of the bed, sometimes sitting on the edge thereof, his finger on the pulse of the dying man. Occasionally, he put his ear down to catch the lessening beats of his heart. Mr. Lincoln's pastor, the Reverend Dr. Gurley stood a little to the left of the bed. Mr. Stanton sat in a chair near the foot on the left, I stood quite near the head of the bed and from that position had full view of Mr. Stanton across the President's body. At my right, Robert Lincoln sobbed on the shoulder of Charles Sumner.

"Stanton's gaze was fixed intently on the countenance of his dying chief. He had, as I said, been a man of steel, throughout the night but as I looked at his face across the corner of the bed and saw the twitching of the muscles I knew that it was only by a powerful effort that he retrained himself. The first indication that the dreaded end had come was at twenty-two minutes past sever when the Surgeon-

General gently crossed the pulse-less hands of Lincoln across the motionless breast, and rose to his feet.

"Dr. Gurlsy stepped forward, and lifting his hands began, "Our Father and our God, "-I snatched a pencil and notebook from my pocket, but my haste defeated my purpose. My pencil point, (I had but one) caught in my coat and broke, and the world lost the prayer,—a prayer which was only interpreted by the sobs of Stanton as he buried his face in the bed clothes. As "Thy will be done, Amen," in the subdued and tremulous tones floated through that little chamber, Mr. Stanton raised his head, the tears streaming down his cheeks. A more agonized expression I never saw on a human countenance as he sobbed out the words, 'He belongs to the ages now.'

"Mr. Stanton directed Major Thomas M. Vincent of the Staff to take charge of the body, called a meeting of the Cabinet in the room where we had passed most of the night, and the assemblages disappeared.

"Going to my apartment, I sat down at once to make a second longhand copy for Mr. Stanton of the testimony I had taken, it occurred to me that wished to retain the one I had written out that night. I had been thus engaged but a brief time when hearing some commotion on the street, I stepped to the window and saw a coffin containing the body of the dead President being placed in a hearse which passed up Tenth St., to F, and thus to the White House, escorted by a Lieutenant and ten privates. As they passed with measured tread and arms reversed, my hand involuntarily went to my head in a solute as then started on their long, long journey back to the prairies and to the hearts he knew and loved so well, the mortal remains of the greatest American of all times, bar none."

Register of Wills
U.S. COURT HOUSE
Washington, D.C.

JAMES TANNER
REGISTER

April 30th, 1923.

J. E. Boos, Esq.,
10 Lexington Avenue,
Albany, New York.

My dear Sir:

In response to your request of the 26th instant, telling me you were gathering a number of expressions from men who personally knew something of Mr. Lincoln, I am sending you herewith something which I believe will far outweigh anything else I might indite at this date. I was impelled to write it some years ago just after Mr. Lincoln's Centennial; as the statement of one who was personally present during that awful night and who saw him draw his last breath it should have an interest beyond almost anything else I could send you.

As our memories are all liable to be treacherous on little things I would say to you that I was particularly favored when I sat down to write the enclosed. Only eight hours after I saw Mr. Lincoln die I sat down and wrote to my mother, then living up in Schoharie County, a long letter descriptive of the events of that night. At her death, back in the 80's, I found that she had religiously preserved all the letters I had sent her from the time I went to war, and among them of course, was this letter telling of the events of that dread night. So, as that letter had been written so soon after the great tragedy I was able to state positively what I did state.

I hope it will please you.

Very truly yours,

James Tanner

---

make a second longhand copy for Mr. Stanton of the testimony I had taken, it occurring to me that I wished to retain the one I had written out that night. I had been thus engaged but a brief time when hearing some commotion on the street, I stepped to the window and saw a coffin containing the body of the dead President being placed in a hearse which passed up Tenth St., to F, and thus to the White House, escorted by a Lieutenant and ten privates. As they passed with measured tread and arms reversed, my hand involuntarily went to my head in salute as then started on their long, long journey back to the prairies and to the hearts he knew and loved so well, the mortal remains of the greatest American of all time, bar none.

James Tanner

JOHN FLAHERTY

Daniel E. Sickles lost a leg in the Peach Orchard when his famous Excelsior Brigade stopped the advance of the Confederates on that part of the field at Gettysburg, and I never met a soldier who belonged to the regiments numbered 70th to 74th New York Volunteers who was not proud of his connection with it.

Gen. Henry E. Tremain was speaking. It was a hot summer day; a July day at Gettysburg.

"Before me," he said, "before you, as we gaze on this monument, there glides a swift panorama, beginning with the turgid Lower Potomac in that placid Winter of 1861-2, and ending only where the fluttering white flag, above the tufts of smoke, on that Spring morning of April, 1865, stopped the clashing charges in the Appomattox battle. Yorktown, Williamsburg, Fair Oaks, Glendale, Malvern Hill, Bristoe Station, Second Bull Run, Fredericksburg, Chancellorsville, Gettysburg, Wapping Heights, Mins Run, Wilderness, Spottslyvania, North Anna, Cold Harbor, Petersburg, Ream Station, Farmville, Sailors Creek, Appomattox, are not to you merely names, to be rolled off in idle talk, but ineffaceable pictures of your mental vision. Nor can I forget the picture of my own 73rd , when, under its orders from Gen. Humphreys to follow me, it was lined up in the bloody attempt to stem the tide which finally rolled over the wounded Graham and his little band at the Peach Orchard corner."

When those words were spoken, the men gathered about the orator were still alive in everyday life and though hair graying, most of them had not passed the half-century mark. Ambition was still strong and life still seemed young.

In 1918, when another great war was squeezing the resources out of nearly every nation of the world, I had the privilege of meeting one of the men who had carried a musket in the 73rd New York, who had fought in many of the battles mentioned by the speaker, and who had returned to Gettysburg to see the Excellsior Brigade Monument dedicated on that hot summer day. He limped; he stooped; he was grey; he was tired, and the ambitions and dreams of that other day were gone.

His life's race was nearly run, but the pride of having stood in battle was as keen as it was when war drums sounded and the bugle called to arms.

He had seen Lincoln, and he was one of the crowd that saw the great leader carried out of the theatre to the house where he died the next morning.

"I had the real pleasure of shaking hands with President Lincoln, April 8, 1865," said John Flaherty; "and on the night of April 14th, I sadly looked on when he was carried from Ford's Theatre after he was shot."

> Mr. John Flaherty of
> 73rd my Vol I had Pleasure of
> Shake Hand With the Great Presedent
> of the U.S. Presedent Lincoln on the
> 8" April 1865 and on the 14 of April
> I saw Carried from Ford Theatre after
> he was Shot

Henry C. Rankin

I often wondered if the territory of Michigan named its capital, Lansing, after the numerous Dutch family that settled in Albany in the early days of the founding of the colony of New York, and how the citizens of Ypsilanti pronounced the name of the town they lived in.

Henry C. Rankin lived in Ypsilanti, and he spent much of his time in Lansing for a few years, where he was a member of the House of Representatives. I believe he was born in the State, because he was a member of the 9th Michigan Volunteers, and toward the end of the war was a member of the 5th United States Veteran Volunteers.

He was attending a Grand Army Encampment in the East, and he related the following while sitting in the Convention Hall after one of the sessions adjourned.

"My company was encamped on one of the turn pikes three miles from Washington on one of the nights of April 14 and 15, 1865. All night of April 14, and the morning of the 15, couriers rode, carrying the sad news of the shooting of the President. It was my duty as Sergeant to announce the death of Lincoln to the company at roll call that eventful morning. Nearly all the men went to their quarters sobbing. Could the Union army have been turned against Lincoln's defamers that morning they would have been swept from the earth at one fell swoop.

"We were not the only ones, hardened men that we were, who shed tears; the sorrow was universal."

The words reminded me of an editorial I had read in a magazine a short time before, and I quoted it to the soldier.

"When the body of Abraham Lincoln lay-in-state in Chicago, on its journey from Washington to Springfield, among the thousands who thronged to the courthouse to peer mournfully into the sad, still face was a little boy nine years old. He had been in the street nearly all day, standing in line with a regiment of school children waiting to take their place in the funeral procession, and he remembers still the furious headache that kept him company during the long hours. At length, however the children swung into the line of march; the courthouse was reached, and the boy stood looking into the dead President's face."

"That boy was the great artist Leonard Volk," said Mr. Rankin; "and the experience of that day never passed from his mind. That was only one little boy, but it was the experience of many thousands along route of the funeral train, many waiting long hours for a glimpse of the man they dearly loved."

Mr. Rankin, like every Union veteran, was proud of his blue uniform, and strong in his praise for Lincoln.

> I was three years in the 9th. Mich. Infty, one year in the 5th U.S. Vet. Vols.
>
> My company was encamped on one of the turnpikes three miles from Washington the night of April 14 and 15, 1865. All night of April 14 and the morning of the 15 couriers rode carrying the sad tidings of the shooting of the President. It was my duty as Sergeant to announce the death of Lincoln to the company at roll call that eventful morning. Nearly all the men went to their quarters sobbing. Could the Union army have been turned against Lincoln's defamers that morning they would have been swept from the Earth at one fell swoop. I did not meet Lincoln personally. Henry C. Rankin
> Spicloute, Michigan

Henry W. Littlefield

It was easy enough to find Independence Hall, but it was nearly two hours work trying to find West Walnut Lane. I was looking for Henry W. Littlefield, an original member of the Sons of the Revolution, and a Lieutenant in the 54th Massachusetts Volunteers in the Civil War.

It was Lincoln's birthday. I had stood on the spot where the President-elect had raised a flag on Washington's natal day in 1861, and I determined I would shake the hand of a man who had touched the Emancipator's-supposing every soldier had seen him,–so I looked up the man on whose bed the President had died.

"Won't you finish reading your mail, Mr. Littlefield," I said, as I was invited to a chair near the window, the day being raw, and dark, and gloomy.

"I have already read the letter, and I was musing over it when you rang the bell. It is a very old letter; not to me, but to the 'Dear Folks at Home,' and was written in the war by Major Ben Thompson of the 32nd W.S. Colored Troops. One of my old comrades in the 44th Massachusetts, the regiment I first enlisted in, sent it to me. He knew I would enjoy reading it, and value it, because it was written just one year after Lincoln made his priceless address at Gettysburg, and about two weeks after the national election. All the soldiers were for the Union, and I well remember how we feared McClellan and his peace at any price Democrats might win. How we cheered when the news came there would be 'No swappin horses in the middle of the stream.' The army got new confidence after that, and the Johnny Rebs soon found it out.

"At Petersburg, they would yell across to us to vote for Little Mac and end the war, and we would yell back that Uncle Abe was going to be re-elected, and he would end it right, before the next summer. 'Grant and Billy Sherman will have every one of you in the stockade, and old Jeff Davis will hang,' we would shout, while all the boys along the line would cheer, but we really believed the people were so tired for the war they might vote Democrat.

"We were tired. Of course we were. But we wanted 'The Smoked Yankees,' as we called the colored troops to be sure of their freedom, and we well knew all our sacrifices would be in vain, because the Democrats intended to let the South go at the very point of Victory, because in less than six months after the Confederacy went down, and the Union was safe. It is nice to hear folks say we fought to save the Union, but most us volunteers fought, not alone to save the Union, but to free the negroes. We did save it! and there was no more worries about another long, dreadful war, and we boys have been justly proud of our share in it ever since.

"This letter brings back a flood of memories. The Major says, 'Last night brought us news of the great victory over treason at home and we all breathe freer. I feel now, that we have shown ourselves able to conquer ourselves, and we shall more surely and speedily conquer our enemies. Particulars begin to filter through the Rebel lines, but all we know as yet is-all gone for Lincoln but New Jersey, Missouri, and Kentucky.'

"These words brought a thrill when I first read them, and I can almost hear the cheers and see the celebrating when the news came to us in an almost identical way. The celebrating kept up all day and far into the night among the troops not in the trenches, and the officers, too, joined in the celebrating.

"Grant will root out the Rebels now,' seemed to be the watchword; and Hang 'Jeff Davis to the Sour Apple Tree,' the favorite song.

"Winter came, and then the Spring campaign, which ended the war. I was stationed in Washington on special duty, and was on a furlough home when the President was assassinated. I was on the Fall River boat on my way from Boston to New York that night and arrived in Washington the afternoon of the 15th.

"I had to show my pass at almost every corner, and when I neared my boarding house, I met my roommate, Billy Clark, terribly excited and worried, who told me we could not use our room because the President had been taken to it from the theatre.

"We hurried into the house, and our landlady, Mrs. Peterson told us we could use an upstairs room that night because she was too upset and tired to change the bedding and rearrange it.

"Billy was a member of the 13th Massachusetts Volunteers, being at the time a clerk in the office of Gen. Auger. We went in our room and looked over everything for a souvenir of the tragedy. I decided to cut two pieces off the linen towel that had been placed under the President's head, and Billy insisted on taking Lincoln's boots, which were still under the bed.

"I gave him one piece to preserve, but I refused to accept one of the boots, Billy taking them home when he was discharged from the army, and he kept them until his death.

"Crowds filled the street in front of the house until long after dark, and we went out and mixed with it, being as excited and as bitter as anybody. We thought no more our room at the time, but we afterward learned great numbers of people would have paid for any scrap we cared to take out of it, so that they might have a souvenir of the house where the President died.

"When I read that soldier's letter it took me back more than 60 years and I just mused and dreamed, many of those old scenes seeming as real as the day they happened. I looked with awe and horror at the blood-stained bed, at the confusion of everything and the mud on the floors, and I wanted to run to get away from it, but I did not know where to run to.

"Billy, who had calmed down, suggested going to our new room, where we sat a few minutes, then came down again and began our search of the lower floor for a memento, deciding to take the towel and boots. To our room we went again, and then to the street, where we stayed until late that night."

The old gentlemen talked more than an hour, and when I left I was real proud to know I had met a man who had seen a little of the tragedy, and who had been in more than one vital battle When I look back to that meeting with him I am surprised how fast time has gone. Everyone connected with that terrible scene lives no more to tell of it."

"On the night of the assassination I was on Long Island Sound. Fall River boat, (Providence, I think) en-route from Boston to New York on my return trip to Washington, which I reached that evening, and Mr. W.T. Clark, my chum was there. Mr. Lincoln's body had been removed from our room. Everything was in confusion. I don't think I laid down anywhere that night. Mr. Clark and I went around to many places,–crowds everywhere.

"Mr. Clark died many years ago. He was married but left no children.

"My Grandfather, four great grand fathers, and one great great grand father, as well as several great and great grand uncles of mine were in the Revolution, have been Son of the Revolution, 50 years ever since it started as a society."

> ON the night of the assassination I was on Long Island Sound, Fall River boat, (Providence, I think,) enroute from Boston to New York on my return trip to Washington, which I reached that evening, and Mr. W. T. Clark, my chum was there. Mr. Lincoln's body had been removed from our room. Everything was in confusion. I don't think I laid down anywhere that night. Mr. Clark and I went around to many places,--crowds everywhere.
>
> Mr. Clark died many years ago. He was married but left no children.
>
> My Grandfather, four greatgrandfathers, and one great great grandfather, as well as several great and great grand uncles of mine were in the Revolution. Have been Son of the Revolution, 50 years, ever since it started as a society.
>
> *Henry W. Littlefield*
> *a Massachusetts Soldier in the Civil War – 1861-1866*

Philadelphia, Pa.
Feb. 27th 1926

John E. Boos
    10 Lexington Av.
        Albany N.Y.

Replying to your request of Feb 16th inst, I can only say, that on the night of the Assassination by John Wilkes Booth of President Abraham Lincoln, in Fords' Theatre Washington, D.C., Mr. Lincoln was carried across the street, and laid on the bed in the room, in the house where William T Clark and I lodged at the time and expired on that bed. Mr. Clark was a Soldier of Co D. 13th Mass. and was a clerk in the Office of General Auger. I never met President Abraham Lincoln. Mr. Clark had the boots Mr Lincoln had on at the time of his death, and Mr. Clark and myself each had a piece of the linen towel which was on the pillow under Mr. Lincoln's head when he died.

Mr. Clark and I were boy friends before the Civil War in 1861-6, in which we both served.

    Henry Warren Littlefield
        44th Mass. Vol. Infantry
First Lieutenant 54th Mass Infantry

49

Calvin L. Vincent

The bullet from the pistol of John Wilkes Booth struck down Abraham Lincoln in the box at Fords Theatre at 10:30 p.m. on the night of April 14, 1865. He never moved from the moment of the wound until his death in the little brick house across the street from the theatre at 7:20 the next morning. His body was immediately taken to the White House, the funeral taking place in the East Room at noon on the 19th. It was then taken to the rotunda of the Capitol, where great crowds passed by the coffin until the morning of the 21st, when they were placed on the funeral car and the long journey to his old home commenced.

Senator Lafayette S. Foster said, "After being gazed upon by myriads of loving eyes, under the dome of this magnificent capitol, the remains of our President were borne in solemn procession through our cities, towns, and villages, all draped in the habiliments of sorrow, the symbols and token of profound and heartfelt grief, to their final resting-place in the capital of his own state."

One of the men who stood guard over the remains, and who marched in the funeral procession in Washington, wrote in his 85th year that:

"I never met the Immortal Lincoln while living. At the time he was assassinated, the regiment to which I belonged, the 8th Illinois Calvary, was stationed at Fairfax Court House, Va., and were immediately called to Washington, where we took part at the funeral as guards of honor. I rode directly beside the remains of the President as he was taken to the railroad station. We were sent in pursuit of Booth, the assassin. We soon struck his trail in Maryland at the home of Dr. Mudd, where he had his leg set. Booth was shot shortly after by other troops.

Need apology of poor writing because 85 years old, 1927.

"Nearly every building in Washington was draped in mourning, and a majority of the citizens wore badges to express their sorrow publicly. When the time was announced for the public to enter the capitol and pass near the dead President, great crowds formed in lines of two and very slowly moved ahead, sometimes waiting hours before they could enter the building."

Calvin L. Vincent was a private in the 109th New York Volunteers, and being in the city at the time, he took his place in the line, and was one of the many who saw Lincoln's face before the funeral train started for his home in Springfield.

Hustler April 11th 1927

Mr John E Boos
    Dear Sir

In answer to your letter of April 7th will say I never met the immortal Lincoln while living. At the time he was assasinated the regt to which I belonged 8th Illinois cavalry was stationed at Fairfax Court House Va and were immediately called to Washington where we took part at Lincolns funeral as guard of honor I rode directly beside the remains of the President as he was taken to the R R station to be sent to Springfield Illinois.

We were then sent in

pursuit of Wilks Boothe the assassin we soon struck his trail in Maryland at the home of Dr Mudd where he had his leg set broken when jumping from the stage after shooting Lincoln. Booth was shot soon after leaving Dr Mudds by other troops

Yours truly
C D Curtis

you must excuse poor writing for I shall soon be 85 years old

.JOHN B. PATRICK

The funeral train moved slowly out of the city of Washington, and upon its arrival in Baltimore, it was met by great crowds, all anxious to look at the face of the dead President, and to pay tribute to his great leadership. Few eyes were dry, everybody feeling his passing was a personal loss.

How different from that morning a little more than four years earlier, when he was taken secretly through that city because of a plot by Rebel sympathizers to do the very act Booth had committed.

When Lincoln called for volunteers to defend the capital, this city, in which long lines of people were now passing before his coffin, mobbed the first regiment to pass through, killing a number of the militia and injuring many more.

The Old Bay State hung the musket of one of those dead men in her capitol as a lasting memorial to the 6th Massachusetts Regiment, and as a reminder of the treatment Maryland mobs gave her citizens shortly after Fort Sumter was captured.

Though Maryland regiments marched under the flag of the Confederacy, the State remained loyal, and many other regiments stood on the battlefields under the flag of the Union. Though men sang, "Maryland, my Maryland," under the Stars and Bars, more men sang it under the Stars and Stripes, and there was a great rejoicing when Lee dropped his flag at Appomattox, and a few days later, the State was plunged into mourning for Abraham Lincoln.

Past Department Commander of the Pennsylvania G.A.R., John B. Patrick was 16 years old when he enlisted, and he was in the great crowd that waited for the funeral train to come into the Maryland city. Mr. Patrick said,–

"I enlisted in June, 1863 in the 2nd Battalion Pennsylvania Volunteers. Shortly after my discharge, I re-enlisted in the 193rd Pennsylvania Volunteers, and when again Discharged, I enlisted as a veteran in the 97th Pennsylvania Veteran Volunteers.

"During this service my company was detailed with the Marshall's office in the city of Baltimore, where we were when the war ended.

"When Lincoln was shot, we were called out to do patrol duty, and served as such until after the internment of the body at Springfield, Ill.

"I was detailed as one of the guard while Lincoln's body lay-in-state when it passed through Baltimore. I never saw President Lincoln living, but saw him in his casket while thousands passed through the Exchange Building to get a last look of all that was mortal of the greatest President that ever presided over the destines of our country."

I enlisted in June, 1863 in Second Battalion 6 Months Penna. Volunteers. Discharged at the end of this service and came home. Shortly after I enlisted for the second time, in 193rd Penna. Vol and from this enlistment was discharged to re-enlist as a veteran in the 97th Regt. Penna. Veteran Volunteers.

During this service my Company was detailed for service with the Marshalls Office in the City of Baltimore, Md. where we were when the War ended.

When Lincoln was shot we were called out to do patrol duty and served as such until after the interment of the body at Springfield, Ills,

I was detailed as one of the guard while Lincoln body lay in State while passing through Baltimore, I never saw President living, but saw him in his casket, while thousands passed through the Exchange Building to get a last look of all that was mortal of the greatest President that ever presided over the destinies of our County

John B. Patrick
Commander, Department of Penna, G. A. R.

Harlan G. Mendenhall

A ten year old boy waited for hours at the railroad station at Coatesville, Pa., on February 23, 1861 to see the train bearing Abraham Lincoln pass through. Four years later he waited again to see a train draped in mourning bear that same President through the town. The boy was Harlan G. Mendenhall, and he wrote many years afterward,–

"In the winter of 1864-5 I lived in Washington, my father being a paymaster in the U.S. Army. I attended with my parents the January reception at the White House and shook hands with Mr. Lincoln. On another occasion, at a night reception at the White House I joined the multitude and again shook hands with him. Later in the year I was home at Coatesville and at the Railroad Station and saw the casket bearing his dead body as the train passed on to Philadelphia."

Dr. Mendenhall was born in Coatesville, April 12, 1851, graduated from Western Theological Seminary in 1874, and was ordained a Presbyterian Minister the following year. He was Pastor of churches at Fort Wayne, Ind., Pittsburg, Pa., Mercersburg, Pa., Grand Forks, N.D., Kansas City, Kan., Brooklyn, N.Y., and died as Pastor Emeritus of the 23rd St., Church of New York City. In 1894 he was given a D.D. degree by Lafayette College, and an S.T.D. by University of Debreczen, Hungary in 1930. In 1869 he was Associate Editor of the Springfield, Mass., Republican, and in 1889 was President of the Jamestown North Dakota College.

Dr. Mendenhall was President of the Presbyterian Ministers Association of N.Y. from 1911 to 1913; President Presbyterian Union of New York, 1918-9; Moderator of the Presbyterian Synod of New York, 1916-7; President Presbyterian Society of New York, 1916-22, and State Clerk of the New York Presbyterians from 1922-1931. In 1919 he was presented from 1922 to 1931. In 1919 he was presented with Medal of Order of Redeemer.

Litchfield, Conn-June 6, 1934

"There was something about Lincoln's personality that was so fascinating and charming it clings and clutches life at this far off period-I have met many men in my life but outside of the family relation this personal touch goes far beyond what I have known in other men. I may be a fanatic but I'm making the above confession."

Yours truly,

"My native town was Coatesville, Pa. On the morning of February 23, Mr. Lincoln passed through this village from Philadelphia to Harrisburg. I was at the railroad station when the train bearing Mr. Lincoln passed. He stood on the rear platform of the train and bowed to the applause of the people.

"In the winter of 1864-5 I lived in Washington, my father being a paymaster in the U.S. Army. I attended withy my parents the January reception at the White House and shook hands with Mr. Lincoln.

"On another occasion at a night reception at the White House I joined the multitude and again shook hands with him. Later in 1865 the Christian Commission had a mass meeting in the hall of the House of Representatives at the Capitol. Mr. Lincoln was present and requested the signing of a hymn of which he was fond, and the request was granted.

"That same year I was again at the Coatesville Railroad Station and saw the casket bearing his dead body as the train passed on to Philadelphia."

PRESBYTERY OF NEW YORK
156 FIFTH AVENUE
NEW YORK CITY

H. G. MENDENHALL
STATED CLERK EMERITUS

Litchfield, Conn--June 6, 34

John E. Boos
[Al]bany, N.Y

[M]r Boos:-

Following your suggestion I have signed and [mailed] the within Lincoln item and thank you for the privilege [of ma]king this record. There was something about Lincoln's [person]ality that was so fascinating and charming it clings and [fills] life at this far off period--I have met many men in my [life b]ut outside of the family relation this personal touch [is] far beyond what I have known in other men. I may be a fanat[ic] [but] I'm making the above confession

Yours truly

H. G. Mendenhall

[You will allow me to return stamps]

 My native town was Coatesville, Pa. On the morning of February 23, Mr. Lincoln passed thro this village from Philadelphia to Harrisburg. I was at the railroad station when the train bearing Mr. Lincoln passed. He stood on the rear platform of the train and bowed to the applause of the people.

In the winter of 1864-5 I lived in Washington, my father being a paymaster in the U. S. Army. I attended with my parents the January reception at the White House and shook hands with Mr. Lincoln.

On another occasion at a night reception at the White House I joined the multitude and again shook hands with him.

Later in 1865 the Christian Commission had a mass meeting in the hall of the House of Representatives at the Capitol. Mr. Lincoln was present and requested the singing of a hymn of which he fond, and the request was granted.

That same year I was again at the Coatesville Railroad Station and saw the casket bearing his dead body as the train passed on to Philadelphia.

Harlem G. Mendenhall

June 6, 1934

P.E. HARRINGTON

When Lincoln left his home in Springfield for the inauguration in February, 1861, the train moved slowly across country, so that the people could see him, and crowds hailed him almost every foot of the way to Philadelphia, where he stayed overnight, so that he might visit the capitol at Harrisburg the next day. When the reception at the capitol was over, he secretly returned to Philadelphia, thence to Washington, because of a threatened plot on his life, and the terrific strain of leading a war-torn nation soon commenced.

Just as peace was about to come over the land, the assassin's bullet struck its mark, and the train started back toward Springfield, as slowly as it had come four years earlier, but with sorrowing crowds taking the place of cheers and well-wishers. Lincoln the President-elect answered the cheers; Lincoln the martyr was beyond the sobs and fears.

At Philadelphia the coffin was tenderly borne to Independence Hall, where it lay-in-state while great crowds lined the streets to see the funeral procession go by. In the early morning of Washington's birthday four years before, he raised a flag to the top of the staff over the historic building amid great enthusiasm, and now, another had lowered it to half-mast as a mourning tribute to the illustrious dead.

One of the crowd was a young officer just turned from the front, and in 1927 he wrote,–

> *"At Philadelphia I saw the stilled face of the great Emancipator, but his spirit lived in the nation. On the night when Lincoln was struck down, the noble order of the Loyal Legion was born, a first-fruit of the immortal spirit.*
>
> *P.F. Harrington*
> *Commander-in-Chief, Military Order of the Loyal Legion, 1927*

At Philadelphia I saw the stilled face of the great Emancipator, but his spirit lived in the Nation.

On the night when Lincoln was struck down, the noble Order of the Loyal Legion was born, a first fruit of that immortal spirit.

One of our Companions, Henry M. Rogers, has noted the lasting influence in these words;—

"We reverently ac-
"knowledge that the
"death of Abraham
"Lincoln, and even
"the manner of his
"death, were neces-
"sary to make the

"teachings of his life
" vividly remembered
" through the ages.
" His death, on Good
" Friday, foreshadowed
" an Easter, a new
" birth to his country."

P. F. Harrington,
Commander-in-Chief,
Military Order of
the Loyal Legion of
the United States.

Headquarters,
Philadelphia,
October 6, 1927.

Charles D. Beldon

There passed away in New York City on July 27, 1919, a man who had talked with Abraham Lincoln. The men who had spoken to the great war President were fast passing on and it was a real honor to grasp the hand of one who had heard the Emancipator's voice. He was only 74,–and I say only, because many men of the Civil War period had lived to far greater age, one of them, Dr. Augustus Beard reaching 101, and he was healthy and on his feet until a few days before his death in 1934.

It was a hot, uncomfortable day, the heavy bag seeming to be a real burden to the elderly gentlemen as he trudged up Broadway in Albany.

"I am going past the station," I said by way of introduction, "and I will be real glad to carry your suitcase."

He willingly handed it over, his pace quickened a little and he felt much better without the load.

"I did not like Albany when I was a young man," he said, "because there were as many Copperheads in the city as there were loyal people, and for two years Governor Seymour really encouraged them in their disloyalty."

"There were a great many peace-at-any-price men," I answered, "but Confederate armies felt the power of the 3rd, 43rd, 44th New York Volunteers, and of the 7th New York Heavy Artillery, nearly all of the men of the latter regiment, nearly all of the men of the latter regiment having enlisted in Albany County, and any student of the Civil War will admit they left their mark on many a hard fought field.

"Well! A person would think you stood at the stone wall at Gettysburg with Albany's 11th New York Battery. You speak as I have heard old soldiers talk while defending the fighting of their regiments at some major battle," he laughingly answered.

"My father was nine years old when President Lincoln was shot, and his father was called a Black Republican because he dared vote for the great war President in 1864, and I imagine my love for him comes from them, because our family were strong admirers of the Union.

"I am wondering," I went on, as we seated ourselves in the station, "if you ever saw Lincoln."

"I was Assistant Secretary of the Committee which held the great Fair in aid of the Sanitary Commission in the Academy of Music, Brooklyn.

"After a most satisfactory Fair continuing about a month, the Committee desired to send a large silk national flag to the President. I, with another, took charge of it. We visited the White House and presented the flag to Mr. Lincoln. He was a sorrowful looking man, but his countenance brightened and was almost beautiful

Statement by Chas. D. Belden M.D.
of Co 13. 13th Reg't N.Y. S.N.G.

I was ass't Secretary of the Committee which held the great Fair in aid of the Sanitary Commission in the Academy of Music Brooklyn.

After a most satisfactory Fair continuing about a month the Committee desired to send a large Silk National flag to President Abraham Lincoln. I with another, Took charge of it. We visited the White House and presented the flag to the President. He was a sorrowful looking man but his countenance brightened and was almost beautiful as he understood our errand and he made a few eloquent remarks.

Not long afterward, as a reporter for the New York Tribune I was appointed to report the reception of the dead body of Lincoln as it arrived in Jersey City and was escorted to the New York City Hall and deposited in the Governors room. I attended to these duties and described the escort. I was with the undertaker as the coffin was opened. It was covered with dust. I assisted in cleaning and rearranging the corpse, clothing and coffin. It was then transferred to the rotunda and the when he understood our errand, and he made a few eloquent remarks. Not long afterward, as a reporter for the New York Tribune, I was appointed to report the reception of the dead body of Lincoln as it arrived in Jersey City, and was on the train when it was escorted to New York City Hall and deposited in the Governor's room. I attended to those duties and described the escort. I was with the undertaker when the coffin was opened. It was covered with dust. I assisted in cleaning and rearranging the corpse, clothing the coffin. It was then transferred to the rotunda and the citizens were permitted to pass the catafalque for a few hours.

"The grief of the nation was most affecting, and the sentiment of intense admiration and respect for that noble statesman and devout Christian philanthropist has increased from that time to now."

That ended our talk. The caller was shouting. "New York Flyer on Track 1," and Dr. Charles D. Belden, shook hands, and in a moment he was hurrying as fast as weary legs would carry him to the train shed.

CHARLES H. PORTER

The funeral train stopped in New York City, that city which caused the President more concern than any spot in the Union during his more than four years in office. Here it was that the most serious draft riots took place, where troops from the front had to be sent to quell them, where Fernendo Wood tried to make an independent city, and where great editors like Horace Greely and James G. Bennett, sometimes praised, but more times criticized Lincoln's methods of conducting the war. Many thought the city more opposed to the administration than in accord with it, but now the head of that government was dead, and the citizens of the great metropolis were overwhelmed with grief.

Great crowds watched the flag-draped coffin pass, and when the City Hall was opened to the public, long lines of people waited for hours to pass the bier and get a last look at the martyr's face.

One of the men in the crowd was Charles H. Porter, an ex-soldier, who afterward moved to Cincinnati, Ohio, and he once wrote,–

"I wish I could state I had met Uncle Abe living, for I think he was the noblest man that ever lived. I was born in Hartford, Conn., in Artillery in Greensburg, Ind., in May, 1861. Corporal Co. A, 17th Indiana. Sergeant in Rigly Battery in 1862. Elected 1st Lieut. Wilder Battery in 1863 resigned in 1864. Broke down in service in East Tennessee. Was in Hartford, Conn., when Lincoln was killed and went to New York to see his remains. Stood waiting in the ranks for hours before I passed coffin."

Charles H. Porter

Dear Sir I do wish I could state I had met-
Uncle Abe living for I think he was the Noblest that ever lived - I was born in Hartford Conn 1836 you know the Porters are part of the History of the U S I enlisted as Private Decatur light Artilly Greensburg Ind May 1861 Corporal Co A 17th Ind next Sergent Rigbys Battery 1862, Elected 1st Lieut Wilder Battery 1863 Resigned 1864 broke down in service at East Tenn Resigned Feb 1864, was in Hartford when he was Killed. Saw his Body in New York after Waiting in Rank for hours

> We are descent from
> John Porters son Windsor
> Porters sister was the Mother
> of the Grant Family
> Worked for Lincoln Election
> belonged to Rail Splitters
> also the first Company
> of Wide awake, Capt
> Terry afterward
> Gen Fort Fisher Fame
>   Sincerly yours
> Charles Henry Porter
> Evanston Avenue
>   Cin Ohio
>
> _ Cincinati

Edward Godfrey

In April, 1932, there passed away in Cookstown, N.J., the last of the men who fought under the great Indian fighters in opening the West.

Writing of the Little Big Horn Battle, an editorial in the Baltimore Sun said,–

"The quite death at the great age of 88 of one of the last survivors of the battle of the Little Big Horn, Gen. Edward S. Godfrey, recalls to the present generation the fact that a half century ago dashing American cavalrymen were still riding out against Red Indians, and in the instance with Gen. Godfrey's name was connected, meeting with disaster as famous as it was tragic.

"Fifty years is a considerable time, if we measure in terms of the individual's life, but a very short time if we think in terms of history. And it will be only 56 years this June that Lieut-Col. George A. Custer, who from the first battle of Bull Run to the last discharge at Appomattax had won distinction as a cavalry officer, led his 7th Calvary against the Sioux. His whole career had been one of daring and romance. When Maximilian became Emperor of Mexico it was Custer whom the Indian patriot, Juarez, sought to lead the Mexicans against the ill-fated Austrian.

"Scouting for Gen. Terry's main force, Custer and his men came upon the Sioux Village on the west bank of the Little Big Horn. Custer misjudged the strength of his foes, and fatally divided his troops. In one-third of them, led by Major Reno, was Godfrey, who had just gone to the long bivouac. Reno's men were repulsed after some 50 of them had been killed, but retreated safely; while Custer and five companies struck into the very center of the Indian line. In less than an hour he had been surrounded and his entire force of 208 soldiers destroyed. Of all who took part in the battle Gen. Godfrey was one of the last. And that lent him a special glamour, for in the late years he was one of the scant band who could remember, not the story merely but the experience of the battle which captured the minds and memories of Americans more than any other incident of the Indian Wars."

The General was not alone in the Indian Wars, he was in the Civil War, and the Spanish-American War, having been granted a Congressional Medal of Honor for distinguished bravery in the battle of Bear Paw Mountains in 1877.

While in Washington he was enthusiastic member of Kit Carson Post, Grand Army of the Republic, being a Quartermaster for a number of years.

Writing to him in 1926 about President Lincoln, he answered and said,–

"I never saw Abraham Lincoln. I was cadet at the United States Military Academy at the time of his assassination.

"The corps of cadets was at Garrisons Station on the Hudson River Railroad when the funeral train arrived. The official salute was given on the arrival and departure of the train. Your allusions to my record in West with Indians prompts me to state that I joined the 7th U.S. Cavalry home for nearly thirty-four years, participating in all its major campaigns and battles"

Robert B. Dickie

The train slowed down at every station between New York and Albany, the sorrowing crowds patiently awaiting its arrival. When the capital was reached, the downtown streets were packed to congestion, and the funeral procession had to halt at times, so that the police and militia could make room so that it could proceed.

Capital Park was surrounded by an iron picket fence, and when the gates were opened, a line of people blocks long moved up State St., and through the Capitol to get a last look at the face of the dead President.

Guards kept the people in line, others stood near the coffin, one of them being Robert B. Dickie, who had recently been discharged from the 2nd New York Volunteers. He said many of the discharged soldiers living in and near Albany volunteered their services, put on their old uniforms, went to the armory to get a mus-

> Robert B Dickie
> 2nd Reg't New York Vols
> 4 Paisley Innce, Pittsfield Mass
> was Garde of Honner at
> Lincolns Funral at Albany N.Y.
> Saw Pres Lincoln at Harrisonlanding
> and Falmouth Va and shoke hands
> with him —
> Aug. 7, 1912.

ket, and did short tricks of guard duty, around, and in the capitol, being relived at the intervals by other volunteers. Every one of them was bitter against the assassin and Jeff Davis, all believing he had had a hand in the plot.

Mr. Dickie had seen the President at Harrison's Landing on one of his visits there, and he was one of the private soldiers to have the honor to shake his hand. The old veteran lived in Pittsfield, Mass., in 1912.

H.R. WRIGHT

H.R. Wright was born in Esperance, and when the century old covered bridge was being torn down, I sat in his office for more than an hour one day listening to his stories of the village and of one of the last big wooden bridges in the state. He left the village when a boy and moved to Schenectady, later coming to Albany, where he conducted a large poultry commission house at the corner of Division St., and Broadway for may years. He later moved to Hudson Ave., above Broadway, the business gradually changing to wholesale groceries. He conducted the business almost to the time of is death, he being more than 80 years old.

He was a Republican in politics, and speaking of Lincoln one day, he related the following story,–

"The day Lincoln's body passed through Schenectady, a great crowd of citizens waited at the station to see the lifeless form of the great man, if it were possible. The funeral train was proceeded by an engine whose bell kept continually ringing. The train was side-tracked, the door was opened and the long line that had formed slowly walked through the funeral car and looked into the face of the dead leader. I was in the crowd, and there was hardly a person without tears."

I was an ardent Wide Awake, though but a boy of 16, and marched in the Lincoln parades in Schenectady. We were called Nigger Lovers and Black Republicans, and were usually greeted with showers of stones at the corners of the prominent streets by the Copperheads, as we called the peace Democrats. I saw, more than once, the effigy of the President being carried on a rail in the parades of the Democrats, but the Republicans never lowered themselves to throw missles at their political opponents. Another of their favorite ideas was an old carriage with a negro in it hugging a white woman.

The day Lincoln's body passed through Schenectady a great crowd of citizens waited at the station to see the lifeless form of the great man, if it were possible. The funeral train was preceeded by an engine whose bell kept continually ringing. The train was sidetracked, the door was opened and the long line that had formed slowly walked through the funeral car and looked into the face of the dead leader. I was in the crowd, and there was hardly a person without tears.

H R Wright

JAMES H. KENNY

The funeral train stopped at Cleveland, where it was met by crowds as large and sorrowful as the crowds were in every city through which it passed. James H. Kenny's father brought him to the city that he might have a chance to pay tribute to the dead,–by his presence at least,–and little did that father think the boy would some day pass the caskets of the two other martyred Presidents, both Union soldiers, the President, Garfield, the General, and McKinley, the Captain were spared by war, but died by the hand of men who thought they could change world history with the assassin's bullet.

Mr. Kenny Lived in Pasadena, Cal., in 1930 and from there he wrote,–

"When Garfield lay-in-state in Cleveland, on the very spot where Lincoln lay, I saw him in his coffin. I was then managing editor of the Cleveland Herald, and knew him well."

1281 Avocado Terrace
Pasadena, Calif.
April 23, 1930

Mr. John E. Boos,
  Albany, N. Y.

My Dear Sir, I am glad
to answer yours as to when
and where I looked upon
the face of Abraham Lin-
coln — in Cleveland, as
he lay in state on his
last journey to his home

I was a mere boy; my
father took me to Cleveland;
we saw him in the
calm dignity of death. —

and that look has ahered us
Ne Ever since. I never saw
him when alive Oliss.

When Garfield lay in the state
in Cleveland; on the very spot
where Lincoln lay — I saw him
in his coffin — I was then the
Managing Editor of the Cleveland
Herald, and knew him well.

I also knew McKinley well.
and went from New York to Washington; where I saw him in his coffin
under the Cedars down at Oak.

I never have seen any
a sight — or sight — as was permitted to be.

Jun 14, 1935 J. Ober H Kenn

Dr. C.R. Pontius

It is strange how clearly the smallest boy remembered the face of Lincoln. Possibly the strenuous times, the long strain of war, the constant fear in the homes where loved ones were in the service, and the actual suffering of many left a vivid impression on their minds when they saw the face of the one man they were sure would bring them safely through. In death, as in life, the face of the leader stamped itself indelibly on their minds, and they could clearly recall it until they, too, passed on.

Dr. C.R. Pontius lived in Fremont, Ohio, and his father took him to Columbus, the lad being under school age at the time, to see the funeral procession. Talking with the kindly Doctor in 1932, he said,–

"When the body of Abraham Lincoln lay in state in the rotunda of the capital at Columbus, Ohio, my father, a farmer, drove twelve miles to Columbus to be one of the many thousands to view the body of the great Emancipator. He very thoughtfully took his young son with him. As we neared the casket, he took me, a tiny boy of four years, on his arm so I could see the body of our dead President. It made wonderful and lasting impression on me. I do not remember seeing a dead person previous to that time. The face of Mr. Lincoln, the scenes of that eventful day in my young life, the soldiers, the hearse drawn by six white horses, a colored man at the head of each horse, made a lasting impression."

Mr John E. Boos. Fremont Ohio
Dear Sir. Dec 17" '32

I am glad to comply with your request and tell you about seeing Mr Lincoln.

When the body of Abraham Lincoln lay in state in the rotunda of the capitol at Columbus Ohio, my father, a farmer, drove twelve miles to Columbus to be one of the many thousands to view the body of the great Emancipator. He very thoughtfully took his young son with him. As we neared the casket, he took me, a tiny boy of four years, on his arm so I could see the body of our dead President. It made a wonderful and lasting impression on me. I do not remember seeing a dead person previous to that time. The face of Mr Lincoln, the scenes of that eventful day in my young life, the soldiers, the hearse drawn by six white horses, a colored man at the head of each horse, made a lasting impression. After trying for several years I secured a picture of the scene I saw that day.

For many years I have been a student of the life of Lincoln. I have visited his birthplace, have a replica of the cabin, and traveled over roads that Lincoln trod; visited his home and tomb in Springfield Ill. New Salem where he lived seven years or more.

Where he worked and died in Washington, his summer home all interested me intensely.

Where Lincoln stood and delivered his address at Gettysburg, to me is hallowed ground.

Usually in the month when his birth is commemorated I am asked by church organizations, or clubs, to talk to them about Lincoln. I have 22 beautiful slides that I use, sometimes, to throw pictures on a screen on such occasions. I am pleased to talk about Lincoln for I think it is in line of Christian work to present Lincoln as one to be emulated.

I regard Abraham Lincoln as the greatest man America, and probably the world, excepting Christ, has ever produced.

Your accumulation of letters is unique and will be most interesting.

Sincerely,

C. R. Pontius M.D.

Cornilius Van Dyck

He was a little slim man who looked like a farmer; sturdy, and very muscular. His hair was mixed with gray, as was the short beard. He was born in Rotterdam, N.Y., on November 13, 1843, and enlisted in the little village as a private in the 134th New York Volunteers. He was through the whole war, taking part in a number of battles, and was wounded at Resaca, Ga., while on the March to the Sea, he being known as one of "Sherman's Bummers." Mr. Van Dyck came to Albany in 1900, and I first met him in the rooms of Lew Benedict Post of the Grand Army, where he told me he was one of the guards when President Lincoln's body lay in state at Indianapolis, Ind.

He died May 20, 1918 and was buried with military honors at Rotterdam.

Cornilius Van Dyck
Sergt Co A 134 NYV
Was gard over Lincons Remains
while lying in State at
Indianapolis Ind
Albany, April 6, 1911.

Charles Blodgett

Though most religious leaders oppose war, those of them who actually marched to battle are very proud of their records and their regiments. Charles W. Blodgett was a Methodist Minister, and during the Civil War he helped defend the country as a private in the 47th Iowa Volunteers. When his term of enlistment expired, he entered the Illinois Military College at Fulton, Ill., and "It was there the train bearing the body of Abraham Lincoln stopped, the casket opened, and I, with thousands of others had a glimpse of his face," said the old minister many years after."

Mr. Blodgett entered the ministry in 1869, and he was active as a pastor more than 50 years. He was also Department Commander of Ohio, Department Chaplin of Iowa, and Chaplain-in-Chief of the Grand Army of the Republic.

Charles H. Blodgett
Private Co F. 47th Iowa
Volunteer Infantry
7th Army Corps
Enlisted in Des Moines Iowa
Educated ti tr University
At the close of Enlistment
was a Student in Illinois
Military College at Fulton
Ills. It was there the
train bearing the body
of President Abraham Lincoln
stopped and the Casket was
exposed
Enlisted in the Methodist
Episcopal Ministry in 1869
and served continuously
for 50 years
Have been Dept Chaplain
of Iowa also of Ohio and
Commander of Dept of Ohio
and at this writing Oct 14
1924 – National Chaplain
G.A.R. Elected in Boston
in August 1924
Charles H. Blodgett
2890 Griegle ave
Hyde Park Cincinnati Ohio

George A. Jewett

George A. Jewett was one of those men whose great ability made him a leader in many different organizations. In 1865 he graduated from Bryant & Strattons College in Chicago, and almost immediately became the manager of the Agriculture Implement House of Des Moines, Iowa, where he stayed until 1873.

He was interested in other concerns until 1881 when he founded Drake University, becoming the Secretary and Trustee for many years, and in 1892, the LL.D. degree was conferred on him. He published the Christian Worker since 1887, was President and General Manager of the Jewett Typewriter Co., for years, and President of the Jewett Lumber Co., from 1906 until his death, this company being the largest of its kind in Des Moines.

He was born in Red Rock, Iowa, September 9, 1847.

I met Mr. Jewett one day in February, 1930, and during our conversation, I asked him if he had ever met President Lincoln, and his answer was,–

"I never saw the great War President, but I had the honor of being one of the guards of honor to March beside the remains in Chicago from the railroad, down about 16th Street where they stopped the train and marched to the Court House where the remains laid in state for two days and nights."

"I was a great believer in Abraham Lincoln, so much so that I worked for the abolition of slavery, drove a team in the underground railway with slaves as a boy. I was in Chicago attending Bryant and Stratton Commercial College when Lincoln was assassinated and the mayor of Chicago came to the Commercial College and said he wanted fifty of us to volunteer to march on the two sides of the hearse and I had the honor of being one of them."

JEWETT BUILDING
DES MOINES, IOWA.
February 3, 1930.

Mr. John E. Boos,
  21 Dudley Heights,
     Albany, N. Y.

Dear Mr. Boos:

        I have yours of December 3rd in reference to a collection of autographs of friends of Abraham Lincoln.

        I did not know Mr. Lincoln but I had the honor of being one of the guards of honor to march beside the remains in Chicago from the railroad, down about 16th street where they stopped the train, and marched to the Court House where the remains laid in State, for two days and nights.

        I was a great believer in Abraham Lincoln, so much so that I worked for the abolition of slavery, drove a team in the underground railway with slaves when a boy. I was in Chicago attending Bryant and Stratton Commercial College when Lincoln was assassinated and the Mayor of Chicago came to the Commercial College and said he wanted fifty of us to volunteer to march on the two sides of the hearse and I had the honor of being one of them.

        Now if any of the facts which I have given you you desire to have on the sheet which you have sent me I will be glad to write it out. Thank you for the opportunity of letting me read your address at the banquet, it was fine.

        Yours truly,

Leo A. Jewett

Peter Yeager

When death came, the President's body was moved to the White House, the funeral services being held in the East Room on Wednesday, April 19th. The remains were then taken to the capitol, the broad street being cleared of traffic while the funeral procession passes. There he lay-in-state, viewed by immense crowds until 6 a.m., of Friday the 21st, when the doors were closed, last prayers said, and at 7 a.m., the procession formed and moved to the station where a train of seven coaches, draped in mourning were waiting to take the great man to his home in Springfield.

A pilot engine moved ahead, all schedules being arranged so that the funeral train could move at a slow rate of speed, giving the crowds that were sure to gather a good chance to see it.

Baltimore was reached at 10 a.m., where a stay of four hours was made, when it again proceeded, stopping a few minutes at some places, to hours at others. Long stops were made at the capitol cities of the states through which it passed, and at Cleveland and Chicago, where even then great crowds were disappointed because they could not look into his face. One newspaper said the scene was like a funeral in every home.

The train came to a stop at Springfield on the morning of May 3rd, and the coffin was borne to the Representative Hall in the State House where it was again opened so that his friends and neighbors could look upon him for the last time, and at 10 a.m. on the 4th, the long procession slowly moved to Oak Ridge Cemetery. There the last services were held and the body placed in a temporary tomb, years later to be placed in permanent resting-place under the fine monument erected to his memory.

Peter Yeager served through the war in the 145th Illinois Volunteers, and he was chosen as one of the guards at the funeral. He was living in Kent., Ill., in 1916, and said,–

"I was one of the Lincoln Guards. Was detailed to go to Springfield and was there on May 3rd, when Lincoln's remains arrived. Met the train and was one of the guards to the State House, where we arrived at 11 a.m. The body lay in state until the next morning. Thousands of people passed through the State House to take a last sad look at our beloved President, passing through two a breast. They moved without a break from 11 a.m. May 3rd to 9 a.m. the next day, when the gates were closed. There were still hundreds of people in line that did not get in. The funeral services were then held. There were one hundred selected signers and the St. Louis German Band furnished the music.

"The funeral procession was over two miles long, and the body was placed in a vault in Oak Ridge Cemetery."

No 1

Kent Illinois March 30th 1914

I was one of the Lincoln Guards Was Detailed to go to Springfield Was there on May First 1865. when Lincolns Remains arived met The train. helped to gard the Remains to the State House Arived at the State House at 11 oclock A.M. the body laid In State till the next morning May 4th Thousands of people passed through the State house to take a last Sad look on our bloved President, the people passed through the State house two In a brest From 11 oclock May 3Rd – to 9 oclock May 4th when the gates of the State House were closed there were still hundreds of people formed In line that did not get to See the remains the funrel Services were held at the State House there there were one Hundred Selected Singers and the St Luis German Bond furnished the musick.

The funeral Procession was over two miles long Lincolns Body was placed In a vault at Oak Ridge Cemetery Springfield Illinois There has Been a Beautiful Monument Erected On a high Elevation at The Cemetery wich I visited Several Years ago and Lincolns Mortal Remains are lying under Its Base to its close I Seaved During the Civil War In Co. E. 146th Illinois Infantry Volinteers Inlisted at the age of 16 Years. Am Now 68 Years Young.
Yours Respectfuly:
  Peter Yeager Kent Illinois

HUGH A. CUMMINGS

A terrific war was drawing to a close, and though despair gripped the hearts of the leaders of the Confederacy, the North was overjoyed, and every loyal mother uttered prayers of thankfulness. Never again would there be fear of division of States. The Union was safe and every family with a son or brother was safe and every family with a son or brother at the front looked forward to his return. Though Grant was given the greater credit for the success of the armies, Lincoln was looked upon as the great leader. He held the faith of the majority of the people, and now that the end was near, they looked to him to bring the country back to peace and prosperity.

When the assassin's bullet struck down the President, it struck the whole North, and the nation sincerely mourned the passing of its Chief Executive. Strong men broke down, and unrestrained tears were shed when the news was told in most homesteads across the whole land.

Hugh A. Cummings had enlisted in the 39th Indiana Volunteers in August, 1861, was discharged in September, 1864, and again enlisted on March 7, 1865 in the 14th Main Volunteers. His regiment was encamped near Savannah, Georgia when a brigade drill was ordered, and when the regiments were formed in line, the dispatch was read of the President's assassination.

"Then it was that brave men were sought low, as every eye filled with tears and everybody was pained with anguish."

Indianapolis, Ind. 2/8 1926.

Mr John E Boos.
　　Albany, N. Y.

Dear Sir:—
　　Yours of 29th Ult. is before me. While I fail to grasp your idea, I will say that it was never my good fortune to see Our Martyred President, Abraham Lincoln. But I <u>do remember</u> of being on Brigade Drill (Something new for us at that time) near Savanna, Georgia, in April, 1865. when we were all formed in line, and someone came and read a dispatch that Abraham Lincoln had been assassinated. Then, it was, that brave men were brought low, as every eye was filled with tears, and every heart was pained with anguish.
　　I was at <u>that time</u> a member of Co. G. 14th Regiment of Maine Volunteers, having enlisted. March 7th 1865. and was discharged about Aug. 24th 1865. But I had served <u>over three years</u> in Co. B, 39th Ind. Infty. changed to the 8th Ind Cavalry, after the Battle of Stone River. Enlisting Aug. 15th 1861, and discharged about Sept 27th 1864. Wishing you success I am, Most Respectfully, Yours.
　　　　Hugh A. Cummings.
　　　　　　122, N. Arsenal Ave.,
　　　　　　　　Indianapolis, Ind.

Joseph Ruff

"I will remember the day the errand boy ran into the shop and gasped, almost out of breath, "The President has been shot!" I was the apprentice boy; as care free as any mischievous boy could be, but the news shocked me, and I watched the papers from day to day as anxiously as any older head, and shed real tears when the announcement came; "President McKinley is dead, and Theodore Roosevelt has just taken the oath to succeed him.

"Looking back to those days I can realize how the soldiers of the Union Army felt when the dispatches came, announcing the assassination of their great leader."

Joseph was a Lieutenant in the 12th Michigan Volunteers, and writing from his home in Albion, Mich., in 1911, he said,–

"It was never my good fortune to see Mr. Lincoln. I should have esteemed it a great pleasure to have met him, but my four years service was spent in the Western Department. I remember well when we were drawn up in line on dress parade and the dispatch was read that the great man who had stood firm through all the four years of Civil War had been cruelly assassinated. Never will I forget the murmur that ran down the whole line when those words were read and the curses the men uttered when they were dismissed. The mourning was universal in the Army."

Albion Mich
June 8th 1911

J. E. Boos Albany N. Y.

Dear Sir Your comunication of the 8th inst – just recieved & in reply would say that it never was my good fortune to see Mr. Lincoln I should have surely esteemed it a a great pleasure to have met so great a Man. but my 4 year & 3 months Service was all Spent in the Western Dept & I have never been in Washington even to this very Day I esteem Mr. Lincoln as one of the greatest Characters of the 19th Century, I remember well when we were drawn up in Line on Dress Parade, & Despatch was read that the great Man, who had stood firm through all the 4 years of civil War with its tremendous sacrifise of Life, had been cruelly assinated

Never will I forget the murmur that ran down the whole line, & Soldier would stand spell bound, & wonder who the fiend could be who could commit such a dastardly act. There was a Universal Mourning among the Army & the whole Nation was in Mourning.

Respectfully Yours
Joseph Ruff
Late Lieut 12th Mich Infty.

J. E. Boos. Albany N.Y.
Dear Sir. your request for Autograph recieved in reply to ever having met Mr. Lincoln I must say that It never was my Priveleyde to see or meet Mr. Lincoln & while it would have been a great Priveleyde & a sweet Memory. yet I am not Debarred in the cherished Memory of this great & good Man. The man I consider the Ideal American. & greatest wish is that we had more like him.
I am Respectfully Yours in
F. C. & L. Joseph Ruff
Late Private Do, D, & Lieut Co."B.
12th Regt. Vet. Vol. Infty.
Albion Mich.

M.D. VANCE

Out in Arkansas they still hate black men, but M.D. Vance did not hate them as much as he wished the South to have the right and power to control them.

The argument was on, an argument of sword and gun, of battle and destruction, of suffering and famine, because the debate had gone beyond legislative halls to the field where the tragedy of armed leaders and the noise of shot and shell took the place of oratory and debate. The South seemed to be in the ascendant for a time, but the tide slowly receded until the Stars and Bars trailed in the dust at Appomattox, and the Confederacy was dead. In less than a week the leader of the Union, as he was of the old, was dead, and the whole North was stunned at the tragedy, while many in the beaten forces like M.D. Vance realized their real friend at the court of reconstruction was gone, the assassin destroying the only one they could go to now that defeat had crushed them.

M.D. Vance was 18 when he enlisted in 1863 at Little Rock, Arkansas, where he lived out his life, being Commander-in-Chief of the United Confederate Veterans in 1926-7.

"I was born June 8, 1845. Was reared on a farm in Carroll and Boom Counties. Educated in Clarke Academy. Joined the Confederate Army in 1863, and surrendered in 1865. Served in Co. D, Hamills Bat. Cabell's Brig, Cavalry, in Price's Div. under Gen. Kirby Smith in the Trans-Miss. Dept. Did not go east of Miss River, hence I never met Gen. Lee."

M.B. LESSIER
(Pittsburgh, Penn. November 25, 1937)

"The first time I heard of Abraham Lincoln and learnt that he was opposed to slavery must have been about 1865 when the Republican party was organized. I was around eleven years of age. Even at this early period my childish mind was disturbed by an inconsistency. I did not understand how we could boast of freedom and equality yet tolerate slavery with the borders of our own country. So I became a Republican sympathizer at once. My father, like most Germans who had lived under the developing democratic influence of 1840-48 in Germany, was inclined to favor a democratic type of party in his adopted land. However he discovered his mistake and also became an enthusiastic admirer of Abraham Lincoln. I felt proud of him when he carried his oil lamp in the Lincoln torch light procession for that to me was equivalent to saying that he did not approve of slavery either.

"How much Abraham Lincoln's personality impressed my childish mind may be culled from the following. Besides being obsessed with the desire to paint pictures I loved music even though I could not play piano like other village boys who could not afford to have instructors. East Birmingham, now the South Side of Pittsburgh, was at that time a scattered village like settlement and did not offer many opportunities. Books were very expensive and limited so I did things without intelligent guidance or assistance. Among other things I made a violin; I deliberately put the picture of Abraham Lincoln on the back then I stained, varnished and polished the surface thus sealing the picture under this shining cover for all time. I did not know or care if Lincoln could play the violin nor did I care whether he had any special fondness for music. Those considerations were of no consequence; my hero was enshrined! I was not long in discovering that while my instrument could be played upon, its construction was very imperfect but by correcting its defects could be very much improved. I knew, too, that it would have been much more appropriate to have the picture of a celebrated musician or a world renowned violinist instead of the picture of the great anti-slavery president on the back of my violin. But in spite of unfriendly advise and adverse criticism I preferred to leave it as it was.

"While it was a monument of my primitive skill and ignorance it illustrated, also, what was more important to me-the great love, esteem and admiration I had for our great humanitarian president. I never had the pleasure of coming in contact with this great man but I have the pleasant recollection of seeing and hearing him when he addressed an enthusiastic crowd that had gathered at the old Monongahela House in Pittsburgh. He spoke from the balcony over the main entrance of the hotel where speakers could easily be seen and heard. I will remember how, a little later, the sad news of the assassination of our greatly beloved Abraham Lincoln came to us early one morning. The telegrapher who received the shocking message was a school friend and a next door neighbor of mine. This Bob Weitbrec at the age of sixteen went to Washington and in a very short time became a capable telegraph operator. He finally was engaged in military telegraph service and was eventually taken prisoner at Fairfax Court which resulted in no harm to him. While in Washington he frequently saw the president who was a welcome visitor in the telegraph operating room where he often went to read messages just as they came in. When there was no distressing news he usually had a funny little story to tell to illustrate some smart or stupid incident. When Bob came home to take employment with the Western Union Telegraph Company he had many stories to relate that were credited to good old Abe. He was on night duty when the great tragedy occurred. He received the message of the assassination in the early morning and his mother, with tears in hear eyes, imparted the sad news to us before the morning papers had been delivered to our homes. No words could express the painful consternation and sorrow that made us almost speechless.

"And so, my dear Mr. Boos, you know how the Lincoln violin came into existence. Perhaps you also know that I am in my ninety-third year. Many things have accumulated during my long period of activity. Some are more important than others but I am now endeavoring to find hospitable homes for all of my keepsakes. I shall be very glad to hear from you and very much obliged if you can recommend an appropriate resting place for my treasured violin."

Pittsburgh, Penna.
November 25, 1937

My dear Mr. Boos,

The first time I heard of Abraham Lincoln and learnt that he was opposed to slavery must have been about 1856 when the Republican party was organized. I was around ele eleven years of age. Even at this early period my childish mind was disturbed by an inconsistency. I did not understand how we could boast of freedom and equality yet tolerate slavery within the borders of our own country. So I became a Republican sympathizer at once. My father, like most Germans who had lived under the developing democratic influence of 1840-48 in Germany, was inclined to favor a democratic type of party in his adopted land. However he discovered his mistake and also became an enthusiastic admirer of Abraham Lincoln. I felt proud of him when he car ried his oil lamp in the Lincoln torch light procession for that to me was equivalent to saying that he did not approve of slavery either.

How much Abraham Lincoln's personality impressed my childish mind may be culled from the following. Besides being obsessed with the desire to paint pictures I loved music even though I could only fiddle or drum upon the piano like other village boys who could not afford to have instructors. East Birmingham, now the South Side of Pittsburgh, was at that time a scattered villagelike settlement and did not offer many opportunities. Books were very expensive and limited so I did things without intelligent guidance or assistance. Among other things I made a violin; I deliberately put the picture of Abraham Lincoln on the back then I stained, varnished and polished the surface thus sealing the picture under this shining cover for all time. I did not know or care if Lincoln could play the violin nor did I care whether he had any special fondness for music. Those considerations were of no consequence; my hero was enshrined! I was not long in discovering that while my instrument could be played upon, its construction was very imperfect but by correcting its defects could be very much improved. I knew, too, that it would have been much more appropriate to have the picture of a celebrated musician or a world renowned violinist instead of the picture of the great anti-slavery president on the back of my violin. But in spite of unfriendly advise and adverse

criticisms I preferred to leave it as it was.
While it was a monument of my primitive skill
and ignorance it illustrated, also, what was more
important to me -- the great love, esteem and admiration I had for our great humanitarian president. I never had the pleasure of coming in contact with this great man but I have the pleasant
recollection of seeing and hearing him when he
addressed an enthusiastic crowd that had gathered
at the old Monongahela House in Pittsburg. He
spoke from the balcony over the main entrance of
the hotel where speakers could easily be seen and
heard. I
well remember how, a little later, the sad news
of the assassination of our greatly beloved
Abraham Lincoln came to us early one morning. The
telegrapher who received the shocking message was
a school friend and a next door neighbor of mine.
This Bob Weitbrec at the age of sixteen went to
Washington and in a very short time became a capable telegraph operator. He finally was engaged
in military telegraph service and was eventually
taken prisoner at Fairfax Court which resulted in
no harm to him. While in Washington he frequently
saw the president who was a welcome visitor in the

telegraph operating room where he often went to read messages just as they came in. When there was no distressing news he usually had a funny little story to tell to illustrate some smart or stupid incident. When Bob came home to take employment with the Western Union Telegraph Company he had many stories to relate that were credited to good old Abe. He was on night duty when the great tragedy occurred. He received the message of the assassination in the early morning and his mother, with tears in her eyes, imparted the sad news to us before the morning papers had been delivered to our homes. No words could express the painful consternation and sorrow that made us almost speechless.

And so, my dear Mr. Boos, you know how the Lincoln violin came into existence. Perhaps you also know that I am in my ninety-third year. Many things have accumulated during my long period of activity. Some are more important than others but I am now endeavoring to find hospitable homes for all my keepsakes. I shall be very glad to hear from you and very much obliged if you can recommend an appropriate resting place for my treasured violin.

Sincerely, W. B. Lewis

Pittsburgh Nov 27"/937

Mr. John E. Boos
Albany. N.Y..
    Dear Mr Boos:

    I have just recently returned to my Pittsburgh home. The response to your request was Typed and cut down to get it all upon the paper you sent me. The Typed copy came to me a few days ago — and is not in the most desirable condition. If you should prefer a more presentable one to go into your collection; I shall be very glad to add my signature to any improved copy you may send to me.

    Sincerely
        M. B. Leisser

Henry R. Rathbone

Fate and Tragedy at the Fords Theatre

Fate seemed to decree that all who entered the box in Fords Theatre on that fatal night of April 14th, 1865 should suffer a sad death. The assassin, John Wilkes Booth, was shot by Boston Corbett in a barn a few days after his revolting crime, and died within two hours.

The shock affected Mrs. Lincoln to such a degree, that she slowly lost her mind, and though her last days were made as happy as possible under the circumstances, none could console her. Her grief was pitiable, and the last few years were spent in her room, which she seldom left, at last taking to her bed, where she died, July 16, 1882.

Miss Clara Harris was the daughter of U.S. Senator Ira Harris; and Major Henry R. Rathbone, the fourth occupant of the box was the Senator's stepson.

When the fatal shot was fired, Major Rathbone grappled with Booth, who stabbed the Major in the arm, and this interference, though it did no more than rip some of Booth's clothing, caused him to hastily jump to the stage below. Hurriedly mounting the rail on the box, his spur caught in a flag, which momentarily held him, causing the spur to strike a portrait of Washington, and he lost his balance when he landed, breaking an ankle.

Major Rathbone had the President removed from the box to the house across the street, then fainted from loss of blood and shock. His wound quickly healed, but the terrible event prayed upon his mind, and he soon became a victim of melancholy periods. He married Miss Harris soon after the tragedy and they took up their residence in the west. Later, he was appointed U.S. Consul to Hanover, Germany, which position he held a number of years. Becoming suddenly insane, he murdered his wife, was sent to the Hildesheim Insane Asylum at Hanover, where he remained violently insane until his death, which occurred August 14, 1912.

He was born July 1, 1837, the son of Mayor Jared L. Rathbone, received his education at Union College, and in 1861, after his graduation, formed a law partnership with John S. Barnes in Albany.

January 1, 1861, his name was placed on the roll of the Albany Zouave Cadets, and during the Civil War was Captain in the 12th U.S. Infantry. He resigned a lawyer in Chicago, and in 1924 was a member of Congress. The following note about the great War President was written by him.

"Whenever the human heart shall sigh for freedom, wherever the oppressed shall rise against the oppressor, wherever man shall seek to establish or to maintain a true rational, constitutional liberty, there they will turn to Abraham Lincoln as their great example, their guide, who will lead them on the pathway of duty to a glorious destiny."

Congress of the United States
House of Representatives
Washington, D. C.

February 23, 1924

Mr. J. E. Boos
10 Lexington Avenue
Albany, N. Y.

My dear Mr. Boos:

I have your favor of February 21, 1924 and, in compliance with your request I am inclosing herewith a little sentiment concerning Abraham Lincoln, which I hope will prove to be what you want.

With kindest regards and best wishes, I am

Sincerely yours,

Henry R. Rathbone

Wherever the human heart shall sigh for freedom, wherever the oppressed shall rise against the oppressor, wherever man shall seek to establish or to maintain a true, rational, constitutional liberty, there they will turn to Abraham Lincoln as their great example their pride, who will lead them on the pathway of duty to a glorious destiny.

Henry R. Rathbone.

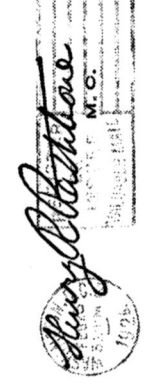

Mr. J. E. Boos
10 Lexington Avenue
Albany, New York

We are actively seeking to purchase correspondence, letters, manuscripts, relics and documents relating to Abraham Lincoln and the Civil War

We offer free appraisal by fax, phone or e-mail and are famous for having the fastest check in the business; by FedEx if you desire.

We also purchase rare stamp and coin clollections, rare books and any documents or relics relating to famous individuals or events in history.

Visit us on the web at
www.UniversityArchives.com

Contact us at:
University Archives
49 Richmondville Avenue • Westport, CT 06880
Toll-free **1-800 237-5692** • (203) 454-0111   Fax (203) 454-3111

If there's one signature collectors recognize, it's ours

A Division of USC, Inc.

Member: ABAA, UACC, Manuscript Society, IADA

Printed in the United States
77525LV00002B/31-42